Redis 4.x Cookbook

Over 80 hand-picked recipes for effective Redis development and administration

Pengcheng Huang
Zuofei Wang

BIRMINGHAM - MUMBAI

Redis 4.x Cookbook

Commissioning Editor: Amey Varangaonkar
Acquisition Editor: Namrata Patil
Content Development Editor: Amrita Noronha
Technical Editor: Jovita Alva
Copy Editor: Safis Editing
Project Coordinator: Shweta H Birwatkar
Proofreader: Safis Editing
Indexer: Mariammal Chettiyar
Graphics: Jisha Chirayil
Production Coordinator: Aparna Bhagat

First published: February 2018

Production reference: 1270218

Published by Packt Publishing Ltd.
Livery Place
35 Livery Street
Birmingham
B3 2PB, UK.

ISBN 978-1-78398-816-7

www.packtpub.com

To my wife, Ting Wang , who's always accepted and supported my hustle, drive, and ambition:
you are and always will be my perfect wife and mother to our kids.
To my parents, I could not have asked for better parents or role models.
To my incoming lovely, child HaoHao, you are a blessing,
a precious little angel to cherish and to love.
- Pengcheng Huang

To my parents: Hongwu Wang and Jiuxiang Yang.
- Zuofei Wang

`mapt.io`

Mapt is an online digital library that gives you full access to over 5,000 books and videos, as well as industry leading tools to help you plan your personal development and advance your career. For more information, please visit our website.

Why subscribe?

- Spend less time learning and more time coding with practical eBooks and Videos from over 4,000 industry professionals

- Improve your learning with Skill Plans built especially for you

- Get a free eBook or video every month

- Mapt is fully searchable

- Copy and paste, print, and bookmark content

PacktPub.com

Did you know that Packt offers eBook versions of every book published, with PDF and ePub files available? You can upgrade to the eBook version at `www.PacktPub.com` and as a print book customer, you are entitled to a discount on the eBook copy. Get in touch with us at `service@packtpub.com` for more details.

At `www.PacktPub.com`, you can also read a collection of free technical articles, sign up for a range of free newsletters, and receive exclusive discounts and offers on Packt books and eBooks.

Foreword

I still remember how surprised I was when for the first time I heard about Redis. It's so elegant and powerful, like a Swiss Army knife for your backend applications, and of course, it's blazing fast. In modern data centers, the unit cost of RAM is getting lower and lower; it's no surprise that Redis is playing an important role in storage stacks of modern applications. Frankly speaking, Redis is way beyond an in-memory cache.

I'm a database engineer. Codis, a distributed Redis middleware, is my first open source project, which is widely used in the community. I'm quite proud of it. Codis provides a proxy-based solution to tackle the scalability problem of Redis and it's an alternative to Redis Cluster. As one of the earliest adopters and developers of Redis in China, I witnessed the increasing popularity of Redis. Still more thanks to Redis that I met my dear friend, Redis expert, and contributor, Pengcheng Huang. When he told me he wanted to write a book about Redis, I told him I would definitely buy one. Finally, he made it, and it's my honor and pleasure to review the early version and write a foreword in this book.

You won't regret choosing this book. Many significant changes and features were introduced after Redis 4.0 was released. Whether you are new to Redis or an experienced Redis developer like me, you'll learn new tricks from this book.

Dongxu Huang

PingCap CTO and Codislabs cofounder

As a contributor and member of the Redisson project as well as a long-time Redis advocate, I have witnessed Redis steadily taking over the world over the years as it evolved from one version to another. After having several conversations with many members of both Redis and Redisson communities, I couldn't help but wonder: wouldn't it be great if there were a canonical book with the most up-to-date information on Redis so that Redis users don't have to trawl through tons of Stack Overflow questions to get the answers they were looking for?

Quite obviously, Pengcheng and Zuofei shared the same vision.

I have known Pengcheng for quite some time. He is a well-known Redis enthusiast in the Redis Chinese community, managing a very active user group full of members ranging from Redis core contributors and tools/library authors, to Redis advocates and everyday users. This book is about what Pengcheng knows best: Redis, or Redis version 4 to be more precise. As one might imagine, he doesn't manage a user group for a living. He serves as a team lead of big data infrastructure and the technical director of Redis in China Minsheng Bank. His responsibility is to ensure that Redis, as one of the most important parts of the bank's infrastructure, is being implemented and managed correctly throughout. It is his work at the bank that had helped plant the seeds that would eventually grow into this book.

As a result, the book covers a wide range of topics and is organized in a logical order, primarily catering to beginners and intermediate users. Beginners, you can find plenty of useful examples, diagrams, and how-to guides to help you read through the entire book. Intermediary readers, you will be very pleased to see that the authors were not shy when diving into the depths of how everything in Redis works, along with recommendations for further reading on each topic.

Personally, I quite like the detailed explanations of each Redis configuration option. I think this book will serve me well as a useful handbook, to be kept at the side of my table for quick reference. I hope you will find this book as enjoyable to read as I have, and that it will prove useful as you explore the many wonderful features of Redis 4.

Rui Gu

Long-time Redis advocate, contributor and core developer, Redisson Team

Contributors

About the authors

Pengcheng Huang has been working as a software engineer and team lead of the Big Data Infrastructure team at China Minsheng Bank (ranked No.29 in the Top 1000 World Banks in 2017) for more than 5 years providing Big data infrastructure services for the whole bank. Also, as the technical director of Redis at the bank, he devotes much of his energy making better use of Redis in the production environment. He is also a Redis contributor. You can reach him on LinkedIn by searching for gnuhpc.

I want to thank my wife for her support and encouragement. Moreover, thanks to the technical reviewers for their valuable feedback:
Domagoj Katavić (Vectra Networks)
Igor Malinovskiy (RedisDesktop)
Zhao Zhao, Lei Fu, Tielei Zhang (Alibaba)
Cong Tang (Tencent)
Luyao Mei (Huobi)
Hailei Zhang (AutoHome)
Peng Liu (HomeLink)
Jianchao Wu (Oppo)
Huaping Huang (MaiMai)
Jinshuai Dou (DiDi)
Jianhong Huang (huangz)

Zuofei Wang is an experienced software engineer living in the San Francisco Bay area. With more than 5 years of experience in the software industry, he has worked on projects with different technologies and is currently employed by Airbnb Inc. Zuofei is passionate about learning new things and sharing his knowledge. He also enjoys reading, traveling, and ham radio in his spare time.

About the reviewers

Domagoj Katavic has a master's degree in electronics and computer engineering. Currently, he works at Vectra Networks, a network security company that identifies real-time cyber attacks.

Previously, he has worked at Planet9 Energy (a UK Energy supplier), Codeanywhere (a cloud IDE), and as an assistant professor at FESB, the University of Split, Croatia.

Ihor Malinovskiy is an addicted programmer from Ukraine. He started his career as a web developer in 2009 and has worked in different domains, such as advertising, healthcare, and cloud software, since then. Ihor is an open source enthusiast and was the core developer in an OpenStack project. In 2013, he started his own product—a desktop GUI for Redis, called Redis Desktop Manager.

Packt is searching for authors like you

If you're interested in becoming an author for Packt, please visit `authors.packtpub.com` and apply today. We have worked with thousands of developers and tech professionals, just like you, to help them share their insight with the global tech community. You can make a general application, apply for a specific hot topic that we are recruiting an author for, or submit your own idea.

Table of Contents

Preface

Redis, as a popular key-value in-memory data store, is gaining more and more attention recently for its high-performance, diversified data types with powerful APIs, high availability, and scalable architecture. It has been successfully ranked at number 9 in the top 10 databases in the DB-Engine Complete Ranking since 2017. Even before that, it had been at the top of the key-value stores ranking provided by DB-Engine for quite a long time. From the early version, 2.x, to the latest version, 4.x, many fantastic features of Redis have been added to help those who want to deliver low-latency services in their business scenarios.

Based on the latest version of Redis 4.x, *Redis Cookbook* offers you both step-by-step recipes and relevant background information. It covers everything from a basic understanding of Redis data types to advanced aspects of Redis such as high availability, clustering, administration, and troubleshooting.

With the concept of *Learning by doing is the best approach* in mind, we have spared no effort to deliver the knowledge of Redis through real use cases in writing the recipes in this book. In other words, this book offers out-of-the-box solutions for many common development and maintenance problems. Especially on your personal computer, you will be able to catch the key points of each recipe easily by following the steps in the *How to do it* section of every recipe. Furthermore, it's not enough for you to know just how to reach your goal with Redis; explanatory notes of the steps you take within a certain task will be provided in the *How it works...* section. We also offer essential relevant information and necessary explanations of the internal workings of Redis in the *There's more...* section. The better you understand how Redis works, the more you can make informed decisions regarding the trade-offs that are involved in engineering. Every recipe is structured in this organized way.

Lastly, we do hope this book gives you a better understanding of Redis and enables you to learn more best practices when you use Redis in your environment.

Who this book is for

This book is for developers, architects, and database administrators who want to start using Redis or improve their Redis knowledge. If you want to design high-performant, scalable database solutions using Redis, this book will guide you towards gaining a comprehensive and in-depth understanding with various kinds of practical recipes. DBAs looking for solutions to common problems encountered during their day-to-day tasks while working with Redis will also find this book useful. The book covers all the aspects of using Redis and provides solutions and hints for everyday usage. Some basic understanding of Redis is expected but is not required to get the best out of this book.

What this book covers

Chapter 1, *Getting Started with Redis*, covers the step-by-step installation of a Redis Server and basic operations, including starting and shutting down the Redis Server, connecting to Redis with redis-cli, and getting server information. The Redis Event Model and Redis protocol are also covered at the end of this chapter.

Chapter 2, *Data Types*, talks about Redis data types and their common operational API commands. All data types that are supported in Redis 4.x (string, list, hash, Set, Sorted Set, HyperLogLog, and Geo) will be covered in this chapter. Basic Redis key management is also discussed.

Chapter 3, *Data Features*, covers a few useful Redis features that make data manipulation easier. It first shows how to use bitmaps, sort, and setting key expiration. You will then be introduced to three important features of Redis: pipeline, transaction, and PubSub. At the end of this chapter, we will demonstrate how to write and debug Lua scripts in Redis.

Chapter 4, *Developing with Redis*, demonstrates how to develop applications with Redis. First, it discusses the usage scenario of Redis and the choice of data types and APIs. Then, it shows examples of developing Java and Python applications with the Redis Client libraries, Jedis and redis-py. Lastly, we will cover examples of using Redis in the Spring Framework and writing a MapReduce/Spark job will also be covered.

Chapter 5, *Replication*, covers the Redis replication mechanism. It shows how to set up a Redis slave and explains how Redis replication works. Then, topics of optimizing and troubleshooting Redis replication will be discussed.

Chapter 6, *Persistence,* introduces the two persistence options in Redis: RDB and AOF. It shows how to enable RDB and AOF persistence in Redis and explains how things work behind the scenes. It also talks about the difference between RDB and AOF and how to utilize the combination of these two options.

Chapter 7, *Setting Up High Availability and Cluster,* covers the high availability of Redis. It demonstrates how to set up Redis Sentinels and Redis Clusters. A few experiments will be shown to explain how Redis Sentinel and Cluster work.

Chapter 8, *Deploying to a Production Environment,* discusses the things to notice when deploying Redis in a production environment. It first talks about the operation system, network, and security concerns. Then, it touches upon the topics of tweaking configuration and logging Redis. Setting up the LRU policy is also included. Lastly, we will look at Redis benchmarking.

Chapter 9, *Administrating Redis,* covers various Redis administration tasks, including updating server settings, using redis-cli, backing up and restoring data, managing memory usage, managing client, and data migration.

Chapter 10, *Troubleshooting Redis,* provides some practical examples on troubleshooting Redis issues. It covers the usage of slow log to identify slow queries and demonstrate common cases of troubleshooting latency, memory, and crash issues.

Chapter 11, *Extending Redis with Redis Module,* discusses how to extend the Redis functionality with the Redis Module. It talks about how the Redis module works and then demonstrates how to build Redis Modules with Redis Modules SDK.

Chapter 12, *The Redis Ecosystem,* talks about third-party components for Redis. A few popular tools, clients, and proxies are also briefly introduced.

Appendix, *Windows Environment Setup,* explains how to configure Windows environment for Redis.

To get the most out of this book

All the examples in this book are to be run on Redis 4.x. A Linux environment is preferred, while macOS X is also supported. If you are using Windows, it is recommended to install and run a Linux OS in VirtualBox or VMWare. You also need JDK 1.8+ and Python 2.7+ or 3.4+ to run the code examples.

Download the example code files

You can download the example code files for this book from your account at
`www.packtpub.com`. If you purchased this book elsewhere, you can visit
`www.packtpub.com/support` and register to have the files emailed directly to you.

You can download the code files by following these steps:

1. Log in or register at `www.packtpub.com`.
2. Select the **SUPPORT** tab.
3. Click on **Code Downloads & Errata**.
4. Enter the name of the book in the **Search** box and follow the onscreen
   instructions.

Once the file is downloaded, please make sure that you unzip or extract the folder using the
latest version of:

- WinRAR/7-Zip for Windows
- Zipeg/iZip/UnRarX for Mac
- 7-Zip/PeaZip for Linux

The code bundle for the book is also hosted on GitHub at `https://github.com/
PacktPublishing/Redis-4.x-Cookbook`. In case there's an update to the code, it will be
updated on the existing GitHub repository.

We also have other code bundles from our rich catalog of books and videos available
at `https://github.com/PacktPublishing/`. Check them out!

Download the color images

We also provide a PDF file that has color images of the screenshots/diagrams used in this
book. You can download it here:
`http://www.packtpub.com/sites/default/files/downloads/Redis4xCookbook_ColorImag
es.pdf`.

Conventions used

There are a number of text conventions used throughout this book.

`CodeInText`: Indicates code words in text, database table names, folder names, filenames, file extensions, pathnames, dummy URLs, user input, and Twitter handles. Here is an example: "Open a Terminal and connect to Redis with `redis-cli`."

A block of code is set as follows:

```
for i in `seq 10`
do
nohup node generator.js hash 1000000 session:${i} &
done
```

Any command-line input or output is written as follows:

```
127.0.0.1:6379> SETBIT "users_tried_reservation" 100 1
(integer) 0
```

Bold: Indicates a new term, an important word, or words that you see onscreen. For example, words in menus or dialog boxes appear in the text like this. Here is an example: "Click **Import Project from Sources** and select the `redis-4.0.1` sub-directory in the `coding` directory."

 Warnings or important notes appear like this.

 Tips and tricks appear like this.

Sections

In this book, you will find several headings that appear frequently (*Getting ready*, *How to do it...*, *How it works...*, *There's more...*, and *See also*).

To give clear instructions on how to complete a recipe, use these sections as follows:

Getting ready...

This section tells you what to expect in the recipe and describes how to set up any software or any preliminary settings required for the recipe.

How to do it...

This section contains the steps required to follow the recipe.

How it works...

This section usually consists of a detailed explanation of what happened in the previous section.

There's more...

This section consists of additional information about the recipe in order to make you more knowledgeable about the recipe.

See also

This section provides helpful links to other useful information for the recipe.

Get in touch

Feedback from our readers is always welcome.

General feedback: Email feedback@packtpub.com and mention the book title in the subject of your message. If you have questions about any aspect of this book, please email us at questions@packtpub.com.

Errata: Although we have taken every care to ensure the accuracy of our content, mistakes do happen. If you have found a mistake in this book, we would be grateful if you would report this to us. Please visit www.packtpub.com/submit-errata, selecting your book, clicking on the Errata Submission Form link, and entering the details.

Piracy: If you come across any illegal copies of our works in any form on the internet, we would be grateful if you would provide us with the location address or website name. Please contact us at copyright@packtpub.com with a link to the material.

If you are interested in becoming an author: If there is a topic that you have expertise in and you are interested in either writing or contributing to a book, please visit authors.packtpub.com.

Reviews

Please leave a review. Once you have read and used this book, why not leave a review on the site that you purchased it from? Potential readers can then see and use your unbiased opinion to make purchase decisions, we at Packt can understand what you think about our products, and our authors can see your feedback on their book. Thank you!

For more information about Packt, please visit packtpub.com.

1
Getting Started with Redis

In this chapter, we will cover the following recipes:

- Downloading and installing Redis
- Starting and shutting down Redis
- Connecting to Redis with redis-cli
- Getting server information
- Understanding the Redis Event Model
- Understanding the Redis protocol

Introduction

Redis is a very popular, memory-based, lightweight key-value database. Strictly speaking, Redis is a data structure server, according to **Matt Stancliff** (@mattsta), one of the most important contributors to Redis (https://matt.sh/thinking-in-redis-part-one). The author of Redis, **Salvatore Sanfilippo** (@Antirez), first called it Redis, which stands for **REmote DIctionary Server** because Redis natively implements various kinds of data structures in memory, and provides a variety of APIs for manipulating these data structures. More importantly, Redis supports high-performance command processing, high availability/scalability architectures, and also data persistence features as a long running data store service.

With the development of high-concurrency and low-latency systems, the use of Redis is becoming more and more widespread. Redis has been ranked in the top ten of the DB-Engine complete ranking (`https://db-engines.com/en/ranking`) since 2017. Before that, it was ranked at the top of the key-value stores ranking (`https://db-engines.com/en/ranking/key-value+store`) for quite a long time.

The goal of this chapter is to guide readers to quickly set up a simple Redis instance and learn about some common operations, such as starting, connecting, and shutting down a Redis Server. Retrieving basic information from a Redis Server is also introduced. Moreover, it's essential to have a better understanding of the event model and communication protocol of Redis before learning Redis. The last two sections of this chapter include a detailed discussion of the event model and protocol of Redis.

Downloading and installing Redis

Redis has an active community on GitHub. Large numbers of pull requests have been made and merged during the years, and the author, **Antirez**, has always given a timely response on the issues section in GitHub. Hence, the release cycles of Redis are very rapid. From the early versions, 2.6/2.8 to 3.0/3.2, which were widely used, and then to the latest 4.x version, each release of Redis offers some essential enhancements and bug fixes. So using the latest version of Redis, if possible, is one of the best practices. In this book, we are adopting the latest version of Redis 4.0.1.

Redis is an open software written in pure C language so that we can install it by compilation. Major operating systems also include Redis binary packages in their software repository, although the Redis version is often a little out of date.

Getting ready...

You can find the download link and basic installation steps at `https://redis.io/download`. If you would like to build Redis by compiling source code in Linux/Unix/macOS, both the gcc compiler and C Standard Library libc are needed in your environment. When it comes to OS repository installation, all you need are an internet connection and the correct repository configuration.

How to do it...

We will demonstrate the compilation installation of Redis in Ubuntu 16.04.2 LTS (Xenial Xerus). The downloading and building steps are as follows:

1. Set up building tools:

   ```
   $ sudo apt-get install build-essential
   ```

2. Create a directory and enter it for Redis:

   ```
   $ mkdir /redis
   $ cd /redis
   ```

3. Then, download Redis:

   ```
   $ wget http://download.redis.io/releases/redis-4.0.1.tar.gz
   ```

4. Untar it and enter the directory:

   ```
   $ tar zxvf redis-4.0.1.tar.gz
   $ cd redis-4.0.1
   ```

5. Create a directory for the Redis configuration file and copy the default configuration file into it:

   ```
   $ mkdir /redis/conf
   $ cp redis.conf /redis/conf/
   ```

6. Building dependencies:

   ```
   $ cd deps
   $ make hiredis lua jemalloc linenoise
   $ cd ..
   ```

   Due to the differences among various operation systems and libraries installed on it, the aforementioned steps will be required when errors occur indicating some dependencies are not satisfied. For example, you may encounter the error message:
   zmalloc.h:50:31: fatal error: jemalloc/jemalloc.h: No such file or directory.
   This step is not a must for most environments, if nothing about dependencies goes wrong.

7. Do the compilation:

```
$ make
```

If everything goes well, the following message will be shown. It means that the compilation has been done successfully:

```
It's a good idea to run 'make test' ;)
make[1]: Leaving directory '/redis/redis-4.0.1/src'
```

8. Install Redis:

```
$ make PREFIX=/redis install
```

The following messages represent the success of installation:

```
Hint: It's a good idea to run 'make test' ;)
    INSTALL install
    INSTALL install
    INSTALL install
    INSTALL install
    INSTALL install
make[1]: Leaving directory '/redis/redis-4.0.1/src'
```

9. Enter the /redis directory and verify that the Redis binary files have been generated:

```
$ ls /redis/bin
redis-benchmark   redis-check-aof   redis-check-rdb   redis-cli
redis-sentinel    redis-server
```

Congratulations! You have completed the Redis compilation installation.

Compared to the compilation installation, using apt-get in Ubuntu to install Redis is much easier. Let's take a look:

1. First, update software repository index:

```
$ sudo apt-get update
```

2. And then start the installation:

```
$ sudo apt-get install redis-server
```

3. When it's finished, check if Redis has been set up in your environment:

```
$ which redis-server
```

How it works...

When it comes to the Redis version selection, bear in mind that Redis follows the standard practice of versioning, which is *major.minor.patch* level. An even-numbered minor stands for a stable release, while an odd-numbered minor means it's an unstable version, although there are a few versions using an odd minor for Redis.

The differences between building Redis by compiling and building via a software repository, are that the former can add optimization or debugging options when compiling, and also own the flexibility of specifying the installation location during installation.

After installation, there are some executable files in the `bin` directory. Their description and remarks are shown in the following table:

File name	Description	Remarks
redis-server	Redis Server	
redis-sentinel	Redis Sentinel	A soft link for `redis-server`.
redis-cli	Redis Console Tool	
redis-check-rdb	Redis RDB Check Tool	
redis-check-aof	Redis **Append Only Files (AOF)** Check Tool	
redis-benchmark	Redis Benchmarking Tool	

There's more...

For Windows, you can obtain the Redis release of Windows, which the Microsoft Open Technologies group used to maintain at: `https://github.com/MicrosoftArchive/redis/releases`.

Just download the `.msi` executable file and give it a double-click to install, keeping the default configurations.

For macOS, there is no big difference from the procedures in Linux. You can also install Redis by issuing the command, `brew install redis` on macOS.

See also

- For the impact of different compilation options on Redis performance, refer to Matt Stancliff's evaluation of Redis performance for different versions by taking different compilation options: `https://matt.sh/redis-benchmark-compilers`

- For security concerns, a non-root user should be used for Redis and the *Securing Redis* recipe in `Chapter 8`, *Deploying to a Production Environment* will have a detailed discussion

- You can further refer to `https://github.com/antirez/redis` for more information

Starting and shutting down Redis

Before accessing Redis, the Redis Server must be started in a proper way. Similarly, under certain circumstances, you have to stop the Redis service. This recipe will show you how to start and stop a Redis Server.

Getting ready...

You need to finish the installation of the Redis Server, as we described in the *Downloading and installing Redis* recipe in this chapter.

How to do it...

The steps for starting and shutting down a Redis Server are as follows:

1. You can start a Redis Server with the default configurations:

```
$ bin/redis-server
```

Your server should now start up as shown in the following screenshot:

```
redis@gnuhpc-desktop:~$ bin/redis-server
24188:C 30 Aug 09:57:44.315 # o000o000o000o Redis is starting o000o000o000o
24188:C 30 Aug 09:57:44.315 # Redis version=4.0.1, bits=64, commit=00000000, modified=0, pid=24188, just started
24188:C 30 Aug 09:57:44.315 # Warning: no config file specified, using the default config. In order to specify a config file use bin/redis-server /path/to/redis.conf

                _._
           _.-``__ ''-._
      _.-``    `.  `_.  ''-._           Redis 4.0.1 (00000000/0) 64 bit
  .-`` .-```.  ```\/    _.,_ ''-._
 (    '      ,       .-`  | `,    )     Running in standalone mode
 |`-._`-...-` __...-.``-._|'` _.-'|     Port: 6379
 |    `-._   `._    /     _.-'    |     PID: 24188
  `-._    `-._  `-./  _.-'    _.-'
 |`-._`-._    `-.__.-'    _.-'_.-'|
 |    `-._`-._        _.-'_.-'    |           http://redis.io
  `-._    `-._`-.__.-'_.-'    _.-'
 |`-._`-._    `-.__.-'    _.-'_.-'|
 |    `-._`-._        _.-'_.-'    |
  `-._    `-._`-.__.-'_.-'    _.-'
      `-._    `-.__.-'    _.-'
          `-._        _.-'
              `-.__.-'

24188:M 30 Aug 09:57:44.328 # WARNING: The TCP backlog setting of 511 cannot be enforced because /proc/sys/net/core/somaxconn is set to the lower value of 128.
24188:M 30 Aug 09:57:44.328 # Server initialized
24188:M 30 Aug 09:57:44.328 # WARNING you have Transparent Huge Pages (THP) support enabled in your kernel. This will create latency and memory usage issues with Redis. To fix this issue ru
n the command 'echo never > /sys/kernel/mm/transparent_hugepage/enabled' as root, and add it to your /etc/rc.local in order to retain the setting after a reboot. Redis must be restarted aft
er THP is disabled.
24188:M 30 Aug 09:57:44.328 * DB loaded from disk: 0.000 seconds
24188:M 30 Aug 09:57:44.328 * Ready to accept connections
```

2. To start a Redis Server using a configuration file, such as the configuration file we copied from the source code package in the installation receipt, type the following:

   ```
   $ bin/redis-server conf/redis.conf
   ```

3. If you have installed Redis from the repository of an operating system, you can start up Redis using the init.d script:

   ```
   $ /etc/init.d/redis-server start
   ```

4. To run redis-server as a daemon in the background at start up, you can edit the configuration file and set the daemonize parameter to yes and start with this configuration:

   ```
   $ vim conf/redis.conf
   daemonize yes
   $ bin/redis-server conf/redis.conf
   ```

   The message Configuration loaded shown in the following screenshot indicates the configuration has already taken place:

```
redis@gnuhpc-desktop:~$ bin/redis-server conf/redis.conf
23527:C 30 Aug 09:10:58.089 # o000o000o000o Redis is starting o000o000o000o
23527:C 30 Aug 09:10:58.089 # Redis version=4.0.1, bits=64, commit=00000000, modified=0, pid=23527, just started
23527:C 30 Aug 09:10:58.089 # Configuration loaded
```

5. Correspondingly, you may use *Ctrl + C* (if Redis started in the foreground), or use `Kill` + `PID` (if you run Redis in the background) to stop the Redis service:

```
$ kill `pidof redis-server`
```

6. The more graceful and recommended way to stop Redis is calling the shutdown command in `redis-cli`:

```
$ cd /redis
$ bin/redis-cli shutdown
```

7. Redis can also be shut down by the `init.d` script, in case you installed it from the repository of the operating system:

```
$ /etc/init.d/redis-server stop
```

How it works...

The term *instance* in Redis represents a `redis-server` process. Multiple instances of Redis can run on the same host, as long as they use different configurations, such as different binding ports, data persistence paths, log paths, and so on.

Starting and stopping the Redis instance are basic operations. There is not much to note when starting Redis, but for a data service, stopping a Redis service deserves more attention, because as a data store service, it is of great importance for you to learn how to stop the Redis Server gracefully in order to maintain data integrity.

The reason why using the `shutdown` command to stop Redis is highly recommended is that if you care about data integrity and have already set persistence for Redis to save your data in memory to disk (the persistence of Redis will be discussed in Chapter 6, *Persistence*), issuing the `shutdown` command not only terminates the process, but also takes a series of other actions.

First, the `redis-server` will stop all the clients, and then one persistence action will be performed if the persistence has been enabled. Afterwards, it will clean the `.pid` file and `socket` file if there are any, and finally quit the process. By adopting this strategy, Redis does its best to prevent any data loss. Conversely, if the `kill` command is used rudely, to terminate the `redis-server` process, data may get lost because it has not been persisted before the server is shut down.

It should be noted that using `kill` or other process management tools to send a `SIGTERM` signal (15 signal) to the Redis process is basically equivalent to the `shutdown` command for gracefully stopping the `redis-server`.

There's more...

Configuration parameters can be added to the command `redis-server` while starting, which is quite useful when deploying multiple instances on a single host. We can have a single configuration file of common configuration parameters used by multiple instances on the same host. Meanwhile, the unique configuration parameters of each instance can be passed in the command line on startup. This way, the cost of maintaining multiple configuration files is eliminated, and instances can be distinguished easily via `ps` or other system commands.

In addition, you can manage your Redis instance using process management tools such as systemd, supervisord, or Monit, which can also prevent you from messing up when you deploy multiple instances on a single host. All we need to pay attention to are the startup configuration parameters mentioned previously and exit signal handling mechanisms.

See also

- Refer to `https://redis.io/topics/signals` to learn more about how Redis handles various kinds of signals, especially finding out the slight but important differences among these signal handling mechanisms. Additionally, refer to `https://redis.io/commands/shutdown` for more details about gracefully shutting down a Redis instance.
- For the process management tool to control the start up/shutdown of Redis, `https://git.io/v5chR` is an example for systemd configuration for a Redis Server.
- Furthermore, you can refer to `Chapter 6`, *Persistence* for persistence of Redis.

Connecting to Redis with redis-cli

In the development and maintenance of Redis, the `redis-cli` in the `bin` directory is the most commonly used tool. This section gives a brief description of its usage so that readers can get a brief idea of how to connect to and use Redis with `redis-cli`.

Getting ready...

You need an up-and-running Redis Server, as we described in the *Starting and shutting down Redis* recipe in this chapter.

How to do it...

The steps for connecting to Redis using `redis-cli` down a Redis Server are as follows:

1. Open a Terminal and connect to Redis with `redis-cli`:

   ```
   $ bin/redis-cli
   127.0.0.1:6379>
   ```

   The pattern of the preceding prompt is `IP:port`, indicating `redis-cli` has connected to this Redis instance successfully.

2. Send some simple commands for testing. More data types and features will be discussed in the following chapters.

3. First, set two string key-value pairs: `foo value1`, `bar value2`:

   ```
   127.0.0.1:6379> set foo value1
   OK
   127.0.0.1:6379> set bar value2
   OK
   ```

4. After that, fetch the values we just set:

   ```
   127.0.0.1:6379> get foo
   "value1"
   127.0.0.1:6379> get bar
   "value2"
   ```

5. Finally, we terminate the Redis instance by sending the `shutdown` command:

```
$ bin/redis-cli
127.0.0.1:6379> shutdown
not connected>
```

6. After shutting down, the Command Prompt changed to `not connected`. Then, we quit from `redis-cli` and make the connection again with `redis-cli`. The following error message will be shown:

```
not connected>quit
$ bin/redis-cli
Could not connect to Redis at 127.0.0.1:6379: Connection refused
Could not connect to Redis at 127.0.0.1:6379: Connection refused
not connected>
```

How it works...

By default, `redis-cli` connects to a Redis instance running on localhost at default port `6379`. You can also specify the hostname/IP address the Redis Server is running on with the `-h` option. Just make sure that the network connectivity between the `redis-cli` side and the Redis Server side has no problem.

`redis-cli` allows you to specify the port with the `-p` option, if your Redis Server is not running on the default port `6379`. This option is also useful if you would like to connect to multiple Redis instances with different binding ports on the same host.

Also, if a Redis instance is protected by password, the `-a` option can be used to set the password when connecting to Redis.

In addition, if a Unix `socket` file is enabled in Redis, you can connect to the Redis Server simply by using the `-s` option.

There's more...

It is often necessary to do some data prototype verification before hooking up your application to Redis. redis-cli is a very useful tool for this. It provides an interactive command-line interface for you to quickly verify your data design. In the daily maintenance of Redis Server, redis-cli also offers a set of commands, including obtaining the metrics, manipulating system states, and performing configuration settings.

See also

- Refer to Chapter 9, *Administrating Redis* for a more detailed discussion on how to manage a Redis instance with redis-cli

Getting server information

The most comprehensive and important information about a Redis instance can be obtained with redis-cli with the INFO command. In this section, we will see how to use the INFO command to fetch these essential statistics.

Getting ready...

You need an up-and-running Redis Server as we described in the *Starting and shutting down Redis* recipe in this chapter.

How to do it...

Follow these steps to get server information of Redis:

1. Connect to a Redis instance and then use the INFO command:

```
$ bin/redis-cli
127.0.0.1:6379> INFO
```

The result looks as follows:

```
# Server
redis_version:4.0.1
```

```
...
# Clients
connected_clients:1
...
# Memory
used_memory:828352
used_memory_human:808.94K
used_memory_rss:9420800
used_memory_rss_human:8.98M
...

# Persistence
loading:0
rdb_changes_since_last_save:0
rdb_bgsave_in_progress:0
rdb_last_save_time:1504223311
...

# Stats
total_connections_received:1
total_commands_processed:1
instantaneous_ops_per_sec:0
...

# Replication
role:master
connected_slaves:0
...

# CPU
used_cpu_sys:0.01
used_cpu_user:0.00
...

# Cluster
cluster_enabled:0
```

2. You can select a specific section by adding an optional `<section>` parameter.

   For example, you will get the memory metrics by sending `INFO memory` in `redis-cli`:

```
# Memory
used_memory:827328
used_memory_human:807.94K
used_memory_rss:9420800
used_memory_rss_human:8.98M
used_memory_peak:828384
used_memory_peak_human:808.97K
used_memory_peak_perc:99.87%
used_memory_overhead:815118
used_memory_startup:765488
used_memory_dataset:12210
used_memory_dataset_perc:19.74%
total_system_memory:67467218944
total_system_memory_human:62.83G
used_memory_lua:37888
used_memory_lua_human:37.00K
maxmemory:0
maxmemory_human:0B
maxmemory_policy:noeviction
mem_fragmentation_ratio:11.39
mem_allocator:jemalloc-4.0.3
active_defrag_running:0
lazyfree_pending_objects:0
```

3. Another way to get information from a Redis instance is by using `redis-cli INFO` directly in a shell command line. In this way, it is quite handy for piping the output to a script for metrics analysis or performance monitoring.

How it works...

The `INFO` command gives you all the current Redis metrics and the pattern of each metric is `metric-name: metric-value`, which can be easily parsed afterwards.

The following table summarizes the description of each section returned by `INFO`:

Section name	Description
Server	Basic information about the Redis Server
Clients	Status and metrics of client connections
Memory	Overall memory consumption metrics

Persistence	Data persistence related states and metrics
Stats	General statistics
Replication	Status and metrics of master-slave replication
CPU	CPU consumption
Cluster	Status of Redis Cluster
Keyspace	Database related statistics

There's more...

It is a common practice to build a Redis monitor application by getting information from the INFO command periodically.

See also

- Refer to the *Health checking in Redis, Troubleshooting latency issues,* and *Troubleshooting memory issues* sections in Chapter 10, *Troubleshooting Redis* for more detailed use of INFO for Redis maintenance operation and troubleshooting
- You can further refer to https://redis.io/commands/INFO, which lists the meanings of all the metrics returned by INFO

Understanding the Redis Event Model

Redis, known for its high performance, makes the most of a single thread, non-blocking I/O model to process requests rapidly. Therefore, understanding the event model of Redis is essential. As a taster for readers to understand the model, this recipe first shows an echo server demo program built on the asynchronous event library of Redis (ae library). Then we provide important insights into the event processing model of Redis by analyzing the core snippet of source code in Redis.

This recipe includes a lot of C programming practices. So if you feel unfamiliar with the C language, you can skip this recipe if you wish and it won't bother you too much as you read along.

Getting ready...

This recipe involves source code building and debugging. So you need to finish the *Downloading and installing Redis* recipe in this chapter first. For better illustration, an IDE that supports the C programming language is needed. The IDE we use here is CLion in Ubuntu Desktop 16.04.3 LTS. While the CLion IDE is not free, a 30-days free trial is enough for us.

You should also prepare the C compiler and development environment. In Ubuntu, you can issue the following command to install the related packages:

```
$ sudo get update && apt-get install build-essential
```

After installation, you should make sure the version of CMake is 3.5 or above:

```
$ cmake --version
cmake version 3.5.1
CMake suite maintained and supported by Kitware (kitware.com/cmake).
```

How to do it...

To understand the Redis Event Model, take the following steps:

1. Untar the source code package of Redis and build some required dependencies manually rather than using CMake:

```
~$ mkdir coding; cd coding
~/coding$ tar xzvf redis-4.0.1.tar.gz
~/coding$ cd redis-4.0.1/deps/
~/coding/redis-4.0.1/deps$ make lua linenoise hiredis
```

The following screenshot indicates the dependencies have been built successfully:

```
make[1]: Entering directory '/redis/coding/redis-4.0.1/deps/hiredis'
cc -std=c99 -pedantic -c -O3 -fPIC  -Wall -W -Wstrict-prototypes -Wwrite-strings -g -ggdb  net.c
cc -std=c99 -pedantic -c -O3 -fPIC  -Wall -W -Wstrict-prototypes -Wwrite-strings -g -ggdb  hiredis.c
cc -std=c99 -pedantic -c -O3 -fPIC  -Wall -W -Wstrict-prototypes -Wwrite-strings -g -ggdb  sds.c
cc -std=c99 -pedantic -c -O3 -fPIC  -Wall -W -Wstrict-prototypes -Wwrite-strings -g -ggdb  async.c
cc -std=c99 -pedantic -c -O3 -fPIC  -Wall -W -Wstrict-prototypes -Wwrite-strings -g -ggdb  read.c
ar rcs libhiredis.a net.o hiredis.o sds.o async.o read.o
make[1]: Leaving directory '/redis/coding/redis-4.0.1/deps/hiredis'
```

Chapter 1

2. Download the CLion IDE and untar the package to `/redis/coding/`:

```
~/coding$ wget
https://download.jetbrains.8686c.com/cpp/CLion-2017.2.2.tar.gz
~/coding$ tar zxvf CLion-2017.2.2.tar.gz
```

3. Download the demo program package for `redis-server` building and debugging.

4. Untar it into the `redis-4.0.1` directory:

```
~/coding$ tar xzvf echodemo.tar.gz -C redis-4.0.1/
```

Make sure the following files, `CMakeLists.txt` and `echodemo` exist in the `redis-4.0.1` directory:

```
redis@gnuhpc-desktop:~/coding/redis-4.0.1$ ls
00-RELEASENOTES  CMakeFiles     COPYING    Makefile            deps      redis.conf       runtest-sentinel  tests
BUGS             CMakeLists.txt INSTALL    README.md           echodemo  runtest          sentinel.conf     utils
CMakeCache.txt   CONTRIBUTING   MANIFESTO  cmake_install.cmake redis.cbp runtest-cluster  src
```

5. Log in to the Ubuntu desktop and open a Terminal to start CLion:

```
~/coding/clion-2017.2.2$ bin/clion.sh
```

6. After accepting the license, you must make sure that the CMake and debugger are both ready as in the following following:

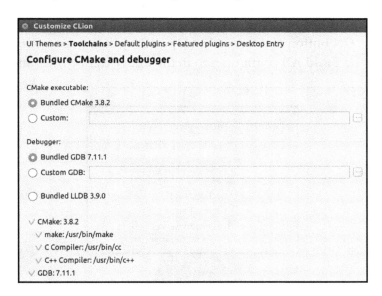

7. Continue with the default options until you reach the following screenshot:

8. Click **Import Project from Sources** and select the `redis-4.0.1` sub-directory in the `coding` directory.

9. Click the **OK** button and then select **Open Project** to open a Redis project.

10. Choose the **Build All** configuration in the upper-right corner and click the **Run** button:

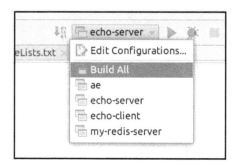

Ignore the error of not specifying an executable target, and click **Run**.

The following logs show you have managed to build both the echo-server/client demo program and redis-server (my-redis-server in this example):

```
/redis/coding/clion-2017.2.2/bin/cmake/bin/cmake --build
/redis/coding/redis-4.0.1/cmake-build-debug --target all -- -j 6
Scanning dependencies of target ae
Scanning dependencies of target my-redis-server
[  1%] Building C object CMakeFiles/ae.dir/src/zmalloc.c.o
...
[ 17%] Building C object CMakeFiles/my-redis-
server.dir/src/blocked.c.o
Scanning dependencies of target echo-server
...
[ 25%] Built target echo-server
[ 26%] Building C object CMakeFiles/my-redis-
server.dir/src/config.c.o
...
[ 31%] Building C object CMakeFiles/my-redis-
server.dir/src/defrag.c.o
[ 32%] Linking C executable echo-client
[ 32%] Built target echo-client
[ 98%] Building C object CMakeFiles/my-redis-
server.dir/src/zmalloc.c.o
[100%] Linking C executable my-redis-server
[100%] Built target my-redis-server
```

11. In case you want to use the command line in the first place to compile the demo, you can perform the following steps:

```
/redis/coding/redis-4.0.1$ cmake
-- The C compiler identification is GNU 5.4.0
...
-- Configuring done
-- Generating done
-- Build files have been written to: /redis/coding/redis-4.0.1
/redis/coding/redis-4.0.1$ make
Scanning dependencies of target my-redis-server
[  1%] Building C object CMakeFiles/my-redis-
server.dir/src/adlist.c.o
[  2%] Building C object CMakeFiles/my-redis-server.dir/src/ae.c.o
...
[ 85%] Building C object CMakeFiles/my-redis-
server.dir/src/zmalloc.c.o
[ 86%] Linking C executable my-redis-server
```

```
[ 86%] Built target my-redis-server
Scanning dependencies of target ae
. . .
[ 92%] Built target ae
Scanning dependencies of target echo-server
. . .
[ 96%] Built target echo-server
Scanning dependencies of target echo-client
. . .
[100%] Built target echo-client
```

12. You can find `echo-server`, `echo-client`, and `my-redis-server` in the `cmake-build-debug` directory under `redis-4.0.1`:

```
redis@gnuhpc-desktop:~/coding/redis-4.0.1/cmake-build-debug$ ls
CMakeCache.txt  CMakeFiles  cmake_install.cmake  dump.rdb  echo-server  libae.a  Makefile  my-redis-server  redis.cbp
```

13. Choose the `echo-server` configuration in the upper-right corner, and click the right arrow button to get it running:

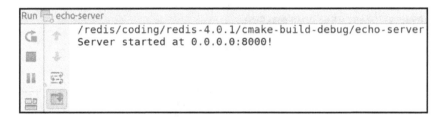

13. Open a Terminal and then connect to the `echo-server` using `nc` (Netcat):

~/coding/redis-4.0.1/cmake-build-debug$ nc 127.0.0.1 8000

14. The message `Hello Client!` will be printed out when the server has started successfully:

```
gnuhpc@gnuhpc-desktop:~$ nc 127.0.0.1 8000
Hello Client!
```

The server logs the connection:

```
/redis/coding/redis-4.0.1/echo-server
Server started at 0.0.0.0:8000!
Accept new connection in acceptProc.
Client info - ip 127.0.0.1 port 34998
AnetNonBlock running successfully
```

15. Type `Hello, please echo!` in nc and press *Enter* to send it out. The same message will be echoed back:

```
gnuhpc@gnuhpc-desktop:~$ nc 127.0.0.1 8000
Hello Client!
Hello, please echo!
Hello, please echo!
```

On the server side, it logs the data, which will be sent back to the client later:

```
Reading Client data from 127.0.0.1:46728!
Size of Data to be writen:20, and the Data is: Hello, please echo!

Sending Client data to 127.0.0.1:46728!
Size of Sent Data:20, and the Data is: Hello, please echo!
```

16. Open another Terminal and then make another connection to the echo-server. A similar result will be obtained on both nc and server side, as shown in the following screenshot:

```
Accept new connection in acceptProc.
Client info - ip 127.0.0.1 port 35004
AnetNonBlock running successfully

Reading Client data from 127.0.0.1:48264!
Size of Data to be writen:13, and the Data is: Hello again!

Sending Client data to 127.0.0.1:48264!
Size of Sent Data:13, and the Data is: Hello again!
```

17. You can debug this server if you wish:

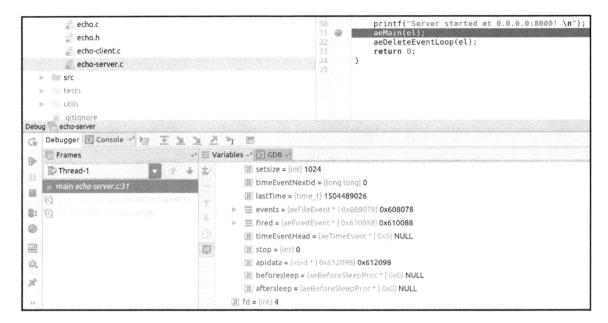

18. You can build and debug `redis-server` (called `my-redis-server` in this example) to dig into the source code in almost the same way as the `echo-server` example. The only thing you have to change is to select the `my-redis-server` run/debug configuration profile:

```
                                              ↓↕  📁 my-redis-server  ▾  ▶  🔧
 echo.c ×   echo-server.c ×   server.c ×   ae.c ×
459 ↳    void aeMain(aeEventLoop *eventLoop) {   eventLoop: 0x776d78
460          eventLoop->stop = 0;
461          while (!eventLoop->stop) {
462              if (eventLoop->beforesleep != NULL)
463                  eventLoop->beforesleep(eventLoop);
464 ⊘              aeProcessEvents(eventLoop, AE_ALL_EVENTS|AE_CALL_AFTER_SLEEP);
465          }
466      }
467
468 ↳    char *aeGetApiName(void) {
469          return aeApiName();
470      }
471
472 ↳    void aeSetBeforeSleepProc(aeEventLoop *eventLoop, aeBeforeSleepProc *beforesleep) {
473          eventLoop->beforesleep = beforesleep;
474      }
```

```
⅀  ⅄  ⅄I  ▦
  ≡ Variables ▸  ▷ GDB ▾
 ⚖  ▼ ≡ eventLoop = {aeEventLoop * | 0x776d78} 0x776d78
        🔢 maxfd = {int} 7
        🔢 setsize = {int} 10128
        🔢 timeEventNextId = {long long} 1
        🔢 lastTime = {time_t} 1504489380
     ▸  ≡ events = {aeFileEvent * | 0x7ffff7f83018} 0x7ffff7f83018
     ▸  ≡ fired = {aeFiredEvent * | 0x776dd8} 0x776dd8
     ▸  ≡ timeEventHead = {aeTimeEvent * | 0x7ac108} 0x7ac108
        🔢 stop = {int} 0
        🔢 apidata = {void * | 0x78aa68} 0x78aa68
        🔢 beforesleep = {aeBeforeSleepProc * | 0x47c2e8} 0x47c2e8
```

How it works...

As mentioned earlier, Redis takes great advantage of the non-blocking, multiplexing I/O model in its main processing single thread, although there are some circumstances where Redis spawns threads or child processes to perform certain tasks.

Redis contains a simple but powerful asynchronous event library called ae to wrap different operating system's polling facilities, such as epoll, kqueue, select, and so on.

So what's a polling facility of an operating system? Let's take a real-life scenario to illustrate it. Imagine you have ordered five dishes in a restaurant. You have to fetch your dishes by yourself at a waiting window, and you want to get them as soon as possible once the dishes get done because you are hungry. You may have three strategies for this scenario:

- You walk to the waiting window all by yourself from time to time in a short period to check whether each dish in the order list is ready.
- You hire five people. Each person walks to the waiting window for you to check whether one of the dishes you ordered is ready.
- You just sit at the table, waiting for the notification. The restaurant provides a dish-ready notification service for free which means that the waiter will tell you which dish is ready, once a dish gets done. When you get the notification, you fetch it by yourself.

Considering the time and efforts it takes, the third option is the best one, obviously.

The polling facility of an operating system works in a similarly way as the third option does. For the simplicity of this section, we only take the epoll API in Linux as an example. First, you can call epoll_create to tell the kernel that you would like to use epoll. Then, you call epoll_ctl to tell the kernel the file descriptors (**FD**) and what type of event you're interested in when an update occurs. After that, epoll_wait gets called to wait for certain events of the FDs you set in epoll_ctl. The kernel will send a notification to you when the FDs get updated. The only thing you have to do is to create handlers for certain events.

The whole multiplexing process is shown as follows:

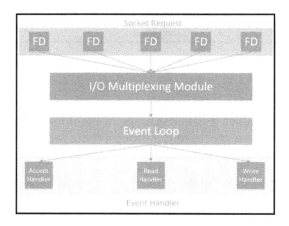

I/O multiplexing model

The ae library in Redis basically follows the preceding procedure to process the requests. In the echo-server example, we create an event loop by calling aeCreateEventLoop firstly. Then a TCP server is built via anetTcpServer for network binding and listening. We call anetNonBlock to set the non-block I/O action for this socket FD. After that, we specify the acceptance event handler acceptProc for the socket FD using the event loop created in aeCreateEventLoop. Once a TCP connection is established, the server will trigger the action in acceptProc. In acceptProc, we use anetTcpAccept to accept the connection request and register readable events of the socket FD for readProc. Then readProc gets called, in which we read the data sent to the server and register the writable event of the socket FD. The event loop then receives the writable event to fire the writeProc to send back the data to the socket client.

Redis works in pretty much the same way as this echo-server does. In the main function of server.c, aeCreateEventLoop, anetTcpServer, and anetNonBlock get called in the initServer method to initialize the server:

```
1812    createSharedObjects();
1813    adjustOpenFilesLimit();
1814    server.el = aeCreateEventLoop(server.maxclients+CONFIG_FDSET_INCR);
1815    if (server.el == NULL) {
1816        serverLog(LL_WARNING,
1817            "Failed creating the event loop. Error message: '%s'",
1818            strerror(errno));
1819        exit(1);
1820    }
1821    server.db = zmalloc(sizeof(redisDb)*server.dbnum);
1822
1823    /* Open the TCP listening socket for the user commands. */
1824    if (server.port != 0 &&
1825        listenToPort(server.port,server.ipfd,&server.ipfd_count) == C_ERR)
1826        exit(1);
1827
1828    /* Open the listening Unix domain socket. */
1829    if (server.unixsocket != NULL) {
1830        unlink(server.unixsocket); /* don't care if this fails */
1831        server.sofd = anetUnixServer(server.neterr,server.unixsocket,
1832            server.unixsocketperm, server.tcp_backlog);
1833        if (server.sofd == ANET_ERR) {
1834            serverLog(LL_WARNING, "Opening Unix socket: %s", server.neterr);
1835            exit(1);
1836        }
1837        anetNonBlock(NULL,server.sofd);
```

The acceptance handler is also set in the `initServer` method, as the following screenshot shows:

```
/* Create an event handler for accepting new connections in TCP and Unix
 * domain sockets. */
for (j = 0; j < server.ipfd_count; j++) {
    if (aeCreateFileEvent(server.el, server.ipfd[j], AE_READABLE,
        acceptTcpHandler,NULL) == AE_ERR)
        {
            serverPanic(
                "Unrecoverable error creating server.ipfd file event.");
        }
}
if (server.sofd > 0 && aeCreateFileEvent(server.el,server.sofd,AE_READABLE,
    acceptUnixHandler,NULL) == AE_ERR) serverPanic("Unrecoverable error creating server.sofd file event.");
```

Once the server is initialized, the `aeMain` method gets called:

```
3842    aeSetBeforeSleepProc(server.el,beforeSleep);
3843    aeSetAfterSleepProc(server.el,afterSleep);
3844    aeMain(server.el);
3845    aeDeleteEventLoop(server.el);
3846    return 0;
```

In the `aeMain` method, `asProcessEvents` is called to process the events continuously:

```
459    void aeMain(aeEventLoop *eventLoop) {
460        eventLoop->stop = 0;
461        while (!eventLoop->stop) {
462            if (eventLoop->beforesleep != NULL)
463                eventLoop->beforesleep(eventLoop);
464            aeProcessEvents(eventLoop, AE_ALL_EVENTS|AE_CALL_AFTER_SLEEP);
465        }
466    }
```

There's more...

It's clear that no thread or sub-process spawns or interacts in the polling process. Therefore, the key benefit of this model is that it's a light context switch I/O model, so that it's not costly for context switching. A number of limitations need to be considered for this processing model. The most common problem you may encounter is latency. In the polling model, Redis won't process any other commands until the one being processed finishes. So keep in mind from now on that an unexpected latency will be the first headache for you when using Redis.

Other polling methods, such as poll, select, and so on, are not discussed here due to the limited area. If you are working on platforms other than Linux, you can debug the source code to learn more about the polling facility on that platform.

See also

- Refer to the *Identifying slow operations/queries using SLOWLOG* and *Troubleshooting latency issues*, sections in `Chapter 10`, *Troubleshooting Redis,* for more detailed approaches to Redis latency troubleshooting
- Refer to `Appendix`, *Windows Environment Setup* if you want to build and debug the source code in Windows
- You can also further refer to the following links:
  - `https://redis.io/topics/internals-eventlib` offers you a deep insight into the event library
  - `https://redis.io/topics/internals-rediseventlib` describes the details of the Redis event library
- If you are working on operating systems other than Ubuntu, you can refer to `https://cmake.org/install/` to install CMake

Understanding the Redis protocol

As we described in the previous recipe, Redis is merely a non-blocking, I/O multiplexing TCP server that accepts and processes requests from clients. In other words, in spite of the complexity within the Redis Server, you can talk to Redis over the TCP connection in various languages. The term *protocol* stands for the language used between a server and a client in the networking communication. As for Redis, **REdis Serialization Protocol** (**RESP**) is the protocol. In this recipe, we'll see how the RESP works in Redis.

One thing should be noted: Even at first glance, it's a little bit advanced for a beginner to go through this recipe. However, we do believe that learning the RESP, as basic knowledge, is not that difficult and it will be of benefit to you, in that understanding the various kinds of clients and proxies implemented in different programming languages will no longer be a mystery to you.

Of course, you can skip this recipe if you like and it won't bother you too much when reading the following chapters.

Getting ready...

You need an up-and-running Redis Server, as we described in the *Starting and shutting down Redis* recipe in this chapter.

The tool, netcat (nc) should be installed. In this recipe, we have the nc command in Ubuntu 16.04.3 LTS for netcat. You can use Cygwin to install netcat if you work under Windows.

How to do it...

To understand the Redis protocol, take the following steps:

1. Send the PING command to the Redis Server with netcat:

   Instead of sending the command PING in redis-cli, let's build the command using RESP:

   ```
   $ echo -e "*1\r\n\$4\r\nPING\r\n" | nc  127.0.0.1 6379
   +PONG
   ```

2. Use the SET and INCR commands to set an integer and increase it by one:

   ```
   $ echo -e "*3\r\n\$3\r\nset\r\n\$5\r\nmykey\r\n\$1\r\n1\r\n" | nc
   127.0.0.1 6379
   +OK
   $ echo -e "*2\r\n\$4\r\nINCR\r\n\$5\r\nmykey\r\n" | nc 127.0.0.1
   6379
   :2
   ```

   You may encounter the following error when you send a non-existent command:

   ```
   $ echo -e "*2\r\n\$3\r\ngot\r\n\$3\r\nfoo\r\n" | nc 127.0.0.1 6379
   -ERR unknown command 'got'
   ```

   Multi-commands can be combined and sent to the Redis Server in a single network transmission:

   ```
   $ echo -e
   "*3\r\n\$3\r\nset\r\n\$3\r\nfoo\r\n\$3\r\nbar\r\n*2\r\n\$3\r\nget\r
   \n\$3\r\nfoo\r\n" | nc 127.0.0.1 6379
   +OK
   $3
   bar
   ```

How it works...

There is a big chance that you will go through these commands in tremendous confusion. As we stated in the *Getting ready* section in this recipe, these commands are the language in which the Redis Server and client talk to each other. It's easy for you to learn them in that there are only five types in RESP.

Let's take a look at each command.

First, we sent *1\r\n\$4\r\nPING\r\n to the Redis Server. The command begins with an asterisk indicating this is an arrays type.

Look at the following:

- 1 stands for the size of this array.
- \r\n (CRLF) is the terminator of each part in RESP.
- The backslash before $4 is the escape character for the $ sign. $4 tells you that the following is a bulk string type of four characters long.
- PING is the string itself.
- +PONG is the string the PING command returned. The plus sign tells you that it's a simple string type.

The next type we talk about is the integer type. Look at :2, which is the result returned by the INCR command. The colon before the number indicates this is an integer.

Sometimes, the server may return an error type message beginning with a minus when a non-existent command has been processed, such as the got command shown previously.

In addition, for the consideration of performance, you may send multiple commands in a single call to the Redis Server using RESP.

To sum up, the client sends commands to a Redis Server as a RESP array of bulk strings. Then the server replies with one of the five aforementioned RESP types accordingly.

See also

- Refer to `https://redis.io/topics/protocol` for a more detailed description of the Redis protocol.
- Various kinds of Redis clients and proxies can be found on GitHub. For example, you can refer to `https://github.com/tonivade/resp-server` for a Java Netty implementation of RESP.
- Another example is `https://github.com/tidwall/resp` which contains reader, writer, and server implementations for the RESP in Golang.

2
Data Types

In this chapter, we will cover the following recipes:

- Using the string data type
- Using the list data type
- Using the hash data type
- Using the set data type
- Using the sorted set data type
- Using the HyperLogLog data type
- Using the Geo data type
- Managing keys

Introduction

Data type is the core concept when it comes to application design and development with Redis. Unlike RDBMS, there is no table or schema you need to worry about in Redis. When it comes to how to organize your data in Redis, the one thing you should consider first is what data types natively supported by Redis fit your scenario best. Moreover, you have no way to manipulate your data in Redis with SQL, as in a relational database. Instead, you issue commands directly on the target data with the API, accompanied by the data. Therefore, another thing you need to think about is whether the operations of a certain data type in Redis can satisfy your business requirements.

In this chapter, we will look at all data types and important operations related to Redis. In order to better illustrate the data types and their operations, a Yelp-like demo application (we'll call it *Relp* for the demo application in this book) design will be shown. Relp is an application for user reviews and recommendations of top restaurants, shopping malls, and other services. Within Relp, you can browse various restaurants in a city, find the top ten gymnasiums within a certain distance, post ratings and review comments for local services, and so on. All the data we are going to store and operate in Relp will be completely usable in Redis.

Using the string data type

The string type is the most common and useful data type in programming languages and applications. It is also the fundamental data type of Redis, in which all keys must be strings. This recipe demonstrates the basic commands to manipulate strings in Redis.

Getting ready...

You need to finish the installation of the Redis Server, as we described in the *Downloading and installing Redis* recipe in `Chapter 1`, *Getting Started with Redis*, and connect to the Redis Server by `redis-cli`.

How to do it...

To understand how to use the string data type, take the following steps:

1. Open a Terminal and connect to Redis with `redis-cli`.
2. To associate a string value to a key, use the `SET` command. In Relp, we can use the restaurant name as the key and its address as the value; for example, if we would like to set the address for the restaurant `"Extreme Pizza"`:

```
127.0.0.1:6379> SET "Extreme Pizza" "300 Broadway, New York, NY"
OK
```

3. String values can be retrieved by simply using the GET command:

```
127.0.0.1:6379> GET "Extreme Pizza"
"300 Broadway, New York, NY"
```

4. Executing GET on a non-existent key will return (nil):

```
127.0.0.1:6379> GET "Yummy Pizza"
(nil)
```

5. The STRLEN command returns the length of the string; for example, if we would like to know the length of the address "Extreme Pizza":

```
127.0.0.1:6379> STRLEN "Extreme Pizza"
(integer) 26
```

6. Executing STRLEN on a non-existent key will return 0:

Redis also provides a couple of commands to manipulate strings directly without using GET to retrieve the value, and SET to assign it back:

- To append to the string value of a key, use the APPEND command:

```
127.0.0.1:6379> APPEND "Extreme Pizza" " 10011"
(integer) 32
127.0.0.1:6379> GET "Extreme Pizza"
"300 Broadway, New York, NY 10011"
```

- To overwrite part of the string value, use SETRANGE; for example, if we would like to update the address of "Extreme Pizza":

```
127.0.0.1:6379> SETRANGE "Extreme Pizza" 14 "Washington, DC 20009"
(integer) 34
127.0.0.1:6379> GET "Extreme Pizza"
"300 Broadway, Washington, DC 20009"
```

How it works...

SET and GET may be the most frequently used commands in Redis. The format of SET is very simple:

```
SET <key> <value>.
```

Redis returns OK if the SET command was executed successfully. The APPEND command appends a string to the end of the existing string and returns the length of the new string. If the key does not exist, Redis will create an empty string for the key at first, then execute APPEND. The SETRANGE command overwrites part of the string, starting at the specified offset, and to the end of the entire string. String offset in Redis starts with 0. SETRANGE returns the length of the new string after the replacement.

There's more...

If there is already a value associated with the key, the SET command overwrites the value. Sometimes we don't want the value to be overwritten blindly if the key exists; one thing we can do is use the EXIST command to test the existence of the key before executing SET. However, Redis provides a command SETNX (short for SET if not exists), which can be used to set the value for a key, but only if the key does not exist, in an atomic operation. SETNX returns 1 if the key was successfully set, and returns 0 if the key already exists, so the old value will not be overwritten:

```
127.0.0.1:6379> SETNX "Lobster Palace" "437 Main St, Chicago, IL"
(integer) 1
127.0.0.1:6379> SETNX "Extreme Pizza" "100 Broadway, New York, NY"
(integer) 0
```

The NX option in the SET command is the same as SETNX. Conversely, there is also an XX option in SET which makes the command only set the key if it already exists.

We can set and get multiple keys for their values at once by using MSET and MGET. The advantage of using MSET is the entire operation is atomic, which means all the keys are set in one trip between client and server. Therefore, we could save the network overhead by using the MSET command rather than issuing multiple SET commands. Here's the format of the MSET and MGET commands:

```
MSET key value [key value...]
MGET key value [key value...]

127.0.0.1:6379> MSET "Sakura Sushi" "123 Ellis St, Chicago, IL" "Green
Curry Thai" "456 American Way, Seattle, WA"
OK

127.0.0.1:6379> MGET "Sakura Sushi" "Green Curry Thai" "nonexistent"
1) "123 Ellis St, Chicago, IL"
2) "456 American Way, Seattle, WA"
3) (nil)
```

It is worth mentioning how strings are encoded in Redis objects internally. Redis uses three different encodings to store string objects and will decide the encoding automatically per string value:

- `int`: For strings representing 64-bit signed integers
- `embstr`: For strings whose length is less or equal to 44 bytes (this used to be 39 bytes in Redis 3.x); this type of encoding is more efficient in memory usage and performance
- `raw`: For strings whose length is greater than 44 bytes

We can use the `OBJECT` command to inspect the internal encoding representation of Redis value objects associated with keys:

```
127.0.0.1:6379> SET myKey 12345
OK
127.0.0.1:6379> OBJECT ENCODING myKey
"int"
127.0.0.1:6379> SET myKey "a string"
OK
127.0.0.1:6379> OBJECT ENCODING myKey
"embstr"
127.0.0.1:6379> SET myKey "a long string whose length is more than 39
bytes"
OK
127.0.0.1:6379> OBJECT ENCODING myKey
"raw"
```

See also

- The `OBJECT` command can do more than encoding inspection, as it also allows us to inspect `refcount` and `idletime` for Redis objects, (https://redis.io/commands/object).
- We are unable to demonstrate all Redis commands for the string data type in this recipe as space is limited. Refer to https://redis.io/commands#string for all Redis string commands.
- Refer to the *Managing keys* section of this chapter for key management, including listing, renaming, and deleting keys.

Using the list data type

The list data type is a very useful type in application development, as a list stores a sequence of objects, and can be also used as a stack or queue. In Redis, the value associated with a key can be a list of strings. A list in Redis is more like a doubly linked list in the data structure world. This recipe demonstrates the basic commands to manipulate lists in Redis.

Getting ready...

You need to finish the installation of the Redis Server, as we described in the *Downloading and installing Redis* recipe in Chapter 1, *Getting Started with Redis*, and connect to the Redis Server by redis-cli.

How to do it...

To understand how to use the list data type, take the following steps:

1. Open a Terminal and connect to Redis with redis-cli.

2. Here, we are going to use a list to store favorite restaurants. To insert two restaurant names to the left end of a list, use LPUSH:

   ```
   127.0.0.1:6379> LPUSH favorite_restaurants "PF Chang's" "Olive
   Garden"
   (integer) 2
   ```

3. To get all restaurant names in the list, use LRANGE:

   ```
   127.0.0.1:6379> LRANGE favorite_restaurants 0 -1
   1) "Olive Garden"
   2) "PF Chang's"
   ```

4. To insert a restaurant name to the right end of a list, use RPUSH:

   ```
   127.0.0.1:6379> RPUSH favorite_restaurants "Outback Steakhouse"
   "Red Lobster"
   (integer) 4
   127.0.0.1:6379> LRANGE favorite_restaurants 0 -1
   1) "Olive Garden"
   2) "PF Chang's"
   3) "Outback Steakhouse"
   4) "Red Lobster"
   ```

5. To insert a new restaurant name after `"PF Chang's"`, use `LINSERT`:

```
127.0.0.1:6379> LINSERT favorite_restaurants AFTER "PF Chang's"
"Indian Tandoor"
(integer) 5
127.0.0.1:6379> LRANGE favorite_restaurants 0 -1
1) "Olive Garden"
2) "PF Chang's"
3) "Indian Tandoor"
4) "Outback Steakhouse"
5) "Red Lobster"
```

6. To retrieve the restaurant name at index position 3 in the list, use `LINDEX`:

```
127.0.0.1:6379> LINDEX favorite_restaurants 3
"Outback Steakhouse"
```

How it works...

As we mentioned previously, a list in Redis is similar to a doubly linked list, so that new elements can be added to a list by using the following three commands:

- `LPUSH`: Prepend elements to the left end of the list
- `RPUSH`: Append elements to the right end of the list
- `LINSERT`: Insert elements before or after a pivotal element in the list

`LPUSH`, `RPUSH`, and `LINSERT` return the length of the list after insertion. It is not necessary to initialize an empty list for a key before pushing elements. If we push elements to the list for a non-existent key, Redis will create an empty list first and associate it with the key. Similarly, we don't need to delete keys whose associated list is empty, as Redis will do the recycling for us.

> If you would like to push elements to a list only if the list exists, you can use the `LPUSHX` and `RPUSHX` commands.

To remove an element from a list, we can use LPOP or RPOP, which removes the first element from the left or right end of the list, and returns its value. Executing LPOP or RPOP on a non_existent key will return (nil):

```
127.0.0.1:6379> LPOP favorite_restaurants
"Olive Garden"
127.0.0.1:6379> RPOP favorite_restaurants
"Red Lobster"
127.0.0.1:6379> LPOP non_existent
(nil)
```

To retrieve elements from a list, we can use the LINDEX command to get one element at a specified index, and the LRANGE command to get a range of elements.

What is the convention of a list index in Redis?
Suppose there are *N* elements in the list; list indexes can be specified as *0 ~ N-1* from left to right and *-1 ~ -N* from right to left. Therefore, *0 ~ -1* represents the entire list. The convention of a Redis list index is very similar to that of a Python list, however, the Python list is more like an array in other programming languages.

The LTRIM command can be used to remove multiple elements in a list while only keeping the range of the list specified by *start* and *end* indexes:

```
127.0.0.1:6379> LRANGE favorite_restaurants 0 -1
1) "PF Chang's"
2) "Indian Tandoor"
3) "Outback Steakhouse"
127.0.0.1:6379> LTRIM favorite_restaurants 1 -1
OK
127.0.0.1:6379> LRANGE favorite_restaurants 0 -1
1) "Indian Tandoor"
2) "Outback Steakhouse"
```

The LSET command can be used to set the value of an element in the list at the specified index:

```
127.0.0.1:6379> LSET favorite_restaurants 1 "Longhorn Steakhouse"
OK
127.0.0.1:6379> LRANGE favorite_restaurants 0 -1
1) "Indian Tandoor"
2) "Longhorn Steakhouse"
```

There's more...

There are blocking versions for the command LPOP and RPOP: BLPOP and BRPOP. They both pop an element from the left or right end of the list, such as the corresponding non-blocking commands, but the client will be blocked if the list is empty. A timeout in seconds has to be specified in these blocking pop commands for the maximum time to wait. Zero timeout means waiting forever. This feature is useful in the job dispatcher scenario, where multiple workers (Redis Clients) are waiting for the dispatcher to assign new jobs. The workers just use BLPOP or BRPOP on a job list in Redis. Whenever there is a new job, the dispatcher pushes the job into the list, and one of the workers will pick it up.

Let's open two more Terminals, which represent two Redis Clients, worker-1 and worker-2, and let them connect to the same Redis Server, using redis-cli. Let the original Redis Client act as the dispatcher.

From both worker clients, execute BRPOP on the same list job_queue to wait for new jobs:

```
worker-1> BRPOP job_queue 0
worker-2> BRPOP job_queue 0
```

From the dispatcher, push a new element into the list:

```
dispatcher> LPUSH job_queue job1
(integer) 1
```

Because worker-1 executed BRPOP before worker-2, worker-1 is unblocked first and gets job1:

```
worker-1> BRPOP job_queue 0
1) "job_queue"
2) "job1"
(170.81s)
```

While worker-2 is still being blocked, let's push two more elements into the list from the dispatcher:

```
dispatcher> LPUSH job_queue job2 job3
```

worker-2 is unblocked and gets job2, while job3 is left in the list, waiting to be picked up:

```
worker-2> BRPOP job_queue 0
1) "job_queue"
2) "job2"
(358.12s)
```

```
dispatcher> LRANGE job_queue 0 -1
1) "job3"
```

Redis uses `quicklist` encoding internally to store list objects. There are two configuration options to tweak the memory storage of the list object:

- `list-max-ziplist-size`: The maximum size of an internal list node in a list entry. In most cases, just leave the default value.
- `list-compress-depth`: The list compress policy. If you are going to use the head and the tail elements of a list in Redis, you can utilize this setting to have a better list compression ratio.

See also

- We did not cover all Redis list commands in this recipe. For a complete command reference, refer to `https://redis.io/commands#list`.

Using the hash data type

The hash data type represents mapping relationships between fields and values, just like maps or dictionaries in some programming languages. The Redis dataset itself can be viewed as a hash, where keys of strings are mapped to data objects such as strings and lists, as we have seen in the previous two recipes. The data objects of Redis can again use hashes, whose fields and values must be strings. To distinguish from Redis keys, we use fields to denote keys in Redis hash-value objects. The hash is a perfect data type for storing an object's properties. In this recipe, we will use hashes to store restaurants' information, such as address, phone number, rating, and so on.

Getting ready...

You need to finish the installation of the Redis Server, as we described in the *Downloading and installing Redis* recipe in `Chapter 1`, *Getting Started with Redis*, and connect to the Redis Server by `redis-cli`.

How to do it...

To understand how to use the hash data type, take the following steps:

1. Open a Terminal and connect to Redis with `redis-cli`.

2. Now, let's set the information properties of the `"Kyoto Ramen"` restaurant using the `HMSET` command:

    ```
    127.0.0.1:6379> HMSET "Kyoto Ramen" "address" "801 Mission St, San
    Jose, CA" "phone" "555-123-6543" "rating" "5.0"
    OK
    ```

3. Use the `HMGET` command to retrieve values in a hash:

    ```
    127.0.0.1:6379> HMGET "Kyoto Ramen" "address" "phone" "rating"
    1) "801 Mission St, San Jose, CA"
    2) "555-123-6543"
    3) "5.0"
    ```

4. To retrieve the value for a single field, use `HGET`:

    ```
    127.0.0.1:6379> HGET "Kyoto Ramen" "rating"
    "5.0"
    ```

5. To test if a field exists in the hash, use `HEXISTS`:

    ```
    127.0.0.1:6379> HEXISTS "Kyoto Ramen" "phone"
    (integer) 1
    127.0.0.1:6379> HEXISTS "Kyoto Ramen" "hours"
    (integer) 0
    ```

6. To get all the fields and values in a hash, the `HGETALL` command can be used:

    ```
    127.0.0.1:6379> HGETALL "Kyoto Ramen"
    1) "address"
    2) "801 Mission St, San Jose, CA"
    3) "phone"
    4) "555-123-6543"
    5) "rating"
    6) "5.0"
    ```

> It is not recommended you use `HGETALL` for large hashes; the reason for this will be explained later.

7. Similarly, there is an HSET command which sets the value for a single field. This command can be used to modify the value for an existing field or add a new field:

```
127.0.0.1:6379> HSET "Kyoto Ramen" "rating" "4.9"
(integer) 0
127.0.0.1:6379> HSET "Kyoto Ramen" "status" "open"
(integer) 1

127.0.0.1:6379> HMGET "Kyoto Ramen" "rating" "status"
1) "4.9"
2) "open"
```

8. To delete fields from a hash, use the HDEL command:

```
127.0.0.1:6379> HDEL "Kyoto Ramen" "address" "phone"
(integer) 2
127.0.0.1:6379> HGETALL "Kyoto Ramen"
1) "rating"
2) "4.9"
```

How it works...

Similar to what we mentioned in the *Using list data type* section, we don't have to initialize an empty hash before adding fields. Redis will do this automatically with HSET and HMSET. Similarly, Redis will do the clean-up work when a hash is empty.

By default, HSET and HMSET will overwrite any existing fields. The HSETNX command, which sets the value of a field only if the field does not exist, can be used to prevent the default overwriting behavior of HSET:

```
127.0.0.1:6379> HSETNX "Kyoto Ramen" "phone" "555-555-0001"
(integer) 0
127.0.0.1:6379> HGET "Kyoto Ramen" "phone"
"555-123-6543"
```

HMGET and HGET will return (nil) for any non-existent key or field:

```
127.0.0.1:6379> HMGET "Kyoto Ramen" "rating" "hours"
1) "4.9"
2) (nil)

127.0.0.1:6379> HGET "Little Sheep Mongolian" "address"
(nil)
```

There's more...

The maximum number of fields that can be put in a hash is 2^{32} -1. If there are a large number of fields in a hash, executing the HGETALL command may block the Redis Server. In this case, we can use HSCAN to incrementally retrieve all the fields and values.

HSCAN is one of the Redis SCAN commands (SCAN, HSCAN, SSCAN, ZSCAN), which incrementally iterate over elements, and therefore do not block the server. The command is a cursor-based iterator, so you need to specify a cursor each time when calling the command, and the starting cursor is 0. When the command is finished, Redis returns a list of elements along with a new cursor, which can be used in the next iteration.

HSCAN can be called in the following format:

- HSCAN key cursor [MATCH pattern] [COUNT number].
- The MATCH option can be used to match fields using a glob-style pattern.
- The COUNT option is just a hint on how many elements should return on each iteration. Redis does not guarantee that the number of elements returned matches the COUNT. The default value of COUNT is 10.

Imagine we have a very big hash in which there are millions, or even more, fields. Let's use HSCAN to iterate over its fields that contain the keyword garden:

```
127.0.0.1:6379> HSCAN restaurant_ratings 0 MATCH *garden*
1) "309"
2) 1) "panda garden"
   2) "3.9"
   3) "chang's garden"
   4) "4.5"
   5) "rice garden"
   6) "4.8"
```

We can use the new cursor 309, which is returned by the server to start a new scan.

```
127.0.0.1:6379> HSCAN restaurant_ratings 309 MATCH *garden*
1) "0"
2) 1) "szechuwan garden"
   2) "4.9"
   3) "garden wok restaurant"
   4) "4.7"
   5) "win garden"
   6) "4.0"
   7) "east garden restaurant"
   8) "4.6"
```

Notice that the new cursor returned by the server is 0, which means the entire scan is completed.

Redis uses two encodings internally to store hash objects:

- ziplist: For hashes whose length is less than list-max-ziplist-entries (default: 512) and the size of every element in the list is less than list-max-ziplist-value (default: 64 bytes) in configuration. ziplist is used to save space for small hashes.
- hashtable: The default encoding when ziplist encoding cannot be used per configuration.

See also

- For SCAN commands in Redis, refer to https://redis.io/commands/scan

Using the set data type

The set data type is a collection of unique and unordered objects. It is often used in applications for membership testing, duplicates removal, and math operations (union, intersection, and difference). Redis value objects can be string set. In this recipe, we will store restaurants' tags in a Redis set and demonstrate basic commands Redis provides to manipulate a set.

Getting ready...

You need to finish the installation of the Redis Server, as we described in the *Downloading and installing Redis* recipe in Chapter 1, *Getting Started with Redis*, and connect to the Redis Server by redis-cli.

How to do it...

To understand how to use the Set data type, take the following steps:

1. Open a Terminal and connect to Redis with redis-cli

2. To add tags for the "Original Buffalo Wings" restaurant, use the following SADD command:

```
127.0.0.1:6379> SADD "Original Buffalo Wings" "affordable" "spicy"
"busy" "great taste"(integer) 4
```

3. To test if an element is in the set, use SISMEMBER:

```
127.0.0.1:6379> SISMEMBER "Original Buffalo Wings" "busy"(integer)
1127.0.0.1:6379> SISMEMBER "Original Buffalo Wings"
"costly"(integer) 0
```

4. To use SREM to remove elements from the set, let's remove "busy" and "spicy" from the restaurant's tags:

```
127.0.0.1:6379> SREM "Original Buffalo Wings" "busy"
"spicy"(integer) 2127.0.0.1:6379> SISMEMBER "Original Buffalo
Wings" "busy"(integer) 0127.0.0.1:6379> SISMEMBER "Original Buffalo
Wings" "spicy"(integer) 0
```

5. To get the number of members in the set, use the SCARD command:

```
127.0.0.1:6379> SCARD "Original Buffalo Wings"
(integer) 2
```

How it works...

Similar to lists and hashes, Redis creates an empty set for us when executing SADD, if the set for the key does not exist. Redis also cleans up empty sets for keys automatically.

There's more...

The maximum number of elements that can be put in a Redis set is $2^{23} - 1$.

There is a command called SMEMBERS that can be used to list all elements in a set, however, similar to what we mentioned for HGETALL in *Using the hash data type*, using SMEMBERS in a large set may block the server, and therefore is not recommended. SSCAN should be used instead for large sets. The usage of SSCAN is very similar to the HSCAN command, which we introduced in *Using the hash data type*.

Redis provides a group of commands for union (SUNION, SUNIONSTORE), intersection (SINTER, SINTERSTORE) and difference (SDIFF, SDIFFSTORE) operations between sets. The commands without the STORE postfix simply return the resulting set of corresponding operations, while the STORE commands store the result into a destination key.

Here's an example of using SINTER and SINTERSTORE. Let's add tags to another restaurant, "Big Bear Wings", and get the common tags of "Original Buffalo Wings" and "Big Bear Wings":

```
127.0.0.1:6379> SMEMBERS "Original Buffalo Wings"
1) "affordable"
2) "great taste"
127.0.0.1:6379> SADD "Big Bear Wings" "affordable" "spacious" "great music"
(integer) 3
127.0.0.1:6379> SINTER "Original Buffalo Wings" "Big Bear Wings"
1) "affordable"

127.0.0.1:6379> SINTERSTORE "common_tags" "Original Buffalo Wings" "Big Bear Wings"
(integer) 1
127.0.0.1:6379> SMEMBERS "common_tags"
1) "affordable"
```

Redis uses two encodings internally to store set objects:

- intset: For sets in which all elements are integers and the number of elements in the set is less than set-max-intset-entries (default: 512) in configuration. intset is used to save space for small hashes.
- hashtable: The default encoding when intset encoding cannot be used per configuration.

Using the sorted set data type

Compared to the data type set introduced in the previous recipe, sorted list is a similar but more complex one in Redis. The word Sorted means each element in this kind of set owns a weight that can be used for sorting, and you can retrieve the elements from the set in order. It's convenient to take advantage of this natively sorted feature in some scenarios for which the sorting is needed all the time. In this recipe, we'll see how to manipulate sorted set.

Getting ready...

You need to finish the installation of the Redis Server, as we described in the *Downloading and installing Redis* recipe in `Chapter 1`, *Getting Started with Redis*, and connect to the Redis Server by `redis-cli`.

How to do it...

To understand how to use the sorted set data type, take the following steps:

1. Open a Terminal and connect to Redis with `redis-cli`.
2. To make a ranking for the local restaurants in Relp, use the following:
   1. The first step we will take is to put the voting rate and the name of each restaurant into a sorted set. The command we use here is `ZADD`:

      ```
      127.0.0.1:6379> ZADD ranking:restaurants 100 "Olive
      Garden" 23 "PF Chang's" 34 "Outback Steakhouse" 45 "Red
      Lobster" 88 "Longhorn Steakhouse"
        (integer) 5
      ```

   2. And then you can retrieve this ranking by using the command `ZREVRANGE`:

      ```
      127.0.0.1:6379> ZREVRANGE ranking:restaurants 0 -1
      WITHSCORES
        1) "Olive Garden"
        2) "100"
        3) "Longhorn Steakhouse"
        4) "88"
        5) "Red Lobster"
        6) "45"
        7) "Outback Steakhouse"
        8) "34"
        9) "PF Chang's"
       10) "23"
      ```

   3. If one user in Relp upvotes a restaurant in Relp, you can use the command `ZINCRBY` to increase the voting to the restaurant in this ranking:

      ```
      127.0.0.1:6379> ZINCRBY ranking:restaurants 1 "Red Lobster"
      "46"
      ```

4. If one user would like to browse the ranking and the number of votings for a specific restaurant, the command ZREVRANK and ZSCORE will return the result:

```
127.0.0.1:6379> ZREVRANK ranking:restaurants "Olive Garden"
(integer) 0

127.0.0.1:6379> ZSCORE ranking:restaurants  "Olive Garden"
"100"
```

5. In case there is another more reliable restaurant ranking from a different data source and the combination for these two rankings is needed, the command ZUNIONSTORE can be used:

```
127.0.0.1:6379> ZADD ranking2:restaurants 50 "Olive Garden"
33 "PF Chang's" 55 "Outback Steakhouse" 190 "Kung Pao
House"
(integer) 4

127.0.0.1:6379> ZUNIONSTORE totalranking 2
ranking:restaurants ranking2:restaurants WEIGHTS 1 2
(integer) 6

127.0.0.1:6379> ZREVRANGE totalranking 0 -1 WITHSCORES
 1) "Kung Pao House"
 2) "380"
 3) "Olive Garden"
 4) "200"
 5) "Outback Steakhouse"
 6) "144"
 7) "PF Chang's"
 8) "89"
 9) "Longhorn Steakhouse"
10) "88"
11) "Red Lobster"
12) "46"
127.0.0.1:6379>
```

How it works...

In the command ZADD, we can only add new elements, by the option NX, to the set if there are already some elements in it:

```
127.0.0.1:6379> ZADD ranking:restaurants NX 50 "Olive Garden"
(integer) 0

127.0.0.1:6379> ZREVRANGE ranking:restaurants 0 -1 WITHSCORES
 1) "Kung Pao House"
 2) "213"
 3) "Olive Garden"
 4) "100"
 5) "Longhorn Steakhouse"
 6) "88"
 7) "Red Lobster"
 8) "46"
 9) "Outback Steakhouse"
10) "34"
11) "PF Chang's"
12) "23"
```

Similarly, the option XX allows you to update the set without adding new elements into it. Please take note that these options can only be applied from Redis 3.0.2 or greater.

Another thing regarding ZADD that should be noted is that it is possible to have multiple different elements with the same score. In this case, a lexicographical order will be followed.

The command ZUNIONSTORE is used to make a union from two sorted set and store the result into a destination key. Different weight, can be used. The command synopsis of ZUNIONSTORE lists as follows:

```
ZUNIONSTORE destination numkeys key [key ...] [WEIGHTS weight [weight ...]]
[AGGREGATE SUM|MIN|MAX]
```

The start and end index in the ZREVRANGE command follows the Redis index convention, as we mentioned in the recipe *Using the hash data type*. So, 0 means the first element, and 1 is the next element, −1 means the last one, and −2 is the last two, and so on. Therefore, a top three restaurants list can be retrieved using the following command:

```
127.0.0.1:6379> ZREVRANGE totalranking 0 2 WITHSCORES
1) "Kung Pao House"
2) "380"
3) "Olive Garden"
```

```
4)  "200"
5)  "Outback Steakhouse"
6)  "144"
```

There's more...

Attention should always be paid to the time and complexity needed when it comes to the complex Redis API. In sorted set, the API `ZINTERSTORE` and `ZUNIONSTORE` are the case.

For your reference, Redis also uses two encodings internally to store sorted set objects, like the data type list mentioned in the *Using the hash data type* recipe :

* `ziplist`: For a sorted set whose length is less than `zset-max-ziplist-entries` (default: `128`) and the size of every element in the set is less than `zset-max-ziplist-value` (default: `64` bytes) in configuration. `ziplist` is used to save space for small lists.
* `skiplist`: The default encoding when `ziplist` encoding cannot be used per configuration.

See also

* We did not cover all Redis sorted set commands due to the space limitation of this book. For a complete command reference, refer to `https://redis.io/commands#sorted_set`.

Using the HyperLogLog data type

Counting distinct values is a common task in various kinds of daily data processing scenarios. In Redis, while it's fine and sometimes necessary to implement distinct counting using set, memory consumption and performance degradation should be taken into consideration when the size of the set increases to tens of millions. If you don't need to retrieve the content of the data set and just want a unique counting value, one thing you can do is to use the **HyperLogLog** (**HLL**) data type in Redis to optimize the memory and performance issues caused by the set. In this recipe, we'll cover how to use HLL in Redis.

Getting ready...

You need to finish the installation of the Redis Server, as we described in the *Downloading and installing Redis* recipe in `Chapter 1`, *Getting Started with Redis*, and connect to the Redis server by `redis-cli`.

How to do it...

To understand how to use the HyperLogLog data type, take the following steps:

1. Open a Terminal and connect to Redis with `redis-cli`.
2. To count the distinct visitors for a restaurant called `Olive Garden` in Relp, we can count once by `PFADD` with one user ID:

```
127.0.0.1:6379> PFADD "Counting:Olive Garden" "0000123"
(integer) 1

127.0.0.1:6379> PFADD "Counting:Olive Garden" "0023992"
(integer) 1
```

3. Then, retrieve how many distinct visitors there are for this restaurant with the `PFCOUNT` command:

```
127.0.0.1:6379> PFCOUNT "Counting:Olive Garden"
(integer) 2
```

Another more complicated example, is that the you would like to show the unique number of visitors for `Olive Garden` in a week in Relp as an indication of weekly popularity; you can keep one HLL per day and merge them into seven days by the `PFMERGE` command to generate the result:

```
127.0.0.1:6379> PFADD "Counting:Olive Garden:20170903" "0023992"
"0023991" "0045992"
(integer) 1
127.0.0.1:6379> PFADD "Counting:Olive Garden:20170904" "0023992"
"0023991" "0045992"
(integer) 1
127.0.0.1:6379> PFADD "Counting:Olive Garden:20170905" "0024492"
"0023211" "0045292"
(integer) 1
127.0.0.1:6379> PFADD "Counting:Olive Garden:20170906" "0023999"
"0063991" "0045922"
(integer) 1
```

```
127.0.0.1:6379> PFADD "Counting:Olive Garden:20170907" "0023292"
"0023991" "0045921"
(integer) 1
127.0.0.1:6379> PFADD "Counting:Olive Garden:20170908" "0043282"
"0023984" "0045092"
(integer) 1
127.0.0.1:6379> PFADD "Counting:Olive Garden:20170909" "0023992"
"0023991" "0045992"
(integer) 1

127.0.0.1:6379> PFMERGE "Counting:Olive Garden:20170903week"
"Counting:Olive Garden:20170903" "Counting:Olive Garden:20170904"
"Counting:Olive Garden:20170905" "Counting:Olive Garden:20170906"
"Counting:Olive Garden:20170907" "Counting:Olive Garden:20170908"
"Counting:Olive Garden:20170909"
OK

127.0.0.1:6379> PFCOUNT "Counting:Olive Garden:20170903week"
(integer) 14
```

How it works...

Each command of HLL in Redis starts with PF, in honor of Philippe Flajolet who is the inventor of the HLL data structure. We won't dive into the detail of HLL algorithms in this book. The advantage of HLL in Redis is that it computes the distinct counts using a fixed amount of memory (less than 12 kb per key for up to 2^{64} cardinalities) and constant time complexity ($O(1)$ per key). However, there is a trade-off regarding HLL algorithms in that the cardinality returned is not exact, with a standard error of less than 1%.

There's more...

HLL is actually stored as string, and it's easy to persist and restore for key-value pairs.

For your reference, HLL in Redis uses two presentations internally to store HLL objects:

- **Sparse**: For an HLL object whose length is less than `hll-sparse-max-bytes` (default: `3000`) in configuration. Sparse representation is more space efficient, while it may cost more CPU in Redis.
- **Dense**: The default encoding when sparse encoding cannot be used per configuration.

See also

- For the more detailed algorithms for HLL, refer to the following paper:

  Flajolet P, Fusy É, Gandouet O, et al. Hyperloglog: *The analysis of a near-optimal cardinality estimation algorithm[C]//AofA: Analysis of Algorithms. Discrete Mathematics and Theoretical Computer Science, 2007: 137-156.*

  ```
  http://algo.inria.fr/flajolet/Publications/FlFuGaMe07.pdf
  ```

Using the Geo data type

Location-based service has gained in popularity as smartphones have become increasingly more common. The Geo API has been introduced officially in Redis, since Release 3.2, to support storing and querying geospatial coordinates for these location-related scenarios. In this recipe, we will explore the Geo data type in Redis.

Getting ready...

You need to finish the installation of the Redis Server, as we described in the *Downloading and installing Redis* recipe in Chapter 1, *Getting Started with Redis*, and connect to the Redis Server by `redis-cli`.

How to do it...

To understand how to use the Geo data type, take the following steps:

1. Open a Terminal and connect to Redis with `redis-cli`.

2. For the demo application Relp, we can add five restaurants in California to a Geo set called `restaurants:CA`, by using GEOADD:

   ```
   127.0.0.1:6379> GEOADD restaurants:CA -121.896321 37.916750 "Olive
   Garden" -117.910937 33.804047 "P.F. Chang's" -118.508020 34.453276
   "Outback Steakhouse" -119.152439 34.264558 "Red Lobster"
   -122.276909 39.458300 "Longhorn Charcoal Pit"
   (integer) 5
   ```

3. Now, get the coordinates for a given member from a Geo set by calling GEOPOS:

```
127.0.0.1:6379> GEOPOS restaurants:CA "Red Lobster"
1) 1) "-119.1524389386177063"
   2) "34.26455707283378871"
```

4. Suppose you are at Mount Diablo State Park, whose longitude/latitude is -121.923170/37.878506, and you would like to know the restaurants within 5 kilometers of your current location:

```
127.0.0.1:6379> GEORADIUS  restaurants:CA  -121.923170 37.878506 5
km
1) "Olive Garden"
```

5. Sometimes, you would like to compare the distance between two restaurants; for this you can call GEODIST API:

```
127.0.0.1:6379> GEODIST restaurants:CA "P.F. Chang's" "Outback
Steakhouse" km
"90.7557"
```

6. The command GEORADIUSBYMEMBER works in a very similar way to GEORADIUS; there is a slight difference in that the location to be measured is a member from the Geo set itself. For example, with GEORADIUSBYMEMBER, we can search for the restaurants in the Geo set whose distance is not 100 km away from "Outback Steakhouse", which is also a member of the Geo set:

```
127.0.0.1:6379> GEORADIUSBYMEMBER restaurants:CA "Outback
Steakhouse" 100 km
1) "Red Lobster"
2) "Outback Steakhouse"
3) "P.F. Chang's"
```

How it works...

When the coordinates are set via GEOADD, they will be internally converted into a 52-bit GEOHASH, which is a Geo-encoding system that is commonly accepted. You should take into consideration that there is a slight difference between the Geo stored and the coordinates returned by GEOPOS, so you should not expect the two to be exactly the same.

In the commands GEORADIUS and GEORADIUSBYMEMBER, you can use the WITHDIST option to obtain the distances. The ASC/DESC option makes the result returned appear in ascending or descending order. In addition, with the option STORE/STOREDIST, you can also store the result returned by GEORADIUS and GEORADIUSBYMEMBER to another Geo set in Redis.

There's more...

The Geo set is actually stored as a sorted set (zset in Redis) and all the commands in a sorted set can be applied to the Geo data type. For example, removing a Geo index from a Geo set can be done by ZREM, and retrieving all the members of a Geo set can be achieved by ZRANGE.

For your reference, the implementation of GEOHASH is based on a 52-bit integer representation (which gives an accuracy of less than 1 meter). When a standard GEOHASH string is needed, you can call GEOHASH to get a string whose length is 11.

For performance concerns, GEORADIUS has the time complexity of $O(N+log(M))$ where N is the number of elements inside the bounding box of the circular area delimited by center and radius, according to the documents of Redis. So, if you want great performance, keep in mind that you should set the radius parameter in one query as small as possible, to cover less points.

See also

- For the uses and encoding designs of GEOHASH, refer to https://en.wikipedia.org/wiki/Geohash
- For a complete command reference, refer to https://redis.io/commands#geo

Managing keys

In this chapter, until now, we have talked about all the data types in Redis. Generally speaking, data in Redis is composed of key-value pairs. Therefore, managing keys is another essential knowledge for application development and administration in Redis. In this recipe, we'll cover keys management.

Getting ready...

You need to finish the installation of the Redis Server, as we described in the *Downloading and installing Redis* recipe in `Chapter 1`, *Getting Started with Redis*, and connect to the Redis Server by `redis-cli`.

In order to show the keys operation clearly, we first populate some fake data into Redis using `fake2db`, with the following steps:

1. Install `fake2db` and the Python Redis driver:

```
$ sudo pip install redis fake2db
Flush all the data of the Redis server:
$ bin/redis-cli flushall
```

2. Populate the testing records to the Redis Server:

```
$ fake2db --rows 10000 --db redis
2017-09-17 16:44:39,393 gnuhpc    Rows argument : 10000
2017-09-17 16:44:46,808 gnuhpc    simple_registration Commits are
successful after write job!
2017-09-17 16:45:10,151 gnuhpc    detailed_registration Commits are
successful after write job!
2017-09-17 16:45:47,224 gnuhpc    companies Commits are successful
after write job!
2017-09-17 16:45:47,919 gnuhpc    user_agent Commits are successful
after write job!
2017-09-17 16:46:15,696 gnuhpc    customer Commits are successful
after write job!
```

How to do it...

To understand how to manage keys , take the following steps:

1. Open a Terminal and connect to Redis with `redis-cli`.
2. To find out how many keys are in Redis, we will perform the following operation:

```
127.0.0.1:6379> DBSIZE
(integer) 50000
```

3. If you are eager to know the keys in the Redis Server, two types of API can be used. The first one is KEYS:

```
127.0.0.1:6379> KEYS *
    1) "detailed_registration:8001"
    2) "company:3859"
    3) "user_agent:4820"
4) "detailed_registration:9330"
...
50000) "company:2947"
(9.30s)
```

4. Another one is SCAN:

```
127.0.0.1:6379> scan 0
1) "20480"
2)    1) "detailed_registration:8001"
      2) "company:3859"
      3) "company:3141"
      4) "detailed_registration:9657"
      5) "user_agent:2325"
      6) "company:1545"
      7) "company:2521"
      8) "detailed_registration:1253"
      9) "user_agent:1499"
     10) "user_agent:3827"
127.0.0.1:6379> scan 20480
1) "26624"
2)    1) "detailed_registration:5263"
      2) "user_agent:2605"
      3) "detailed_registration:1316"
      4) "user_agent:1683"
      5) "customer:894"
      6) "simple_registration:6411"
      7) "company:3638"
      8) "detailed_registration:1665"
      9) "customer:9344"
     10) "company:7028"
      ....
```

5. Under some circumstances, you may need to delete keys in Redis with the DEL command or UNLINK:

```
127.0.0.1:6379> DEL "detailed_registration:1665"
"simple_registration:6411" "user_agent:1683"
(integer) 3
127.0.0.1:6379> UNLINK "company:1664"
(integer) 1
```

6. To tell if one key exits, use the EXISTS command, as follows:

```
127.0.0.1:6379> EXISTS "simple_registration:7681"
(integer) 1
127.0.0.1:6379> EXISTS "simple_registration:99999"
(integer) 0
```

7. Find the data type of a key using the TYPE command:

```
127.0.0.1:6379> TYPE "company:3859"
hash
```

8. You can call RENAME to rename a key:

```
127.0.0.1:6379> RENAME "customer:6591" "customer:6591:renamed"
OK
```

How it works...

Keys management in Redis is quite simple. However, some APIs may become performance killers.

Firstly, you may find that if there are quite a large number of keys in Redis, calling KEYS will make the Redis Server block for a while until all the keys have returned (it took 6.8 s in our example). If you understood the core concept in the recipe *Understanding the Redis Event Model* in Chapter 1, *Getting Started with Redis*, you will know that during one command execution in Redis, all the other commands the server has already received have to wait to be processed. Therefore, calling the KEYS command is a dangerous action for the performance of a production environment. For this issue, the command SCAN, like HSCAN or SSCAN as mentioned in the previous recipes, can be used to iterate the keys in the Redis Server without blocking the server.

A similar extra caution deserving of your attention is the DEL command. If the key to be deleted is a data type other than string, you may encounter server latency when the number of elements in the key is large. To prevent this disaster, using UNLINK instead is a good idea. It will perform the deletion in another thread rather than the main event loop thread, so it won't block the event handling.

In addition, RENAME seems harmless at first glance. However, RENAME will delete the target key if it has already existed. As mentioned earlier, DEL may cause high latency. Therefore, the best practice for renaming is to unlink the target key if it exists, and then do the renaming.

There's more...

The command DUMP/RESTORE can be used for serialization and deserialization. You can use these two commands to make partial backups for Redis.

See also

- For a complete command reference, refer to
  https://redis.io/commands#generic

3
Data Features

In this chapter, we will cover the following recipes:

- Using bitmaps
- Setting expiration on keys
- Using SORT
- Using pipelines
- Understanding Redis transactions
- Using PubSub
- Using Lua
- Debugging Lua

Introduction

We introduced six data types that Redis supports in Chapter 2, *Data Types*. Besides these essential data types, which are commonly used in development, Redis also provides several useful data features to make your life easier if you understand how to use them correctly.

We will go over the following features in this chapter:

- **Bitmaps**: In this recipe, we will show how bitmaps can be used in lieu of strings to save memory space under some circumstances.
- **Expiration**: As Redis is an in-memory data store and usually used as the cache, it is imperative to set expiration for transient data. In this recipe, we will show how to set expiration for Redis keys, and what will happen when keys expire.

- **Sorting**: Sorting is supported when retrieving values from Redis lists, sets, and sorted sets. We will show the usage of the SORT command in this recipe.
- **Pipeline**: In this recipe, you will see how to use the Redis pipelines and why this is a great feature for optimizing the performance of multiple Redis operations.
- **Transactions**: Redis supports transactions such as RDBMS, but Redis transactions are different, as will be explained in detail in this recipe.
- **PUBSUB**: Redis can be used as a message-exchanging channel. You will learn the Redis commands of the Publish/Subscribe feature and its application scenarios in this recipe.
- **Writing/Debugging Lua in Redis**: Lua is a scripting language designed to be embedded into other applications. Lua can be used in Redis to bundle a couple of operations and make the entire execution atomic. In this recipe, you will learn how to write, execute, and debug simple Lua scripts for Redis.

Using bitmaps

A bitmap (also known as a bit array, or bit vector) is an array of bits. A Redis bitmap is not a new data type; its actual underlying data type is string. Since a string is inherently a binary blob, it can be viewed as a bitmap. A bitmap saves enormous memory space for storing boolean information under certain circumstances.

In this recipe, we will use a bitmap to store a flag, whether or not a user has ever used a feature in Relp. Suppose that in Relp every user has a unique and incremental id, which can be denoted by the bitmap offset. The flag, which is a boolean attribute, can be denoted by the bit value in the bitmap.

Getting ready...

You need to finish the installation of the Redis Server as we described in the *Downloading and installing Redis* recipe in Chapter 1, *Getting Started with Redis*.

How to do it...

The steps for using bitmaps are as follows:

1. Open a Terminal and connect to Redis with `redis-cli`
2. Use `SETBIT` to set the bit value in a bitmap at the specified offset.

   For example, when a user whose ID is `100` has tried the restaurant reservation feature in Relp, we set the corresponding bit:

   ```
   127.0.0.1:6379> SETBIT "users_tried_reservation" 100 1
   (integer) 0
   ```

3. To retrieve the bit value from a bitmap at the specified offset, the `GETBIT` command can be used.

   For example, we would like to know if the user whose ID is `400` has ever tried online orders:

   ```
   127.0.0.1:6379> GETBIT "users_tried_online_orders" 400
   (integer) 0
   ```

4. To return the number of bits set to `1` in the bitmap, use the `BITCOUNT` command.

   Suppose we would like to know how many users have ever tried a specific feature, `BITCOUNT` is here to help:

   ```
   127.0.0.1:6379> BITCOUNT "users_tried_reservation"
   (integer) 1
   ```

5. `BITOP` is the command to perform bitwise operations between bitmaps. The command supports four bitwise operations: `AND`, `OR`, `XOR`, and `NOT`. The result will be stored in a destination key. For example, if we want to know the user ids of those who tried both the *restaurant reservation feature* and the *online orders feature*:

   ```
   127.0.0.1:6379> BITOP AND
   "users_tried_both_reservation_and_online_orders"
   "users_tried_reservation" "users_tried_online_orders"
   (integer) 13
   127.0.0.1:6379> BITCOUNT
   "users_tried_both_reservation_and_online_orders"
   (integer) 0
   ```

How it works...

The bitmap structure in Redis is shown in the following graph:

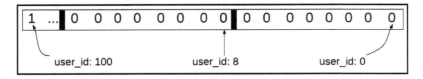

There's more...

In the preceding example, we could also use a Redis set to count the number of users. Let's take a look at the difference between using a bitmap and a set in this example from a memory usage perspective.

As we've seen, every user needs one bit in the bitmap, regardless of whether the user has ever used the feature or not. Suppose there are two billion users on Relp; we need to allocate two billion bits, which is roughly 250 MB, in memory. If we use a Redis set to implement the same counting functionality, we only need to store the users who have used the Relp feature in the set.

Suppose we store the user ids as 8-byte integers. If a Relp feature is very popular and 80% of Relp users (1.6 billion) have used it, we need to allocate space for 1.6 billion 8-byte integers, which is roughly 12.8 GB in memory. A bitmap has advantages over a set in terms of space saving when the number of elements in the set is extremely large.

However, if a Relp feature is not so popular, using a set may be more beneficial. For example, if only 1% of the users (20 million) have used a feature, using a set would need 160 MB space, while using a bitmap still needs 250 MB space. The bitmap is very sparse in this case, as presumably the bits that are set in the bitmap are distributed evenly.

In addition, setting bits in a sparse bitmap may block the Redis Server for some time. This will happen when the bit to be set has a very large offset and the existing bitmap is small, because Redis has to immediately allocate memory to enlarge the bitmap.

See also

- For a more detailed introduction to a Redis bitmap and its usage, refer to the bitmap section of `https://redis.io/topics/data-types-intro`

Setting expiration on keys

In the recipe *Managing keys* in `Chapter 2`, *Data Types*, we learned that Redis keys can be deleted by using the `DEL` or `UNLINK` command. Besides deleting keys manually, we can also ask Redis to delete keys automatically by setting the timeout on keys. In this recipe, we will illustrate how to set the timeout on Redis keys and explain the key expiration mechanism in Redis.

Getting ready...

You need to finish the installation of the Redis Server as we described in the *Downloading and Installing Redis* recipe in `Chapter 1`, *Getting Started with Redis*.

How to do it...

To show how to set expiration on keys, we store the IDs of five restaurants that are closest to the user's current location in a Redis list. As the user's location may change frequently, we should set a timeout on this Redis list. After the timeout has expired, we will fetch the restaurant list again using the current location:

1. Create a Redis list of restaurant IDs at key `closest_restaurant_ids`:

   ```
   127.0.0.1:6379> LPUSH "closest_restaurant_ids"
   109 200 233 543 222
   (integer) 5
   ```

2. Set the timeout on the key to 300 seconds by using the `EXPIRE` command:

   ```
   127.0.0.1:6379> EXPIRE "closest_restaurant_ids" 300
   (integer) 1
   ```

3. We can use the `TTL` command to check the remaining time before the key expires:

   ```
   127.0.0.1:6379> TTL "closest_restaurant_ids"
   (integer) 269
   ```

4. Wait for 300 seconds till the key has expired; executing `EXISTS` on the key will return 0.

   ```
   127.0.0.1:6379> EXISTS "closest_restaurant_ids"
   (integer) 0
   ```

How it works...

When a timeout is set on a Redis key, the expiration time for the key will be stored as an absolute UNIX timestamp. Therefore, even if the Redis Server is down for some time, the expiration timestamp won't be lost and the key will still expire when the server is up again and the clock has passed the UNIX timestamp.

When a key has expired and the client tries to access it, Redis will delete the key from memory immediately. The way Redis deletes a key is known as **expiring passively**. What if a key has expired but it will never be accessed again? Redis also *actively* deletes expired keys by running a probabilistic algorithm periodically. Specifically, Redis randomly picks 20 keys associated with the timeout. Expired keys will be deleted immediately. If more than 25% of the selected keys have expired and been deleted, Redis will randomly pick 20 keys again and repeat the process. By default, this process runs 10 times per second, but it's configurable by the hz value in the configuration file.

There's more...

The timeout of a key can be cleared in the following ways:

- Using the PERSIST command to make it a persistent key.
- The value at the key is replaced or deleted. Commands that will clear the timeout include SET, GETSET, and *STORE. Altering elements from a Redis list, set, or hash will not clear the timeout because the operation does not replace the value object at the key.
- The key is renamed by another key which does not have a timeout.
- The TTL command returns -1 if the key exists but has no associated expire and returns -2 if the key does not exist.

The EXPIREAT command is similar to EXPIRE but takes an absolute UNIX timestamp at which the key is to expire.

In addition, with effect from Redis 2.6, PEXIRE and PEXIREAT can be used to specify the timeout for keys in millisecond granularity.

Since when an expired key will be deleted by Redis *actively* is unpredictable, it is possible that some expired keys are never deleted. We can proactively trigger the *passive expiration* by executing the SCAN command if there are too many expired keys that are not cleaned up.

See also

- The official reference of the EXPIRE command can be found here: https://redis.io/commands/expire

Using SORT

We have already learned in Chapter 2, *Data Types* that elements in a Redis list or set are unordered, and elements in a Redis sorted set are ordered by their scores. Sometimes we may need to get a sorted copy of a Redis list or set in some order, or sort elements in a Redis sorted set by an order other than scores. Redis provides a convenient command called SORT for this purpose. In this recipe, we will take a look at the SORT command and its examples.

Getting ready...

You need to finish the installation of the Redis Server as we described in the *Downloading and installing Redis* recipe in Chapter 1, *Getting Started with Redis*.

How to do it...

The steps for using SORT are as follows:

1. Open a Terminal and connect to Redis with redis-cli.
2. If all elements are numeric, we can simply run the SORT key to sort the elements in ascending order. Suppose in Relp we store a user's favorite restaurant IDs in a Redis set:

```
127.0.0.1:6379> SADD "user:123:favorite_restaurant_ids" 200 365 104
455 333
(integer) 5
127.0.0.1:6379> SORT "user:123:favorite_restaurant_ids"
1) "104"
2) "200"
3) "333"
4) "365"
5) "455"
```

3. If there are non-numeric elements and we want to sort them by lexicographical order, we need to add the ALPHA modifier. Suppose we store restaurant names in the set:

```
127.0.0.1:6379> SADD "user:123:favorite_restaurants" "Dunkin
Donuts" "Subway" "KFC" "Burger King" "Wendy's"
(integer) 5
127.0.0.1:6379> SORT "user:123:favorite_restaurants" ALPHA
1) "Burger King"
2) "Dunkin Donuts"
3) "KFC"
4) "Subway"
5) "Wendy's"
```

4. Adding the DESC modifier to the SORT command will return elements in descending order. By default, the SORT command will sort and return all elements, but we can limit the number of returned elements by using the LIMIT modifier with a starting offset (number of elements to skip) and count (number of elements to return). For example, we only need to get three restaurants in a user's favorite list:

```
127.0.0.1:6379> SORT "user:123:favorite_restaurants" ALPHA LIMIT 0
3
1) "Burger King"
2) "Dunkin Donuts"
3) "KFC"
```

There's more...

Sometimes we do not want to sort elements by their values, but by their weights that are defined in some external keys. For example, we may need to sort the user's favorite restaurants by ratings defined in keys like restaurnat_rating_200, where 200 is the restaurant ID. This can also be done in SORT:

```
127.0.0.1:6379> SET "restaurant_rating_200" 4.3
127.0.0.1:6379> SET "restaurant_rating_365" 4.0
127.0.0.1:6379> SET "restaurant_rating_104" 4.8
127.0.0.1:6379> SET "restaurant_rating_455" 4.7
127.0.0.1:6379> SET "restaurant_rating_333" 4.6
127.0.0.1:6379> SORT "user:123:favorite_restaurant_ids" BY
restaurant_rating_* DESC
1) "104"
2) "455"
```

```
3) "333"
4) "200"
5) "365"
```

In some scenarios, the values from external keys are more useful. In our previous example, we are more interested in getting restaurant names rather than restaurant IDs. Suppose we store restaurant names in keys like `restaurant_name_200`, where `200` is the restaurant ID; we could use the `GET` option in `SORT` to get the restaurant names:

```
127.0.0.1:6379> SET "restaurant_name_200" "Ruby Tuesday"
127.0.0.1:6379> SET "restaurant_name_365" "TGI Friday"
127.0.0.1:6379> SET "restaurant_name_104" "Applebee's"
127.0.0.1:6379> SET "restaurant_name_455" "Red Lobster"
127.0.0.1:6379> SET "restaurant_name_333" "Boiling Crab"
127.0.0.1:6379> SORT "user:123:favorite_restaurant_ids" BY
restaurant_rating_* DESC GET restaurant_name_*
1) "Applebee's"
2) "Red Lobster"
3) "Boiling Crab"
4) "Ruby Tuesday"
5) "TGI Friday"
```

The `GET` option can be used multiple times, and `GET #` means get the element itself.

The `SORT` operation also has a `STORE` option, which stores the sorting result as a list at the specified key. Here is an example of using the `STORE` option:

```
127.0.0.1:6379>SORT "user:123:favorite_restaurant_ids" BY
restaurant_rating_* DESC GET restaurant_name_* STORE
user:123:favorite_restaurant_names:sort_by_rating
(integer) 5
```

Lastly, we would like to mention that the time complexity of `SORT` is $O(N+M*log(M))$, where N is the number of elements in the list or set, and M is the number of elements to be returned. Given the time complexity of a `SORT` operation, Redis Server performance may be degraded when sorting large amounts of data.

See also

- The official Redis `SORT` command reference can be found at
  `https://redis.io/commands/sort`

Using pipelines

In the recipe *Understanding Redis protocol* in Chapter 1, *Getting Started with Redis* we learned that Redis Clients and servers communicate via the RESP protocol. A typical communication process between the client and the server can be viewed as the following:

1. The client sends a command to the server
2. The server receives the command and puts it in the execution queue (as Redis is a single-threaded execution model)
3. The command gets executed
4. The server returns the execution result to the client

The entire time of this process is termed as **round-trip time** (**RTT**). As we can see, the time for step 2 and step 3 depends on the Redis Server, while the time for step 1 and step 4 totally depends on the network latency between the client and the server. If we need to execute multiple commands, network transmission might take a great amount of time, in comparison with the command execution time on the server, which is often very short.

The process can be expedited by using the Redis pipeline. The basic idea of the Redis pipeline is that the client bundles multiple commands and sends them in one shot, instead of waiting for the execution result of each individual command; it asks the server to return the results after all commands have been executed. The total execution time is drastically reduced because step 1 and step 4 happen only once for executing multiple commands.

We will demonstrate a simple example of using pipelines in this recipe.

Getting ready...

You need to finish the installation of the Redis Server as we described in the *Downloading and installing Redis* recipe in Chapter 1, *Getting Started with Redis*.

Use the following command to install dos2unix tools in Ubuntu:

```
sudo apt-get install dos2unix
```

In macOS, you can install dos2unix tools using the following command:

```
brew install dos2unix
```

How to do it...

The steps for using `pipeline` are as follows:

1. Open a Terminal and execute the following:

    ```
    ~$ cat pipeline.txt
    set mykey myvalue
    sadd myset value1 value2
    get mykey
    scard myset
    ```

    Each line in this text file has to be terminate with an `rn` and not with `n`. To achieve this, the command `unix2dos` can be used:

    ```
    $ unix2dos pipeline.txt
    ```

2. To send the commands in the pipeline, you can use `redis-cli` with the `--pipe` option:

    ```
    ~$ cat pipeline.txt | bin/redis-cli --pipe
    All data transferred. Waiting for the last reply...
    Last reply received from server.
    errors: 0, replies: 4
    ```

How it works...

The `--pipe` option in `redis-cli` will send all the commands from stdin in one shot, avoiding the cost of RTT significantly.

Furthermore, the commands can be in the format of a raw RESP protocol by which the client communicates with the Redis Server. For the preceding example, the following operation can do the same job:

```
$ cat datapipe.txt
*3\r\n$3\r\nSET\r\n$5\r\nmykey\r\n$7\r\nmyvalue\r\n*4\r\n$4\r\nSADD\r\n$5\r
\nmyset\r\n$6\r\nvalue1\r\n$6\r\nvalue2\r\n*2\r\n$3\r\nGET\r\n$5\r\nmykey\r
\n*2\r\n$5\r\nSCARD\r\n$5\r\nmyset\r\n
$ echo -e "$(cat datapipe.txt)" | bin/redis-cli --pipe
All data transferred. Waiting for the last reply...
Last reply received from server.
errors: 0, replies: 4
```

Also, with the `--pipe` option of `redis-cli`, you are able to send all the commands in a raw protocol to the server together. For an explanation of the RESP protocol, please refer to the recipe *Understanding Redis protocol* in `Chapter 1`, *Getting Started with Redis*.

There's more...

We demonstrated how to use a pipeline to send multiple commands to the Redis Server in raw RESP. A pipeline is usually used in Redis Clients of a specific programming language. We will show the details in `Chapter 4`, *Developing with Redis*.

See also

- A good explanation of a pipeline from the official Redis documentation can be found here: `https://redis.io/topics/pipelining`

Understanding Redis transactions

A transaction in a relational database is a group of operations performed as an atomic action within a it. This means the group of operations must either complete or fail as a whole. However, the concept of transactions in Redis is a different story. In this recipe, we'll take a look at Redis transactions, and find out the differences in transactions between Redis and RDBMS.

Getting ready...

You need to finish the installation of the Redis Server as we described in the *Downloading and installing Redis* recipe in `Chapter 1`, *Getting Started with Redis*.

How to do it...

To understand Redis transactions, there is a scenario where we are going to organize a coupon codes seckilling, a quick sell out online, for a certain restaurant in Relp. There are only five coupon codes for this seckilling and we have a key, `counts:seckilling`, as a counter to hold the count of available coupon codes.

Here is the pseudo-code for this counter implementation:

```
//Initiate the count of coupon codes:
SET("counts:seckilling",5);

Start decreasing the counter:
WATCH("counts:seckilling");
count = GET("counts:seckilling");
MULTI();
if count > 0 then
            DECR("counts:seckilling",1);
            EXEC();
            if ret != null then
                    print "Succeed!"
                else
                    print "Failed!"
else
    DISCARD();
print "Seckilling Over!"
```

How it works...

Overselling is often a headache for seckilling application design. The reason why the overselling happens is that there was a race condition at the time you retrieved the counter; the number might be valid for the business scenario, but before you decreased the counter, the counter may have been modified by other requests. In our example, we use a Redis transaction to avoid such a situation.

First, we call a WATCH command on the key to set a flag indicating if the key has been changed before the EXEC command; if so, we just discard the whole transaction. Then, we get the value of the counter.

Second, we start a transaction by calling the MULTI command, and if the counter is an invalid value, the transaction is stopped directly by the DISCARD command. Otherwise, we can move on to decrease the counter.

After that, we try to execute the transaction. Due to the WATCH command used before, Redis will check if the value of counts:seckilling has been modified. If the value is changed, the transaction aborts. The abort is considered as a second killing failure.

As we can see, we have successfully ensured that the overselling error could not happen by taking advantage of the transaction feature in Redis.

There's more...

The differences between transactions in Redis and RDBMS merit attention.

The key difference is that there is no rollback feature in a Redis transaction. Generally speaking, two types of error may occur in a Redis transaction while different handling mechanisms are taken:

1. The first one is a syntax error for a command. In this case, because the error is detected while queuing the commands, the entire transaction will fast-fail and none of the commands in this transaction will be processed:

    ```
    127.0.0.1:6379> MULTI
    OK
    127.0.0.1:6379> SET FOO BAR
    QUEUED
    127.0.0.1:6379> GOT FOO
    (error) ERR unknown command 'GOT'
    127.0.0.1:6379> INCR MAS
    QUEUED
    127.0.0.1:6379> EXEC
    (error) EXECABORT Transaction discarded because of previous errors.
    ```

2. Another case is when, although all commands have been queued successfully, the error occurs in the middle of execution. Other commands afterward will continue to execute without a rollback. We'll use the following transaction as an example:

    ```
    127.0.0.1:6379> MULTI
    OK
    127.0.0.1:6379> SET foo bar
    QUEUED
    127.0.0.1:6379> INCR foo
    QUEUED
    127.0.0.1:6379> SET foo mas
    QUEUED
    127.0.0.1:6379> GET foo
    QUEUED
    127.0.0.1:6379> EXEC
    1) OK
    2) (error) ERR value is not an integer or out of range
    3) OK
    4) "mas"
    ```

See also

- For a detailed discussion of transactions in Redis, refer to: `https://redis.io/topics/transactions`
- For transaction commands, refer to: `https://redis.io/commands#transactions`

Using PubSub

Publish-Subscribe (**PubSub**) is a classic messaging pattern which has a long history, as far back as 1987 according to Wikipedia. To explain it in simple terms, publishers, who want to publish the events, send messages to a PubSub channel, which delivers the events to each subscriber who has an interest in this channel. Many popular messaging middleware, like Kafka and ZeroMQ, take advantage of this pattern to build a message delivery system, and so does Redis. In this recipe, we'll explore the PubSub pattern of Redis.

Getting ready...

You need to finish the installation of the Redis Server as we described in the *Downloading and Installing Redis* recipe in `Chapter 1`, *Getting Started with Redis*.

How to do it...

To show how to use PubSub, take a recommendation message-pushing system as an example.

Open three consoles to simulate two subscribers in console-A (SUBer-1) and console-B (SUBer-2), and also one publisher in console-C (PUBer):

1. Subscribe the Chinese restaurant channel in SUBer1:

```
127.0.0.1:6379> SUBSCRIBE restaurants:Chinese
Reading messages... (press Ctrl-C to quit)
1) "subscribe"
2) "restaurants:Chinese"
3) (integer) 1
```

2. Subscribe the Chinese and Thai restaurant channels in SUBer2:

```
127.0.0.1:6379> SUBSCRIBE restaurants:Chinese restaurants:Thai
Reading messages... (press Ctrl-C to quit)
1) "subscribe"
2) "restaurants:Chinese"
3) (integer) 1
1) "subscribe"
2) "restaurants:Thai"
3) (integer) 2
```

3. Publish a message to the Chinese restaurant channel in PUBer:

```
127.0.0.1:6379> PUBLISH restaurants:Chinese "Beijing roast duck
discount tomorrow"
(integer) 2
```

4. Two subscribers will get this message:

```
1) "message"
2) "restaurants:Chinese"
3) "Beijing roast duck discount tomorrow"
```

5. Publish a message to the Thai channel in PUBer:

```
127.0.0.1:6379> PUBLISH restaurants:Thai "3$ for Tom yum soap in
this weekend!"
(integer) 1
```

6. Only SUBer-2, who has subscribed to the Thai channel, will get this message:

```
1) "message"
2) "restaurants:Thai"
3) "3$ for Tom yum soap in this weekend!"
```

How it works...

The SUBSCRIBE command is called to monitor the available messages in a specific channel. One client can subscribe many channels at one time using SUBSCRIBE, and also can subscribe channels that match a given pattern using PSUBSCRIBE. To unsubscribe channels, UNSUBSCRIBE can be used.

The PUBLISH command is for sending a message to a specific channel. All the subscribers subscribing to the channel will receive this message.

Another important command is PUBSUB, which does the channel management job. For instance, one may retrieve the current active channels by issuing the PUBSUB CHANNELS   command, as follows:

```
127.0.0.1:6379> PUBSUB CHANNELS
1) "restaurants:Chinese"
2) "restaurants:Thai"
```

There's more...

For the life cycle of a channel, SUBSCRIBE will create the channel automatically if the given channel has not been subscribed before. And, once there is no active subscriber on the channel, the channel will be deleted at the same time.

Considerable attention must be paid so that there is nothing persisted in Redis PubSub. That means that no messages, channels, or the relationships for PubSub, will be saved on disk. If the server exits for some reason, all these objects will be gone.

Moreover, in the message delivery and processing scenarios, if there is no subscriber for a channel, the message pushed will be dropped. In other words, there is no mechanism to guarantee message delivery. In addition, each message pushed into the channel by a publisher is only processed by one of the subscribers in Redis.

In conclusion, the PubSub feature in Redis is not appropriate for important message delivery scenarios, though one may benefit from its quick speed for trivial communications.

In addition, Redis keyspace notifications, a feature based on PubSub, allow clients to subscribe to a Redis channel and receive *published* events on Redis commands or data changes. If you are interested in this feature, you can check out the documentation listed in the next section.

See also

- For a detailed discussion of PubSub in Redis, refer to: https://redis.io/topics/pubsub
- For a list of transaction commands, refer to: https://redis.io/commands#pubsub
- For the keyspace notifications feature, refer to: https://redis.io/topics/notifications

Using Lua

Lua, a lightweight script language, has been introduced into Redis since version 2.6. Similar to the transactions in Redis mentioned in the recipe *Understanding Redis transactions*, a Lua script is executed atomically, while more powerful features and programming logic can be implemented in Lua as a server-side script language. In this recipe, we'll see how to write and execute a Lua script in Redis.

Getting ready...

You need to finish the installation of the Redis Server as we described in the *Downloading and Installing Redis* recipe in Chapter 1, *Getting Started with Redis*.

How to do it...

The steps for using Lua are as follows:

1. We'll use a Lua script to update a JSON string object in Redis.
2. Open a console and create a Lua script, as follows:

```
$ mkdir /redis/coding/lua; cd /redis/coding/lua
$ cat updatejson.lua
local id = KEYS[1]
local data = ARGV[1]
local dataSource = cjson.decode(data)

local retJson = redis.call('get', id)
if retJson == false then
    retJson = {}
else
```

```
        retJson = cjson.decode(retJson)
end
for k,v in pairs(dataSource) do
        retJson[k] = v
end
redis.call('set', id, cjson.encode(retJson))
return redis.call('get',id)
```

3. To execute the Lua script, you can use `redis-cli` to evaluate the script file:

```
bin/redis-cli --eval updatejson.lua users:id:992452 , '{"name":
"Tina", "sex": "female", "grade": "A"}'
"{"grade":"A","name":"Tina","sex":"female"}"
```

4. If you'd like to call this script later, you can register it to the Redis Server:

```
bin/redis-cli SCRIPT LOAD "`cat updatejson.lua`"
"45a40b129ea0655db7e7be992f344468559f3dbd"
```

5. After registration, you can execute the Lua script by specifying the unique SHA-1 identifier returned when the script was registered. Here, we update the grade to "C" for the user `users:id:992452`:

```
bin/redis-cli EVALSHA 45a40b129ea0655db7e7be992f344468559f3dbd 1
users:id:992452 '{"grade": "C"}'
"{"grade":"C","name":"tina","sex":"female"}"
```

How it works...

First, we create a Lua script `updatejson.lua`. In the Lua script, KEY and ARGV are arguments for the EVAL command. At the beginning of this script, we get one KEY as the key that we'd like to process and one ARGV as the content that we'd like to update for the JSON string. After that, the JSON content passed into the script is deserialized.

Then, we retrieve the value of the specified key by calling the GET command using the `redis.call()` function, and then we look at the value returned by the GET command. If the value is `false`, which indicates the key doesn't exist, we set it as an empty table. Otherwise, we can decode the value as a JSON string.

Then, we start iterating the data to set the key and value in the `retJson` variable. At the end of this script, we set back the value as a JSON string and return the final value.

To execute a Lua script, `redis-cli` with the `--eval` option can be used. In this example, we pass the user ID and the user information to be updated into `redis-cli`:

```
users:id:992452 , '{"name": "Tina", "sex": "female", "grade": "A"}'
```

The user ID is used as the element of `KEYS[]` in the Lua script, and the user information is considered as the element of `ARGV[]`. In addition, a comma separates `KEYS[]` from `ARGV[]` items. In the Lua script, the index of both the `KEYS[]` array and the `ARGV[]` array is started from 1. Instead of using `redis-cli`, you can also use the `EVAL` command in your program to execute a Lua script.

We don't actually need to specify the Lua script every time we want to execute it. In this case, the `SCRIPT LOAD` command helps us to cache the script in the Redis Server process. An SHA-1 string is returned, which will be used as a unique identifier of this script in the `EVALSHA` command when you want to execute it.

There's more...

You may wonder how to choose between Lua and Redis transactions in Redis, since both are capable of executing a group of operations as a whole. Generally speaking, it's better to choose Lua rather than transactions when you need a complex logical judgment or a processing loop for your business scenario.

Similar to Redis transactions, attention must also be paid to the execution time of your Lua script. The Redis Server won't process any commands when executing a Lua program. So, we must make sure that the Lua script can be executed as soon as possible. Once the execution time of a Lua script exceeds 5 seconds by default (set `lua-time-limit` in the Redis configuration to change it), you can call `SCRIPT KILL` to kill it. If any write command has already been called in your script, you have to send `SHUTDOWN NOSAVE` to shut down your Redis Server without performing persistence. If the execution time is less than 5 seconds, the `SCRIPT KILL` command will also be blocked until the timeout is reached.

For Lua script management, you can tell if a script exists by calling `SCRIPT EXISTS` with the SHA-1 ID.

The last thing to note is that because the script is only saved in a script cache of a Redis Server process, which will be gone during rebooting, you have to reload the Lua scripts after you restart the Redis Server.

See also

- For the complete manual for Lua 5.1, refer to `https://www.lua.org/manual/5.1/`
- For Lua commands in Redis, refer to `https://redis.io/commands#scripting`

Debugging Lua

Debugging allows you to detect, diagnose, and eliminate errors in a program. Generally speaking, debugging a program involves logic checking and variable-value viewing. For Lua in Redis, a debugging tool was introduced in version 3.2 to make the debugging process much easier, and there are some functions that can help you to print logs for debugging. In this recipe, we'll see how to achieve these debugging steps in Redis.

Getting ready...

You need to finish the installation of the Redis Server as we described in the *Downloading and installing Redis* recipe in `Chapter 1`, *Getting Started with Redis*.

For logging in Redis, you have to set the following configurations in `redis.conf`:

```
logfile "/redis/log/redis.log"
loglevel debug
```

Then, you can start the Redis Server with the configuration file, as we have shown in the *Starting and shutting down Redis* recipe in `Chapter 1`, *Getting Started with Redis*.

How to do it...

Let's take the Lua script introduced in the previous recipe to show how to debug a Lua script of Redis as an example:

1. Open a console and update the script, as follows:

```
$ mkdir /redis/coding/lua; cd /redis/coding/lua
$ cat updatejsondebug.lua
local id = KEYS[1]
local data = ARGV[1]
redis.debug(id)
redis.debug(data)
```

```
local retJson = redis.call('get',  id)
local dataSource = cjson.decode(data)

if retJson == false then
  retJson = {}
else
  retJson = cjson.decode(retJson)
end
redis.breakpoint()

for k,v in pairs(dataSource) do
  retJson[k] = v
end

redis.log(redis.LOG_WARNING,cjson.encode(retJson))
redis.call('set',  id,  cjson.encode(retJson))

return redis.call('get',id)
```

2. Set the user profile with the user ID 992398 by redis-cli:

```
$ bin/redis-cli set users:id:992398
"{"grade":"C","name":"Mike","sex":"male"}"
```

3. To test if we can modify the schema of the JSON to record grade changes by this Lua script, we start debugging by the --ldb option in redis-cli:

```
$ bin/redis-cli --ldb --eval updatejsondebug.lua users:id:992398 ,
'{"grade": {"init":"C","now":"A"}}'
Lua debugging session started, please use:
quit    -- End the session.
restart -- Restart the script in debug mode again.
help    -- Show Lua script debugging commands.

* Stopped at 1, stop reason = step over
-> 1    local id = KEYS[1]
```

4. Type s to proceed with the script step by step, and debug information will be printed out by the redis.debug() function:

```
lua debugger> s
* Stopped at 3, stop reason = step over
-> 3    redis.debug(id)
lua debugger> s
<debug> line 3: "users:id:992398"
* Stopped at 4, stop reason = step over
-> 4    redis.debug(data)
```

```
lua debugger> s
<debug> line 4: "{"grade": {"init":"C","now":"A"}}"
* Stopped at 6, stop reason = step over
-> 6   local retJson = redis.call('get',  id)
```

5. Type s to move on.

   When a Redis command is called in a Lua script, the debugger will show the complete command and also the result. We can use p VARIABLE to print out the value of the variable in Lua script:

```
lua debugger> s
<redis> get users:id:993298
<reply> "{"grade":"C","name":"Mike","sex":"male"}"
* Stopped at 7, stop reason = step over
-> 7 local dataSource = cjson.decode(data)
lua debugger> p retJson
<value> "{"grade":"C","name":"Mike","sex":"male"}"
```

6. Then, continue executing the script. The execution will stop at the next breakpoint we set using the redis.breakpoint() function in the script:

```
lua debugger> c
* Stopped at 16, stop reason = redis.breakpoint() called
-> 16 for k,v in pairs(dataSource) do
```

7. Type w to browse the whole script you are debugging. After viewing the whole script, we set a breakpoint using b LINENUMBER to check the result before setting it back. Then, use c to continue the execution till the breakpoint in the previous step:

```
lua debugger> b 21
   20   redis.log(redis.LOG_WARNING,cjson.encode(retJson))
  #21   redis.call('set', id, cjson.encode(retJson))
   22
lua debugger> c
* Stopped at 21, stop reason = break point
->#21   redis.call('set', id, cjson.encode(retJson))
```

   The function redis.log() will write the corresponding log information into your Redis Server log file, which is redis.log under /redis/log directory in this example:

```
15549:M 26 Sep 09:20:52.442 #
{"grade":"C","name":"Mike","sex":"male"}
```

8. Then, continue the execution of the script till the breakpoint:

```
lua debugger> c
"{"grade":{"now":"A","init":"C"},"name":"Mike","sex":"male"}"
(Lua debugging session ended -- dataset changes rolled back)
```

How it works...

The debugging process is quite self-explanatory, and there is no need to memorize all the commands in `ldb`; the `help` command in `ldb` will help.

It's important to know that by forking a process to talk to the debug session, the Redis Server won't get blocked during debugging. Also, this mechanism means all the changes made in debug mode, by default, will be rolled back. Another option, `--ldb-sync-mode`, will make your server unavailable when you are debugging. So, make sure you really need to do so when you set the debug mode to sync.

We'll discuss Redis logging in detail in the *Logging* recipe in Chapter 8, Deploying to a Production Environment.

There's more...

When you try to view a variable's value in a Lua script in Redis, your first thought may be to print the variable out directly with the `print()` function in Lua. While it's quite straightforward and works fine, you have to note that you won't see the log if the server is running in daemonize mode, because the message generated by `print()` will be shown in the `stdout` of your `redis-server` process. So, if the server is started in daemonize mode, the `stdout` will be discarded.

See also

- For a complete manual for **Redis Lua debugger (LDB)**, refer to https://redis.io/topics/ldb
- For the script debug command of Lua in Redis, you can refer to https://redis.io/commands/script-debug
- If you are interested in more debugging techniques, you can find them at https://redislabs.com/blog/5-6-7-methods-for-tracing-and-debugging-red is-lua-scripts/

4
Developing with Redis

In this chapter, we will cover the following recipes:

- When to use Redis in your application
- Using the correct data types
- Using the correct Redis API
- Connecting to Redis with Java
- Connecting to Redis with Python
- Connecting to Redis with Spring Data Redis
- Writing a MapReduce job for Redis
- Writing a Spark job for Redis

Introduction

We learned the data types and many useful features of Redis in Chapter 2, *Data Types* and Chapter 3, *Data Features*. In this chapter, we'll focus on the topic of application development with Redis.

First, we start by introducing some common Redis use cases to give you a brief idea of how Redis works in the real world.

After that, some guidelines will be provided for how to choose correct value types and APIs. It's very essential to follow these guidelines when developing applications with Redis because unlike most RDBMSes, you barely do anything to optimize the processing power of Redis by only tweaking the configuration on the server side. Using proper data types and APIs at the very beginning of application design is the key factor for making full use of the high performance of Redis and avoiding its pitfalls at the same time.

After the design guidelines, we are going to show how to develop an application with Redis using Java and Python. Spring Data Redis is also covered for web application development.

Lastly, the last two recipes in this chapter will cover how to utilize Redis in the big data world.

When to use Redis in your application

As you have already seen the powerful features of Redis in previous chapters, you may be wondering what Redis can do in an application and when it should be used. In this recipe, we will show a few real-world application scenarios where Redis is a better choice than other storage solutions. Hopefully you will get more ideas for using Redis in your applications.

Session store

In a modern website architecture, there are multiple web servers behind one or more load balancers. Sessions usually need to be stored in external storage systems. If any of the web servers go down, another server can retrieve the sessions from the external storage and continue to serve traffic. Redis is a perfect session store because it has very low access latency compared to a RDBMS. Also, key expiration support in Redis can be naturally adopted for session timeout management.

Analytics

Redis can also be used for analytical and statistical purposes. For example, if we want to count how many users have viewed a restaurant in our application, we can simply use the INCR command to increase the counter when the restaurant has been viewed. We don't need to worry about the race conditions because all Redis commands are atomic. More advanced counters or a statistical data capturing system can be built with Redis data types such as hash, Sorted Set, and HyperLoglog.

Leaderboards

With the help of the Sorted Set in Redis, we can easily implement a leaderboard. As we have shown in the *Using the Sorted Set data type* recipe in `Chapter 2`, *Data Types* we can create a Sorted Set of restaurants; the score of the Set is the user vote number. Therefore, the `ZREVRANGE` command returns restaurants by popularity. The same functionality can also be implemented in an RDBMS such as MySQL, but the SQL query will be much slower than Redis.

Queues

Remember the blocking `PUSH`/`POP` commands for a Redis list we introduced in the *Using list data type* recipe of `Chapter 2`, *Data Types*. As we demonstrated in that recipe, a Redis list can be used to implement a simple job queue. The widely-used **Resque** project, which is a Redis-backed Ruby library for job queuing, is based on this idea. With the `RPOPLPUSH` command, we can also implement reliable queues using Redis lists.

Latest N records

Suppose we would like to get the ten restaurants that have been most recently added to our application. If using a RDBMS, we would have to run a SQL query, such as the following:

```
SELECT * FROM restaurants ORDER BY created_at DESC LIMIT 10
```

We can take advantage of a Redis list to solve this problem:

1. Maintain a Redis list, `latest_restaurants`.
2. Whenever a new restaurant is added, do `LPUSH latest_restaurants` and `LTRIM recent_restaurants 0 10`. In this way, the Redis list will always contain the latest ten restaurants.

Caching

Since Redis is an in-memory data storage system, using Redis as a cache in front of an RDBMS usually expedites the database query process. Here is a simple use case: Before querying the RDBMS, we first look up the record in Redis. If the record does not exist in Redis, we query the RDBMS and put the record into Redis. When writing to the RDBMS, we also write the record to Redis. Records in the cache are associated with a timeout or eviction policy such as **Least Recently Used** (**LRU**) in order to limit the cache usage.

There's more...

As some of the previous use cases illustrated, certain tasks that are slow or hard to accomplish in an RDBMS can be done easily and quickly in Redis. However, Redis is not the option for all storage needs. Firstly, because the default Redis distribution stores all data in memory (some cloud-based Redis services provide the option of using an SSD as the data storage backend), if the size of data exceeds the memory size Redis cannot hold all the data. Secondly, Redis transactions are not fully **Atomicity, Consistency, Isolation, and Durability (ACID)**-compliant. If ACID transactions are needed, Redis cannot be used. An RDBMS or an other database system should be used in those scenarios.

See also

- For the meaning of ACID, refer to `https://en.wikipedia.org/wiki/ACID`
- For the project Resque, refer to `https://github.com/resque/resque`

Using the correct data types

In `Chapter 2`, *Data Types*, we learned that Redis provides rich data types to fulfill business needs. So, when we develop an application with Redis it's of great importance for us to become familiar with these data types first. This includes not only being aware of the semantic differences between them, but also identifying their strengths and weaknesses when we are going to implement certain business scenarios with them. Although it's not hard to choose one or more data types to meet our requirements when designing the application, there is always room for optimization when we consider the performance and memory consumption.

In this recipe, we'll go through a user data storing design example to show how to use correct data types for less memory consumption.

Getting ready...

You need to finish the installation of the Redis Server as we described in the *Downloading and installing Redis* recipe in Chapter 1, *Getting Started with Redis*.

You need to use the FLUSHALL command to flush all the data in your Redis instance before moving on to the next section.

Use the following command to install the dos2unix tools in Ubuntu:

```
sudo apt-get install dos2unix
```

In macOS, you can install the dos2unix tools using the following command:

```
brew install dos2unix
```

How to do it...

To show how to choose the correct data types, we would like to save the user information of Relp in Redis. As a prototype design verification, we are going to populate some sample data for 10,000 users from Redis to check if we are using the best strategy to store user information in Redis. This means that while satisfying the business needs of the application, we will try to use as little memory as possible. For illustration purposes, the following information will be stored for one user:

- id: user ID
- name: user name
- sex: m/f
- register_time: sign-up timestamp
- nation: the nationality of the user

1. We check the memory consumption of an empty Redis instance:

```
127.0.0.1:6379> INFO MEMORY
# Memory
used_memory:827512
used_memory_human:808.12K
```

2. The first thought that comes to mind is to store each piece of information as a string key-value pair:

```
$ cat populatedata0.sh
#!/bin/bash
DATAFILE="string.data"
rm $DATAFILE >/dev/null  2>&1
NAMEOPTION[0]="Jack"
NAMEOPTION[1]="MIKE"
NAMEOPTION[2]="Mary"
SEXOPTION[0]="m"
SEXOPTION[1]="f"
NATIONOPTION[0]="us"
NATIONOPTION[1]="cn"
NATIONOPTION[2]="uk"
for i in `seq -f "%010g" 1 10000`
do
    namerand=$[ $RANDOM % 3 ]
    sexrand=$[ $RANDOM % 2 ]
    timerand=$[ $RANDOM % 30 ]
    nationrand=$[ $RANDOM % 3 ]
    echo "set \"user:${i}:name\" \"${NAMEOPTION[$namerand]}\"" >>
$DATAFILE
    echo "set \"user:${i}:sex\" \"${SEXOPTION[$sexrand]}\"" >>
$DATAFILE
    echo "set \"user:${i}:resigter_time\" \"`date +%s%N`\"" >>
$DATAFILE
    echo "set \"user:${i}:nation\"
\"${NATIONOPTION[$nationrand]}\"" >> $DATAFILE
    sleep 0.00000${timerand}
done
unix2dos $DATAFILE
$ bin/redis-cli FLUSHALL
OK
$ bash populatedata0.sh
unix2dos: converting file string.data to DOS format ...
$ cat string.data | redis-cli --pipe
All data transferred. Waiting for the last reply...
Last reply received from server.
errors: 0, replies: 40000
```

3. Check the memory consumption using INFO MEMORY within redis-cli:

```
127.0.0.1:6379> INFO MEMORY
# Memory
used_memory:4231960
used_memory_human:4.04M
```

4. The first optimization we are going to do is to store the user information as a JSON string:

```
$ cat populatedata1.sh
#!/bin/bash
DATAFILE="json.data"
... (omit all the variables declared above)

for i in `seq -f "%010g" 1 10000`
do
    namerand=$[ $RANDOM % 3 ]
    sexrand=$[ $RANDOM % 2 ]
    timerand=$[ $RANDOM % 30 ]
    nationrand=$[ $RANDOM % 3 ]
    echo "set \"user:${i}\"
'{\"name\":\"${NAMEOPTION[$namerand]}\",sex:\"${SEXOPTION[$sexrand]
}\",resigter_time:`date
+%s%N`,nation:\"${NATIONOPTION[$nationrand]}\"}'" >> $DATAFILE
    sleep 0.00000${timerand}
done

unix2dos $DATAFILE

$ bin/redis-cli FLUSHALL
OK

$ bash populatedata1.sh
unix2dos: converting file string.data to DOS format ...

$ cat json.data | redis-cli --pipe
All data transferred. Waiting for the last reply...
Last reply received from server.
errors: 0, replies: 10000
```

5. By checking the memory consumption, we found that around 43% *((4.04-2.29)/4.04)* of the memory space has been saved:

```
127.0.0.1:6379> INFO MEMORY
# Memory
used_memory:2398896
used_memory_human:2.29M
```

6. After that, we use a `Lua` script, which was introduced in `Chapter 3`, *Data Features*, to serialize the raw JSON string with the `msgpack` lib:

```
$ cat setjsonasmsgpack.lua
--EVAL 'this script' 1 some-key '{"some": "json"}'
local key = KEYS[1];
local value = ARGV[1];
local mvalue = cmsgpack.pack(cjson.decode(value));
return redis.call('SET', key, mvalue);

$ cat populatedata2.sh
#!/bin/bash
DATAFILE="msgpack.data"

rm $DATAFILE >/dev/null 2>&1
... (omit all the variables declared above)

for i in `seq -f "%010g" 1 10000`
do
    namerand=$[ $RANDOM % 3 ]
    sexrand=$[ $RANDOM % 2 ]
    timerand=$[ $RANDOM % 30 ]
    nationrand=$[ $RANDOM % 3 ]
        echo
"user:00000${i}{\"name\":\"${NAMEOPTION[$namerand]}\",\"sex\":\"${S
EXOPTION[$sexrand]}\",\"resigter_time\":`date
+%s`,\"nation\":\"${NATIONOPTION[$nationrand]}\"}" >> $DATAFILE
        sleep 0.00000${timerand}
done

unix2dos $DATAFILE

$ bin/redis-cli FLUSHALL
OK

$ bash populatedata2.sh
unix2dos: converting file msgpack.data to DOS format ...

$ cat msgpack.data | while read CMD; do  var1=$(cut -d' ' -f1 <<<
```

```
$CMD); var2=$(cut -d' ' -f2 <<< $CMD) ; /bin/redis-cli --eval
setjsonasmsgpack.lua  $var1 , $var2; done
```

7. We have saved around 49% *((4.04-2.06)/4.04)* of memory using `msgpack` serialization:

```
127.0.0.1:6379> INFO MEMORY
# Memory
used_memory:2159048
used_memory_human:2.06M
```

8. Then we continue trying to optimize the design by using a hash data type:

```
$ cat populatedata3.sh
#!/bin/bash
DATAFILE="hash.data"

... (omit all the variables declared above)

for i in `seq -f "%010g" 1 10000`
do
    namerand=$[ $RANDOM % 3 ]
    sexrand=$[ $RANDOM % 2 ]
    timerand=$[ $RANDOM % 30 ]
    nationrand=$[ $RANDOM % 3 ]
    echo "hset \"user:${i}\" \"name\" \"${NAMEOPTION[$namerand]}\"
\"sex\" \"${SEXOPTION[$sexrand]}\" \"resigter_time\" `date +%s%N`
\"nation\" \"${NATIONOPTION[$nationrand]}\"" >> $DATAFILE
    sleep 0.00000${timerand}
done

unix2dos $DATAFILE
$ bin/redis-cli FLUSHALL
OK

$ bash populatedata3.sh
unix2dos: converting file hash.data to DOS format ...

$ cat hash.data | redis-cli --pipe
All data transferred. Waiting for the last reply...
Last reply received from server.
errors: 0, replies: 10000
```

9. Check the memory again. Oops, it seems that compared with the previous optimization mechanism with `msgpack`, more memory was used this time, and nearly the same amount of memory is needed as the JSON string design:

```
127.0.0.1:6379> INFO MEMORY
# Memory
used_memory:2399352
used_memory_human:2.29M
```

10. We find that, although we use the hash data type to store the user data, compared to the JSON string method the keys count is not eliminated. So, we move on to trying to reduce the number of keys by partitioning the user ID. First, we modify the configuration for the max entries and value of hash to use `ziplist`:

```
$ vim conf/redis.conf
hash-max-ziplist-entries 1000
hash-max-ziplist-value 64
```

11. Restart the Redis Server to make the net configurations work. After that, we start our prototype verification:

```
$ cat populatedata4.sh
#!/bin/bash
DATAFILE="hashpartition.data"

PLENGTH=3

... (omit all the variables declared above)

for i in `seq -f "%010g" 1 10000`
do
    namerand=$[ $RANDOM % 3 ]
    sexrand=$[ $RANDOM % 2 ]
    timerand=$[ $RANDOM % 30 ]
    nationrand=$[ $RANDOM % 3 ]
    LENGTH=`echo ${#i}`
    LENGTHCUT=`echo $((LENGTH-PLENGTH))`
    LENGTHEND=`echo $((LENGTHCUT+1))`
    VALUE1=`echo $i | cut -c1-${LENGTHCUT}`
    VALUE2=`echo $i | cut -c${LENGTHEND}-${LENGTH}`
    echo "hset \"user:${VALUE1}\" $VALUE2
'{\"name\":\"${NAMEOPTION[$namerand]}\",\"sex\":\"${SEXOPTION[$sexrand]}\",\"resigter_time\":`date
+%s%N`,\"nation\":\"${NATIONOPTION[$nationrand]}\"}'" >> $DATAFILE
    sleep 0.00000${timerand}
```

```
done

unix2dos $DATAFILE

$ bin/redis-cli FLUSHALL
OK

$ bash populatedata4.sh
unix2dos: converting file hashpartition.data to DOS format ...

$ cat hashpartition.data | redis-cli --pipe
All data transferred. Waiting for the last reply...
Last reply received from server.
errors: 0, replies: 10000
```

12. Check the memory for the hash partition. It can clearly be seen that around 52% *((4.04-1.94)/4.04)* of memory has been saved via this optimization:

```
127.0.0.1:6379> INFO MEMORY
# Memory
used_memory:2032160
used_memory_human:1.94M
```

13. Lastly, we try to combine the hash partition and `msgpack` serialization to see what we can achieve:

```
$ cat populatedata5.sh
#!/bin/bash
DATAFILE="hashpartitionmsgpack.data"
PLENGTH=3

rm $DATAFILE >/dev/null  2>&1

... (omit all the variables declared above)

for i in `seq -f "%010g" 1 10000`
do
    namerand=$[ $RANDOM % 3 ]
    sexrand=$[ $RANDOM % 2 ]
    timerand=$[ $RANDOM % 30 ]
    nationrand=$[ $RANDOM % 3 ]
    LENGTH=`echo ${#i}`
    LENGTHCUT=`echo $((LENGTH-PLENGTH))`
    LENGTHEND=`echo $((LENGTHCUT+1))`
    VALUE1=`echo $i | awk '{print substr($1,1,"'$LENGTHCUT'")}'`
    VALUE2=`echo $i | awk '{print substr($1,"'$LENGTHEND'","'$PLENGTH'")}'`
```

```
        echo "user:${VALUE1} $VALUE2
{\"name\":\"${NAMEOPTION[$namerand]}\",\"sex\":\"${SEXOPTION[$sexra
nd]}\",\"resigter_time\":`date
+%s%N`,\"nation\":\"${NATIONOPTION[$nationrand]}\"}" >> $DATAFILE
sleep 0.00000${timerand}
done


unix2dos $DATAFILE


$ bin/redis-cli FLUSHALL
OK


$ bash populatedata5.sh
unix2dos: converting file hashpartitionmsgpack.data to DOS format
...


$ cat hashpartitionmsgpack.data | while read CMD; do  var1=$(cut -
d' ' -f1 <<< $CMD); var2=$(cut -d' ' -f2 <<< $CMD) ; var3=$(cut -d'
' -f3 <<< $CMD); /redis/bin/redis-cli --eval
setjsonashashmsgpack.lua  $var1 $var2 , $var3; done
```

14. It's amazing to find out that after the optimizations, the sample data only takes `1.34M`, which is only 33% *(1.34/4.04)* of the memory consumption of the initial design:

```
127.0.0.1:6379> INFO MEMORY
# Memory
used_memory:1403272
used_memory_human:1.34M
```

How it works...

When you are going to design an application with Redis, one thing you should bear in mind is that there isn't always only one data type that can fit your business scenario. That means different requirements for storage and query performance lead to different designs. Your job when designing is to dig out which data type is best for you via various prototype verifications as in the previous example.

In this example, first we make a basic design, which is a simple mapping of a key to a value per attribute of a user. We do this in the first step as a baseline of the memory usage for the follow-up reference.

After that, we try to reduce the memory usage in two different ways. One is trying to reduce the number of keys. The reason we do this is that Redis uses some internal data structures to maintain a key. By reducing the number of keys, there is less cost for internal data structures, so a lot of memory space can be saved. For this purpose, using a JSON string as the value for one user and using the hash data type are tried in the preceding example.

Special attention should be paid to the partitioning of a hash key. We are going to store 1000 entries in a hash key. So, the first thing we have done is modify the configuration hash-max-ziplist-entries to 1000 to make sure the internal encoding for the value of our hash key is ziplist. From the *Using hash data type* recipe in Chapter 2, *Data Types*, we said that, if the length of a hash in Redis is less than hash-max-ziplist-entries and the size of every element in the list is less than hash-max-ziplist-value, the ziplist, a more memory effective data structure, is used for internal hash object encoding. A restart of the Redis Server is needed. We partition the key by the first seven digits of a user ID and the rest of a user's information is stored as a JSON string. So, one partition is organized as follows, and each partition (except "user:0000000" and "user:0000010") contains 1000 entries:

```
$ bin/redis-cli hgetall "user:0000007"
088
{"name":"Mary","sex":"f","resigter_time":1506942816344887079,"nation":"uk"}
...
331
{"name":"Mary","sex":"f","resigter_time":1506942817274215585,"nation":"us"}

$ bin/redis-cli hlen "user:0000007"
(integer) 1000
```

The final number of keys for this example is 11, which is much fewer than the initial count of keys (40000):

```
$ bin/redis-cli dbsize
(integer) 11
```

Another way to reduce the memory usage is compressing the value of the key. The cmsgpack library in the lua script plays an important role in achieving this goal.

The final design combines the two methods.

Another easy way to reduce the memory usage is to decrease the length of the key. For example, we can use regt instead of "resigter_time" for short. You can try this strategy out to see how much memory space you could save.

There's more...

More examples can be listed, such as counting the unique visitors to your website; you can use set, bitmaps, or HyperLogLog to achieve your goal. You have to choose the correct data types. The more familiar you are with the Redis data types, the more ways you will find to implement your application.

Apart from the memory consumption concern, you should pay attention to the performance of manipulating the data type you choose. A space-time tradeoff must be considered all the time. Be cautious not to overdesign the memory optimization. For the performance concerns of an application design with Redis, the next recipe will give you some useful tips.

See also

- For more memory optimization details, refer to
  `https://redis.io/topics/memory-optimization`
- The engineering blog in Instagram describes a successful memory saving use case; please refer to
  `https://engineering.instagram.com/storing-hundreds-of-millions-of-simple-key-value-pairs-in-redis-1091ae80f74c`
- The engineering blog for Deliveroo, which is a British online food delivery company, describes another successful practice on session key storage in Redis; please refer to
  `https://deliveroo.engineering/2016/10/07/optimising-session-key-storage.html`

Using the correct Redis APIs

In `Chapter 2`, *Data Types* and `Chapter 3`, *Data Features*, we showed that Redis provides many powerful APIs to manipulate the various kinds of data type. When you are going to develop your application with Redis, similar to the selection of data types mentioned in the previous *Using the correct data types* recipe, there is always more than one Redis API for you to implement certain business needs. To guarantee the performance of a Redis instance, extreme caution must be taken when you make the decision on which API you will use.

In this recipe, we'll take a look at several examples to learn how to use correct APIs to achieve a good performance in Redis.

Getting ready...

You need to finish the installation of the Redis Server as we described in the *Downloading and installing Redis* recipe in `Chapter 1`, *Getting Started with Redis*.

We need to use the `FLUSHALL` command to flush all the data in your Redis instance before moving on to the next section.

Use the following command to install the dos2unix tools in Ubuntu:

```
sudo apt-get install dos2unix
```

In macOS, you can install the dos2unix tools using the following command:

```
brew install dos2unix
```

How to do it

To show how to use the correct Redis APIs, the steps are as following:

1. At the beginning of this example, we will import the data from 1 million users into a hash key in Redis with two APIs: `HSET` and `HMSET`. For better illustration, we execute the following script, which connects to the Redis Server and populates the user data on another host, which is considered an application server. You may have to wait for quite a long time, so run this script and then take a break and get back to catch the result:

```
$ cat hmset-vs-hset.sh
#!/bin/bash
HSETFILE="hset.cmd"
HMSETFILE="hmset.cmd"

rm $HSETFILE $HMSETFILE

... (omit all the variables declared above)
printf "hmset \"user\" " >> $HMSETFILE
for i in `seq -f "%010g" 1 1000000`
do
    namerand=$[ $RANDOM % 3 ]
    sexrand=$[ $RANDOM % 2 ]
    timerand=$[ $RANDOM % 30 ]
    nationrand=$[ $RANDOM % 3 ]
    echo "hset \"user\" ${i}
'{\"name\":\"${NAMEOPTION[$namerand]}\",\"sex\":\"${SEXOPTION[$sexr
```

```
and]}\",\"resigter_time\":`date
+%s%N`,\"nation\":\"${NATIONOPTION[$nationrand]}\"}'" >> $HSETFILE
    printf " ${i}
'{"name":"${NAMEOPTION[$namerand]}","sex":"${SEXOPTION[$sexrand]}",
"resigter_time":`date
+%s%N`,"nation":"${NATIONOPTION[$nationrand]}"}' " >> $HMSETFILE
      sleep 0.00000${timerand}
done

unix2dos $HSETFILE
unix2dos $HMSETFILE

time cat $HSETFILE |/redis/bin/redis-cli -h $SERVER
sleep 10
time cat $HMSETFILE |/redis/bin/redis-cli -h $SERVER

$ bin/redis-cli FLUSHALL
OK

$ bash hmset-vs-hset.sh
...

real    0m4.557s
user    0m0.696s
sys     0m1.284s
OK
(0.51s)

real    0m0.750s
user    0m0.224s
sys     0m0.496s
```

2. As soon as we have finished importing the data, we try to get all the data of this hash key "user" using HGETALL and time this operation. Before issuing HGETALL, we open another Terminal to start a latency test by using the --latency option in redis-cli:

```
$ bin/redis-cli --latency
min: 0, max: 1, avg: 0.11 (136 samples)
```

3. We fetch all the user data by calling HGETALL:

```
$ bin/redis-cli HGETALL user
```

4. High latency is detected during the processing of HGETALL in Redis:

```
$ bin/redis-cli --latency
min: 0, max: 57, avg: 0.13 (2474 samples)
```

5. Stop the latency test by pressing *Ctrl* + *C* and restart it:

```
$ bin/redis-cli --latency
min: 0, max: 1, avg: 0.08 (186 samples)
```

6. Instead of using HGETALL, we try to iterate all the user data with HSCAN this time:

```
$ cat hscan.sh
#!/bin/bash
cr=0
key=$1

rm ${1}.dumpfile
while true; do
    cr=`/redis/bin/redis-cli HSCAN user $cr MATCH '*' | {
        read a
        echo $a
        while read x; read y; do
            echo $x:$y >> ${1}.dumpfile
        done
    }`

    echo $cr
    if [ $cr == "0" ]; then
        break
    fi
done

$ bash hscan.sh user
```

7. During the iteration, no surprising latency is detected:

```
$ bin/redis-cli --latency
min: 0, max: 1, avg: 0.09 (13423 samples)
```

How it works...

When you are going to design an application with Redis, two principles should be taken into consideration. The first principle is that you should make every effort to combine data manipulation to eliminate the **round-trip time** (**RTT**). The concept of RTT was introduced when we discussed the pipeline feature in the *Using pipeline* recipe of `Chapter 3`, *Data Features*. Redis is known for its high speed in processing requests. So, if you can reduce the RTT, a dramatic performance improvement will be obtained. Taking advantage of pipelining is a good idea, while some data APIs of Redis can reduce the RTT natively. Our first part of the previous example is a good example of this. Compared to setting the hash values one by one using `HSET`, using `HMSET` to set them in one go is obviously a better way to do the same job if all the data can be prepared before setting. 83.5% *(1-0.750/4.557)* of time has been saved!

Another principle you should bear in mind is that Redis is mainly a single-threaded data store service, which means you should choose Redis commands with extreme caution and bear in mind their time complexity. The Redis documentation shows the time complexity of every API. For example, you can find out the time complexity of `HGETALL` in the documents of Redis as follows:

Time complexity: O(N)

where *N* is the size of the hash.

Here, the time complexity is marked using the Big O notation. We won't talk a lot about the Big O notation except that it's a widely accepted term to describe the performance or complexity of an algorithm. For your quick reference, the following graph shows the common Big O notation growing speed:

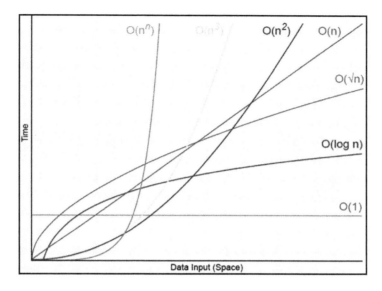

Source: `https://github.com/sf-wdi-31/algorithm-complexity-and-big-o`

In our example, after setting the data into a hash key of Redis, we tried to fetch all the data using HGETALL. A horrifying latency is caught, which is often a nightmare for an online Redis data service. The reason why this happened is that HGETALL has an *O(n)* time complexity in which *n* is the size of the hash. In our example, *n* is 100000 which is quite a big number for Redis with respect to its processing speed. While processing this command, the Redis server is unable to respond to any other requests. A better way to achieve the same goal is to use HSCAN to iterate the hash key. This API will gradually iterate the hash key, eliminating the spike of latency effectively.

There's more...

In addition, commands such as KEYS *, FLUSHDB, DEL, and HDEL may block the Redis Server. Generally speaking, you should pay special attention to Redis APIs that have a time complexity worse than or equal to *O(n)*.

See also

- If you would like to find out what operations slow down your Redis Server, you can use a slow log to record the `slow` commands processed in the Redis Server. For more details, refer to the Identifying slow operations/queries using slow log recipe in Chapter 10, *Troubleshooting Redis*.
- More latency troubleshooting mechanisms will be introduced in the *Troubleshooting latency* section of Chapter 10, *Troubleshooting Redis*.
- For the Big O notation, refer to: `https://en.wikipedia.org/wiki/Big_O_notation` to find out more details.

Connecting to Redis with Java

In order to use Redis in Java applications, we need a Redis Java client. There are a couple of choices that can be found under the **Clients** section on the Redis homepage. In this recipe, we will introduce Jedis, which is an open source and easy to use Redis Java client.

Getting ready...

You need to finish the installation of the Redis Server as we described in the *Downloading and installing Redis* recipe in Chapter 1, *Getting Started with Redis*.

You need to install the **Java Development Kit (JDK)**, version 1.8.

A Java IDE such as IntelliJ IDEA or NetBeans is recommended but not required.

How to do it...

To show how to connect Redis with Java, the first requirement for using Jedis in our Java application is including the library in the project. We can either download the Jedis library JAR file and add its path to `CLASSPATH`, or use build tools such as Maven, Gradle, or Bazel to manage the library dependencies. In examples of this recipe, we use Gradle to include Jedis as a dependency of our project.

Add the following line to the `dependencies` section of `build.gradle`:

```
compile group: 'redis.clients', name: 'jedis', version: '2.9.0'
```

Connecting to the Redis Server

Create a Java class, `JedisSingleDemo`, with the following code:

```java
import redis.clients.jedis.Jedis;
import java.util.List;

public class JedisSingleDemo {
    public static void main(String[] args) {
        //Connecting to localhost Redis server
        Jedis jedis = new Jedis("localhost");

        //String operations
        String restaurant = "Extreme Pizza";
        jedis.set(restaurant, "300 Broadway, New York, NY");
        jedis.append(restaurant, " 10011");
        String address = jedis.get("Extreme Pizza");
        System.out.printf("Address for %s is %s\n", restaurant, address);

        //List operations
        String listKey = "favorite_restaurants";
        jedis.lpush(listKey, "PF Chang's", "Olive Garden");
        jedis.rpush(listKey, "Outback Steakhouse", "Red Lobster");
        List<String> favoriteRestaurants = jedis.lrange(listKey, 0, -1);
        System.out.printf("Favorite Restaurants: %s\n", favoriteRestaurants);

        System.exit(0);
    }
}
```

The demo application will print the following lines:

```
Address for Extreme Pizza is 300 Broadway, New York, NY 10011
Favorite Restaurants: [Olive Garden, PF Chang's, Olive Garden, PF Chang's,
Indian Tandoor, Longhorn Steakhouse, Outback Steakhouse, Red Lobster,
Outback Steakhouse, Red Lobster]
```

Using pipeline in Jedis

Let's create another Java class, `JedisPipelineDemo`:

```java
import redis.clients.jedis.Jedis;
import redis.clients.jedis.Pipeline;
import redis.clients.jedis.Response;

public class JedisPipelineDemo {
    public static void main(String[] args) {
        //Connecting to localhost Redis server
        Jedis jedis = new Jedis("localhost");

        //Create a Pipeline
        Pipeline pipeline = jedis.pipelined();
        //Add commands to pipeline
        pipeline.set("mykey", "myvalue");
        pipeline.sadd("myset", "value1", "value2");
        Response<String> stringValue = pipeline.get("mykey");
        Response<Long> noElementsInSet = pipeline.scard("myset");
        //Send commands
        pipeline.sync();
        //Handle responses
        System.out.printf("mykey: %s\n", stringValue.get());
        System.out.printf("Number of Elements in set: %d\n", noElementsInSet.get());
        System.exit(0);
    }
}
```

The output of the program is:

```
mykey: myvalue
Number of Elements in set: 2
```

Using transactions in Jedis

Let's create a Java class, JedisTransactionDemo:

```java
import redis.clients.jedis.Jedis;
import redis.clients.jedis.Response;
import redis.clients.jedis.Transaction;
import java.util.Set;

public class JedisTransactionDemo {
    public static void main(String[] args) {
        //Connecting to localhost Redis server
        Jedis jedis = new Jedis("localhost");

        //Initialize
        String user = "user:1000";
        String restaurantOrderCount = "restaurant_orders:200";
        String restaurantUsers = "restaurant_users:200";
        jedis.set(restaurantOrderCount, "400");
        jedis.sadd(restaurantUsers, "user:302", "user:401");

        //Create a Redis transaction
        Transaction transaction = jedis.multi();
        Response<Long> countResponse = transaction.incr(restaurantOrderCount);
        transaction.sadd(restaurantUsers, user);
        Response<Set<String>> userSet = transaction.smembers(restaurantUsers);
        //Execute transaction
        transaction.exec();

        //Handle responses
        System.out.printf("Number of orders: %d\n", countResponse.get());
        System.out.printf("Users: %s\n", userSet.get());
        System.exit(0);
    }
}
```

The output of the program is:

```
Number of orders: 401
Users: [user:1000, user:401, user:302]
```

Running Lua scripts in Jedis

Create a Lua script, updateJson.lua, and put it into the Java resources folder. The content of the Lua script can be found in the *Using Lua* recipe in Chapter 3, *Data Features*.

Create a Java class, `JedisLuaDemo`:

```
1    package com.packtpub.redis_cookbook;
2
3    import redis.clients.jedis.Jedis;
4    import java.io.BufferedReader;
5    import java.io.InputStream;
6    import java.io.InputStreamReader;
7    import java.util.Collections;
8    import java.util.List;
9    import java.util.stream.Collectors;
10
11   public class JedisLuaDemo {
12       public static void main(String[] args) throws Exception {
13           //Connecting to localhost Redis server
14           Jedis jedis = new Jedis("localhost");
15
16           String user = "users:id:992452";
17           jedis.set(user, "{\"name\": \"Tina\", \"sex\": \"female\", \"grade\": \"A\"}");
18
19           //Register Lua script
20           InputStream luaInputStream =
21               JedisLuaDemo.class
22                   .getClassLoader()
23                   .getResourceAsStream("updateJson.lua");
24           String luaScript =
25               new BufferedReader(new InputStreamReader(luaInputStream))
26               .lines()
27               .collect(Collectors.joining("\n"));
28           String luaSHA = jedis.scriptLoad(luaScript);
29
30           //Eval Lua script
31           List<String> KEYS = Collections.singletonList(user);
32           List<String> ARGS = Collections.singletonList("{\"grade\": \"C\"}");
33           jedis.evalsha(luaSHA, KEYS, ARGS);
34
35           System.out.printf("%s: %s\n", user, jedis.get(user));
36           System.exit(0);
37       }
38   }
```

The output of the program is:

```
users:id:992452: {"grade":"C","name":"Tina","sex":"female"}
```

Using a connection pool in Jedis

Create a Java class, JedisPoolDemo:

```java
import redis.clients.jedis.Jedis;
import redis.clients.jedis.JedisPool;
import redis.clients.jedis.JedisPoolConfig;

import java.util.HashMap;
import java.util.Map;

public class JedisPoolDemo {
    public static void main(String[] args) {
        //Creating a JedisPool of Jedis connections to localhost Redis server
        JedisPool jedisPool = new JedisPool(new JedisPoolConfig(), "localhost");

        //Get a Jedis connection from pool
        try (Jedis jedis = jedisPool.getResource()) {
            String restaurantName = "Kyoto Ramen";
            Map<String, String> restaurantInfo = new HashMap<>();
            restaurantInfo.put("address", "801 Mission St, San Jose, CA");
            restaurantInfo.put("phone", "555-123-6543");
            jedis.hmset(restaurantName, restaurantInfo);
            jedis.hset(restaurantName, "rating", "5.0");
            String rating = jedis.hget(restaurantName, "rating");
            System.out.printf("%s rating: %s\n", restaurantName, rating);
            //Print out hash
            for (Map.Entry<String, String> entry: jedis.hgetAll(restaurantName).entrySet()) {
                System.out.printf("%s: %s\n", entry.getKey(), entry.getValue());
            }
        }
        System.exit(0);
    }
}
```

The output of the program is:

```
Kyoto Ramen rating: 5.0
rating: 5.0
phone: 555-123-6543
address: 801 Mission St, San Jose, CA
```

How it works...

In the first application, JedisSingleDemo, we connect to the Redis Server by creating a Jedis instance with the server hostname. The default port is 6379 if it's not specified. The Jedis class also has a couple of other constructors, in which we can specify the server port, connection timeout, and so on.

Once we get the Jedis instance, we can call its functions to send commands to the Redis Server. The function names are just the same as the Redis command names we introduced in previous chapters.

In the *Using pipeline* recipe of Chapter 3, *Data Features*, we learned how to use the Redis pipeline feature by manually constructing raw RESP strings. Using a Redis pipeline with the help of Jedis is much easier, as Jedis will take care of the construction of raw RESP strings for us.

In JedisPipelineDemo, we use the pipelined() method to create a Jedis pipeline instance, then we can add commands to the pipeline the same way as when we execute commands directly. The difference here is that responses from commands are Response<T> objects, which are not available until the pipeline is sent to the server and executed. The sync() is the method for sending the pipeline to server, after which, responses can be retrieved.

Similar to creating a pipeline, in JedisTransactionDemo the multi() method is used to create a Redis transaction instance and exec() executes the transaction. Responses are deferred till the transaction execution finishes.

In JedisLuaDemo, we first read updateJson.lua from resources as a string, then register the Lua script using scriptLoad() to get the SHA. We use evalsha() to execute the Lua script; KEYS and ARGS are of the Java string list type and passed into evalsha() as arguments.

The Jedis instance we created in previous examples is not thread-safe, which means the same Jedis instance should not be shared in different threads. Instead of creating a Jedis instance for each thread, we can also use JedisPool, which is a thread-safe pool of Jedis connections. Whenever we need a connection, we request one from the pool; once we have done the work, we return the connection to the pool. Therefore, we can save the overhead of creating and closing a connection, as connections in the pool are already established.

Jedis connections requested from the JedisPool must be returned to the pool by calling close(). Since the Jedis class implements the AutoClosable interface, we can also use the try-resource block to close a connection and return it to the pool.

See also

- This recipe just briefly scratches the surface of using Jedis in Java applications. Since Jedis is an open source project, to learn things we did not cover in this recipe (pub/sub, replication, and so on), you can refer to the Jedis GitHub page: https://github.com/xetorthio/jedis.

Connecting to Redis with Python

There are a couple of Python clients for connecting to Redis. In this recipe, we will briefly introduce how to use the Python Redis client, redis-py.

Getting ready...

You need to finish the installation of the Redis server as we described in the *Downloading and installing Redis* recipe in Chapter 1, *Getting Started with Redis*.

You need to have Python 2.6+ or 3.4+ installed.

How to do it...

To show how to connect to Redis with Python, first of all, we need to install the redis-py library. With the help of PyPI, redis-py can be easily installed by running:

```
pip install redis
```

Connecting to the Redis Server

Now let's create RedisDemo.py with the following code:

```
1    from __future__ import print_function
2    import redis
3
4    # Create connection to localhost Redis
5    client = redis.StrictRedis(host="localhost", port=6379)
6
7    # String Operations
8    restaurant = "Extreme Pizza"
9    client.set(restaurant, "300 Broadway, New York, NY")
10   client.append(restaurant, " 10011")
11   address = client.get("Extreme Pizza")
12   print("Address for " + restaurant + " is: " + address)
13
14   # List operations
15   listKey = "favorite_restaurants"
16   client.lpush(listKey, "PF Chang's", "Olive Garden")
17   client.rpush(listKey, "Outback Steakhouse", "Red Lobster")
18   favoriteRestaurants = client.lrange(listKey, 0, -1)
19   print("Favorite Restaurants: ", favoriteRestaurants)
```

The demo application will print the following lines:

```
Address for Extreme Pizza is 300 Broadway, New York, NY 10011
Favorite Restaurants: [Olive Garden, PF Chang's, Olive Garden, PF Chang's,
Indian Tandoor, Longhorn Steakhouse, Outback Steakhouse, Red Lobster,
Outback Steakhouse, Red Lobster]
```

Using pipelines

Redis pipelines can be implemented very easily with `redis-py`.

Let's create another file `RedisPipelineDemo.py`:

```
 1    from __future__ import print_function
 2    import redis
 3
 4    # Create connection to localhost Redis
 5    client = redis.StrictRedis(host="localhost", port=6379)
 6
 7    # Create a pipeline
 8    pipeline = client.pipeline()
 9
10    # Add commands to pipeline
11    pipeline.set("mykey", "myvalue")
12    pipeline.sadd("myset", "value1", "value2")
13    pipeline.get("mykey")
14    pipeline.scard("myset")
15
16    #Send commands
17    response = pipeline.execute()
18    print(response)
```

In this example, we will get a list that contains the responses of the SET, SADD, GET, and SCARD commands respectively:

```
[True, 0, 'myvalue', 2]
```

Running Lua scripts

`redis-py` provides a very convenient `register_script()` function to register Lua scripts. `register_script()` will return a `Script` instance, which can be used as a function to invoke Lua scripts later. In the *Using Lua* recipe of Chapter 3, *Data Features*, we used SCRIPT LOAD and EVALSHA to cache a Lua script and reuse it. Let's see how we can do it in `redis-py`:

The content of `updateJson.lua` can be found in the *Using Lua* recipe of Chapter 3, Data Features.

Create `RedisLuaDemo.py` with the following code:

```
1    from __future__ import print_function
2    import redis
3
4    # Create connection to localhost Redis
5    client = redis.StrictRedis(host="localhost", port=6379)
6
7    user = "users:id:992452"
8    client.set(user, '{"name": "Tina", "sex": "female", "grade": "A"}')
9
10   # Read the lua scripts from file
11   with open("updateJson.lua") as f:
12       lua = f.read()
13
14       #Create Redis Script instance
15       updateJson = client.register_script(lua)
16
17       #Invoke lua script using the script instance
18       updateJson(keys=[user], args=['{"grade": "C"}'])
19
20       print(client.get(user))
```

The output of the program will be the updated JSON value:

`{"grade":"C","name":"Tina","sex":"female"}`

How it works...

To use the `redis-py` library, first of all we need to import the module with `"import redis"`. `"redis.StrictRedis()"` in line 6 of `RedisDemo.py` creates a `StrictRedis` instance that connects to the localhost Redis Server. Methods in `StrictRedis` can be used to send commands to the Redis Server. Most method names and their syntax are the same as the Redis commands we introduced in Chapter 2, *Data Types* and Chapter 3, *Data Features*. The few exceptions will be explained later in this recipe.

In `RedisPipelineDemo.py`, the `pipeline()` method will create a Redis pipeline instance, then we can add commands to the pipeline in the same way as when we execute commands directly. Calling `execute()` will send the commands to the server and return the responses of commands in sequence.

By default, redis-py will wrap the commands in a pipeline with the MULTI and EXEC commands, making the commands a transaction and executing them atomically. This can be disabled by setting the argument transaction to False in the execute() method:

```
pipeline.execute(transaction=False)
```

In the RedisLuaDemo.py example, we first read the content of the Lua script from an external file, then register the script by calling register_script(). The returned instance can be used as a function; KEYS[] and ARGV[] in Lua scripts can be passed into the function as keys and args arguments to invoke the script.

There's more...

Methods in the StrictRedis class almost follow the official Redis commands in terms of command name and syntax, with a few exceptions:

1. The DEL command is renamed delete as del is a reserved keyword in Python
2. MULTI/EXEC commands are not there as they are implemented in the pipeline class.
3. The SELECT command is not implemented because of thread-safe problems, which will be explained later.
4. SUBSCRIBE/LISTEN is implemented as in the PubSub class.

In redis-py, there is also a class with the name, Redis. It is a subclass of StrictRedis to provide backward compatibility with older redis-py versions. Their very small differences can be found on the GitHub page of redis-py.

The StrictRedis instance in redis-py is thread-safe, because internally there's a connection pool that manages connections to the Redis Server. By default, each instance has its own connection pool. This behavior can be overridden by passing a connection pool instance as the connection_pool argument when creating a new StrictRedis or Redis instance. The connection pool instance can be created by calling redis.ConnectionPool() and it must be created before the StrictRedis or Redis instance:

```
>>> connectionPool = redis.ConnectionPool(host="localhost", port=6379)
>>> client = redis.StrictRedis(connection_pool=connectionPool)
```

See also

- We are not able to cover everything for `redis-py` in this recipe. As it is an open source project, more details of this library can be found on its GitHub page:

  `https://github.com/andymccurdy/redis-py`

Connecting to Redis with Spring Data Redis

In the previous two recipes, we have shown how to connect to Redis with Java and Python. Now it's time to talk about web applications. When it comes to web development in the Java world, Spring from Pivotal is the most famous framework and takes advantage of the MVC pattern for developing robust Java web applications easily and rapidly. For Redis, with the Spring Data Redis library, we can manipulate Redis in Spring out-of-the-box.

In this recipe, we'll create a demo project that implements **create/read/update/delete** (**CRUD**) operations of a user model to show you how to connect to Redis with the Spring Data Redis library.

Getting ready...

You need to finish the installation of the Redis Server as we described in the *Downloading and installing Redis* recipe in `Chapter 1`, *Getting Started with Redis*. You need to use the `FLUSHALL` command to flush all the data in your Redis instance before moving on to the next section.

An IDE is recommended for this recipe. Here we use Intellij IDEA (Community Edition, Intellij for short). You can download Intellij at:
`https://www.jetbrains.com/idea/download/`.

The JDK (8 or above) is also needed for code compilation and running.

Due to space limitations in this book, we won't talk about all the details of this demo project. Only the code and settings associated with Redis will be discussed in the following two sections. For the complete project, you can refer to the sample code along with this book.

How to do it...

To show how to connect to Redis with Spring Data Redis, the steps are as following:

1. Create a new Project in IDEA and use **Spring Initializer**:

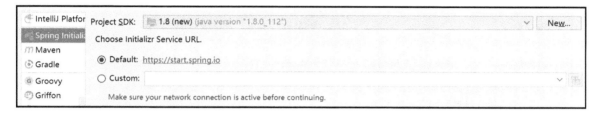

2. Press **Next** to move on and fill in the metadata of the project
3. Select the dependencies for this demo and then finish the creation of the project:

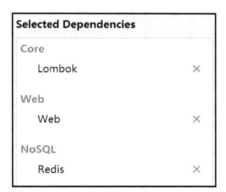

4. First, we create a user model class User as the data representation

5. After that, an application configuration class is constructed in which the address and port of the Redis Server are loaded and then a `RedisTemplate` instance is created:

```
@Configuration
public class AppConfig {
    private @Value("${redis.host}") String redisHost;
    private @Value("${redis.port}") int redisPort;

    @Bean
    JedisConnectionFactory jedisConnectionFactory(){
        JedisConnectionFactory factory = new JedisConnectionFactory();
        factory.setHostName(redisHost);
        factory.setPort(redisPort);
        factory.setUsePool(true);
        return factory;
    }

    @Bean
    RedisTemplate<String, User> redisTemplate(){
        RedisTemplate<String, User> template = new RedisTemplate<>();
        template.setKeySerializer(new StringRedisSerializer());
        template.setHashKeySerializer(new StringRedisSerializer());
        template.setHashValueSerializer(new Jackson2JsonRedisSerializer<>(User.class));
        template.setConnectionFactory(jedisConnectionFactory());
        return template;
    }

}
```

6. To encapsulate data operations in Redis, we make a service interface called
   `UserService` and then implement it for the CRUD of the user data:

```
@Service
public class UserServiceImpl implements UserService {
    private static final String USERKEY = "user";

    private HashOperations<String, Object, Object> operations;

    @Autowired
    private RedisTemplate<String,User> redisTemplate;

    @PostConstruct
    public void initOperations() { this.operations = redisTemplate.opsForHash(); }

    @Override
    public User save(User user) {
        this.operations.put(USERKEY, user.getId(),user);
        return user;
    }

    @Override
    public User findById(String id) { return (User) this.operations.get(USERKEY,id); }

    @Override
    public User update(User user) {
        save(user);
        return user;
    }

    @Override
    public void delete(String id) { this.operations.delete(USERKEY,id); }
}
```

7. To create the RESTful API for the operations of the user, we use a Spring
   `RestController`:

```
@RestController
@RequestMapping("/rest/user")
public class UserController {
    @Autowired
    private UserService userRepository;

    @PostMapping("/{id}")
    public User add(@PathVariable String id, @RequestParam String name,
                    @RequestParam String sex, @RequestParam String nation){
        return userRepository.save(
                new User(id,name,sex,nation, Instant.now().getEpochSecond())
        );
    }

    @GetMapping("/{id}")
    public User findById(@PathVariable String id) { return userRepository.findById(id); }


    @PutMapping("/{id}")
    public User updateUserById(@PathVariable String id,
                            @RequestParam String name, @RequestParam String sex,
                            @RequestParam String nation, @RequestParam long register_time){
        return userRepository.update(
                new User(id,name,sex,nation,register_time)
        );
    }

    @DeleteMapping("/{id}")
    public void deleteUserById(@PathVariable String id) { userRepository.delete(id); }
}
```

8. After finishing the coding, we run the demo and test the API using Swagger-ui at
   `http://127.0.0.1:8080/swagger-ui.html`:

User Demo

Redis Cookbook Spring Data Redis Demo

user-controller : User Controller   Show Hide   List Operations   Expand Operations

DELETE	/rest/user/{id}	deleteUserById
GET	/rest/user/{id}	findById
POST	/rest/user/{id}	add
PUT	/rest/user/{id}	updateUserById

9. For a simple test, we create a user by calling `/rest/user/{id}` with the POST method:

Parameters				
Parameter	Value	Description	Parameter Type	Data Type
id	0000088211	id	path	string
name	Mike	name	query	string
sex	Male	sex	query	string
nation	US	nation	query	string

10. After the creation of a user called `Mike`, we view the user data with `redis-cli`:

```
127.0.0.1:6379> hgetall user
1) "0000088211"
2)
{\"id\":\"0000088211\",\"name\":\"Mike\",\"sex\":\"Male\",\"nation\":\"US\",\"register_time\":1507448493}"
```

How it works...

For Spring Data Redis, the first instance you should create is the `RedisTemplate`, which will be used for Redis data manipulation. Before the `RedisTemplate` is instantiated, a `JedisConnectionFactory` is needed for the settings of the host and the port of Redis. For more reliable connection management, we also enabled the connection pool of the Redis clients.

After getting the `RedisTemplate` instance, we set the serializer of the key, hash key, and hash value respectively. For the key and hash key of the hash data in this demo, we just use plain text. For the hash value, the JSON format is used for better data organization.

Since we have prepared the `RedisTemplate` instance and its related settings, we can use it to implement the CRUD of the user data in Redis in the Spring Service.

In the final steps, we create the RESTful API as an interface to manipulate the user data.

In the stage of testing, we use Swagger to post the data of a user via the REST API and verify the data in Redis with `redis-cli`.

See also

- For more details about Spring Redis Data, please refer to its main page `https://projects.spring.io/spring-data-redis/`.

- We used Swagger, a popular web development tool, in the testing phrase. If you are interested in it, you can find out more about it at `https://swagger.io/`.

Writing a MapReduce job for Redis

If you are a big data engineer, Redis can play an important role in your application design and development. In a batch job scenario, you can retrieve data in Redis to perform some complex computing algorithms in a distributed way. For an online query, you may store the resulting dataset on a Redis Server to achieve better performance.

In the last recipes of this chapter, we'll show you how to manipulate data in Redis using MapReduce and Spark, both of which are extremely popular distributed computing frameworks in the big data world.

Getting ready...

You need to finish the installation of the Redis Server as we described in the *Downloading and installing Redis* recipe in Chapter 1, *Getting Started with Redis*. You need to use the `FLUSHALL` command to flush all the data in your Redis instance before moving on to the next section.

The requirements of IDE and JDK are the same as in the previous recipe, *Connecting to Redis with Spring Data Redis*.

A Hadoop cluster is needed but not a must. For demo purposes, you can debug and run the `MapReduce` job in a local environment instead.

Basic knowledge of `MapReduce` is needed for this recipe.

How to do it...

To show how to write a `MapReduce` job for Redis, suppose every user in Relp has some credit that can be used to pay for services in the application. As a promotion, we are going to add $10 to the credit balance of each user in Relp to encourage the user to use Relp. We would like to make it in a distributed way using the `MapReduce` framework.

1. First, we prepare sample data using the shell script, `preparedata_mr.sh`:

```
$ bash preparedata_mr.sh
OK
unix2dos: converting file mr.data to DOS format ...
All data transferred. Waiting for the last reply...
Last reply received from server.
errors: 0, replies: 10000
```

2. We can explore the data with `redis-cli`:

```
127.0.0.1:6379> SCAN 0
1) "7"
2)   1) "user:0000006"
     2) "user:0000000"
     3) "user:0000008"
     4) "user:0000004"
     5) "user:0000003"
     6) "user:0000002"
     7) "user:0000007"
     8) "user:0000001"
     9) "user:0000009"
    10) "user:0000005"
127.0.0.1:6379> SCAN 7
1) "0"
2) 1) "user:0000010"
```

3. Open IDEA and create a new project using Maven as the support framework

4. Press **Next** to move on and fill in the metadata of the project

5. Add `MapReduce` and other related dependencies in `pom.xml`:

```xml
<dependency>
    <groupId>org.apache.hadoop</groupId>
    <artifactId>hadoop-client</artifactId>
    <version>2.6.5</version>
</dependency>
```

6. After that, we create a user model class, `User`, as the bean of the JSON data

7. To retrieve the data from Redis, we customize the `InputFormat` for a `MapReduce` job:

```
public class RedisHashInputFormat extends InputFormat<Text, Text> {
    private static final int IDLENGTH = 10;
    public static final String REDIS_HOST_CONF = "mr.redishashinputformat.host";
    public static final String REDIS_HASH_PREFIX_CONF = "mr.redishashinputformat.hashprefix";
    public static final String REDIS_BEGIN_CONF = "mr.redishashinputformat.begin";
    public static final String REDIS_END_CONF = "mr.redishashinputformat.end";
    public static final String REDIS_PLENGTH_CONF = "mr.redishashinputformat.plength";

    public List<InputSplit> getSplits(JobContext jobContext) throws IOException, InterruptedException {
        val host = jobContext.configuration.get(REDIS_HOST_CONF);
        val hashPrefix = jobContext.configuration.get(REDIS_HASH_PREFIX_CONF);
        val begin = Integer.parseInt(jobContext.configuration.get(REDIS_BEGIN_CONF));
        val end = Integer.parseInt(jobContext.configuration.get(REDIS_END_CONF));
        val pLength = Integer.parseInt(jobContext.configuration.get(REDIS_PLENGTH_CONF));

        // Create an input split for each host
        val splits = [];
        var initKey="";
        for (val i : [begin, end]){
            val number = StringUtils.LeftPad(i, IDLENGTH, padChar: '0');
            val key = number[:IDLENGTH-pLength];
            if(initKey ≠ key){
                splits += new RedisHashInputSplit(host, hashPrefix,key);
                initKey = key;
            }
        }

        Log.info("Input splits to process: ${splits.size()}");
        return splits;
    }
}
```

8. For each partition of the hash keys, we use a custom `InputSplit` to create a split to get the data:

```
public class RedisHashInputSplit extends InputSplit implements Writable {
    private String host;
    private String prefix;
    private String key;

    public void write(DataOutput out) throws IOException {
        out.writeUTF(host);
        out.writeUTF(prefix);
        out.writeUTF(key);
    }

    public void readFields(DataInput in) throws IOException {
        this.host = in.readUTF();
        this.prefix = in.readUTF();
        this.key = in.readUTF();
    }

    public long getLength() throws IOException, InterruptedException {
        return 0;
    }

    public String[] getLocations() throws IOException, InterruptedException {
        return [host];
    }
}
```

9. In every split, we extend a `RecordReader` to iterate the data in Redis using the Jedis library:

```java
public class RedisHashRecordReader extends RecordReader<Text, Text> {
    private Iterator<Map.Entry<String, String>> keyValueMapIter = null;
    private Text rrKey = new Text(), rrValue = new Text();
    private float processedKVs = 0, totalKVs = 0;
    private Map.Entry<String, String> currentEntry = null;
    private String prefix,host,key;
    private Jedis jedis;

    public void initialize(InputSplit split, TaskAttemptContext taskAttemptContext)
            throws IOException, InterruptedException {
        host = split.locations.first();
        prefix = split.prefix;
        key = split.key;
        String hashKey = prefix+":"+key;

        jedis = new Jedis(host);
        Log.info("Connect to $host");
        jedis.connect();
        jedis.client.setTimeoutInfinite();

        totalKVs = jedis.hlen(hashKey);
        keyValueMapIter = jedis.hgetAll(hashKey).entrySet().iterator();
    }

    public boolean nextKeyValue() throws IOException, InterruptedException {
        if (keyValueMapIter.hasNext()) {
            currentEntry = keyValueMapIter.next();
            rrKey.set(key+currentEntry.key);
            rrValue.set(currentEntry.value);
            return true;
```

10. After fetching the data, we set a mapper to add $10 of credit to the balance of each user:

```
public class RedisOutputMapper extends Mapper<Object, Text, Text, Text> {
    public static final String REDIS_BALANCE_CONF = "mr.redishashinputformat.blance";
    private Text outkey = new Text();
    private Text outvalue = new Text();

    @Override
    protected void map(Object key, Text value, Context context)
            throws IOException, InterruptedException {
        val addBalance = Long.parseLong(context.configuration.get(REDIS_BALANCE_CONF));
        val mapper = new ObjectMapper();
        val user = mapper.readValue(value.toString(), User.class);

        user.balance = addBalance+user.balance;
        // Set our output key and values
        outkey.set(key);
        outvalue.set(mapper.writeValueAsString(user));

        context.write(outkey, outvalue);
    }

    public static void setBalance(Job job, String balance) {
        job.configuration.set(REDIS_BALANCE_CONF,balance);
    }
}
```

11. To write the data back to the Redis Server, we extend OutputFormat and RecordWriter:

```
public class RedisHashRecordWriter extends RecordWriter<Text, Text> {
    private static final int IDLENGTH = 10;
    private final int pLength;
    private final String prefix;
    private Jedis jedis;

    public RedisHashRecordWriter(
            String host, String pLength, String prefix) {
        this.pLength = Integer.parseInt(pLength);
        this.prefix = prefix;
        jedis = new Jedis(host);
        jedis.connect();
    }

    public void write(Text key, Text value)
            throws IOException, InterruptedException {
        String key1 = key.toString().substring(0,IDLENGTH-pLength);
        String key2 = key.toString().substring(IDLENGTH-pLength);
        jedis.hset( key: prefix+":"+key1,key2,value.toString());
    }

    public void close(TaskAttemptContext taskAttemptContext)
            throws IOException, InterruptedException {
        jedis.close();
    }
}
```

12. In the end, we create a `main()` function class:

```
job.jarByClass = Application.class;
job.setMapperClass(RedisOutputMapper.class);

RedisOutputMapper.setBalance(job,balance);

job.inputFormatClass = RedisHashInputFormat.class;
RedisHashInputFormat.setRedisHost(job, host);
RedisHashInputFormat.setHashPrefix(job, hashPrefix);
RedisHashInputFormat.setBegin(job, begin);
RedisHashInputFormat.setEnd(job, end);
RedisHashInputFormat.setPLength(job, pLength);

job.outputFormatClass = RedisHashOutputFormat.class;
RedisHashOutputFormat.setRedisHost(job, host);
RedisHashOutputFormat.setPLength(job, pLength);

job.outputKeyClass = Text.class;
job.outputValueClass = Text.class;

//Wait for job completion
return (job.waitForCompletion( verbose: true) ? 0 : 1);
```

13. Submit the job:

```
. . .
2017-10-10 11:54:42,154 INFO   [main] mapreduce.Job
(Job.java:monitorAndPrintJob(1374)) -  map 100% reduce 0%
2017-10-10 11:54:42,154 INFO   [main] mapreduce.Job
(Job.java:monitorAndPrintJob(1385)) - Job job_local736372500_0001
completed successfully
2017-10-10 11:54:42,184 INFO   [main] mapreduce.Job
(Job.java:monitorAndPrintJob(1392)) - Counters: 18
. . .
```

14. To check if the job is done, we get the hash value using `hget` in `redis-cli`:

```
127.0.0.1:6379> hget "user:0000001" 123
"{\"name\":\"Jack\",\"sex\":\"m\",\"rtime\":1507607748117668688,\"n
ation\":\"uk\",\"balance\":103}"
```

How it works...

To generate some data for demonstration purposes, sample user data is populated into Redis via the script. We partitioned the sample data with the first seven characters of the user ID and stored it as a hash structure.

Due to the characteristics of the sample data in our MapReduce application, we first customized the InputFormat by extending the InputFormat class to create the InputSplit for each partition of the user data. One InputSplit is for one hash key.

In each split, a RedisHashRecordReader, which is a sub-class of RecordReader, is initiated to fetch the data of a hash key correspondingly. During the initiation of the RecordReader, the Jedis library is used to make a connection to the Redis Server, get the length of the hash key by calling the HLEN command, and get all the data of the hash key using the HGETALL command. An iterator is provided afterwards.

A mapper is used to add the balance to each user. At the end, we use the custom OutputFormat and RecordWriter to write the resulting user data to Redis according to the original rule of partitions.

After finishing the coding, we submit the MapReduce job and check the result. All the balances of the user data have been increased by 10 as expected.

See also

- How to get a local MapReduce job running is beyond the scope of this book; you can refer to the guide at: https://goo.gl/3VvYwA

Writing a Spark job for Redis

In the previous recipe, we talked about how to write a MapReduce job to read and write data in Redis. With the development of large-scale computing, over the years Apache Spark has gained more popularity than MapReduce. Apache Spark is an open source, big data distributed, computing engine. Compared to MapReduce, it provides better performance as well as more powerful and user-friendly APIs.

When it comes to using Redis in a Spark job, a connector for manipulating data in Redis with Spark is provided by Redis Labs. In this recipe, we'll show you how to use the Spark-Redis connector library to read and write data in Redis.

Getting ready...

You need to finish the installation of the Redis Server as we described in the *Downloading and installing Redis* recipe in `Chapter 1`, *Getting Started with Redis*. You need to use the `FLUSHALL` command to flush all the data in your Redis instance before moving on to the next section.

The requirements of IDE and JDK are the same as in the *Connecting to Redis with Spring Data Redis* recipe. Only Scala APIs are available for Spark-Redis at the time of writing, so Scala v2.11 and the Scala plugin in IDEA are mandatory. In addition, basic knowledge of Spark and Scala is required for this recipe.

You can submit your job to a standalone Spark cluster or a Yarn cluster. For demo purposes, you can debug and run the Spark job in local mode instead.

How to do it...

In the previous recipe, we assumed each user has a balance. To show how to write a Spark job for Redis, in this example, we are going to compute the sum of the balances of all users in Relp:

1. The first step we're going to take is to prepare the sample data using the shell script, `preparedata_mr.sh`:

```
$ bash preparedata_mr.sh
OK
unix2dos: converting file mr.data to DOS format ...
All data transferred. Waiting for the last reply...
Last reply received from server.
errors: 0, replies: 10000
```

2. We can explore the data with `redis-cli`:

```
127.0.0.1:6379> SCAN 0
1) "7"
2)   1) "user:0000006"
     2) "user:0000000"
     3) "user:0000008"
     4) "user:0000004"
     5) "user:0000003"
     6) "user:0000002"
     7) "user:0000007"
     8) "user:0000001"
     9) "user:0000009"
    10) "user:0000005"
127.0.0.1:6379> SCAN 7
1) "0"
2) 1) "user:0000010"
```

3. Open IDEA, create a new Scala project, and fill in the metadata of the project
4. Add Maven as the support framework of the project
5. Add Spark-Redis-related dependencies and the repository in `pom.xml`:

```
<properties>
    <maven.compiler.source>1.8</maven.compiler.source>
    <maven.compiler.target>1.8</maven.compiler.target>
</properties>

<dependencies>
    <!-- https://mvnrepository.com/artifact/RedisLabs/spark-redis
-->
    <dependency>
        <groupId>RedisLabs</groupId>
        <artifactId>spark-redis</artifactId>
        <version>0.3.2</version>
    </dependency>
    <dependency>
        <groupId>org.apache.spark</groupId>
        <artifactId>spark-core_2.11</artifactId>
        <version>2.1.0</version>
    </dependency>

    <dependency>
        <groupId>org.apache.spark</groupId>
        <artifactId>spark-streaming_2.11</artifactId>
        <version>2.1.0</version>
    </dependency>
```

```
        <dependency>
            <groupId>org.apache.spark</groupId>
            <artifactId>spark-sql_2.11</artifactId>
            <version>2.1.0</version>
        </dependency>

        <dependency>
            <groupId>redis.clients</groupId>
            <artifactId>jedis</artifactId>
            <version>2.9.0</version>
        </dependency>
    </dependencies>
```

6. After that, we create an object `SumBalance` which extends the App trait.

7. In the body of `SumBalance`, we first create a `SparkConf` variable with the running mode and the Redis host configuration settings:

```
val conf = new SparkConf()
    .setMaster("local")
    .setAppName("Spark Redis Demo")
    .set("redis.host", "192.168.1.7")
```

8. After getting the `SparkConf` variable, we initialize the `SparkSession` and then get the `SparkContext` for Spark-Redis use:

```
//Initialize the sparksession
 val sparkSession = SparkSession.builder.
   master("local")
   .config(conf)
   .appName("spark session example")
   .getOrCreate()

 //Fetch the sparkcontext for spark-redis library
 val sc = sparkSession.sparkContext
```

9. To read hash data from Redis, we use the API `fromRedisKeyPattern`:

```
// Read Hash data from Redis
 val userHashRDD= sc.fromRedisKeyPattern("user*").getHash()
```

10. Before we compute the sum of the balances, we first parse the JSON data:

```
import sparkSession.implicits._
 val ds = sparkSession.createDataset(userHashRDD)

 //Preparing the schema of the JSON data
 val schema = StructType(Seq(
   StructField("name", StringType, true),
   StructField("sex", StringType, true),
   StructField("rtime", LongType, true),
   StructField("nation", StringType, true),
   StructField("balance", DoubleType,true)
 ))

 // Parse the json data and rename the columns
 val namedDS = ds
   .withColumnRenamed("_1","id")
   .withColumnRenamed("_2","jsondata")
   .withColumn("jsondata",from_json($"jsondata", schema))
```

11. As soon as we have prepared the data, it's time to do the math. After computing the sum, we prepare the data for writing the sum, as a simple string key value pair, back to Redis for an online query:

```
//Generating the result [String, String] RDD
 val totalBalanceRDD =
namedDS.agg(sum($"jsondata.balance")).rdd.map(total
=>("totalBalance",total.get(0).toString()))
```

12. Finally, we write the result to Redis using the `toRedisKV` API provided by Spark-Redis:

```
/Write the result back to Redis`
 sc.toRedisKV(totalBalanceRDD)
```

13. To test if the job works as expected, we submit the job:

```
. . .
17/10/10 21:02:28 INFO TaskSchedulerImpl: Removed TaskSet 1.0,
whose tasks have all completed, from pool
17/10/10 21:02:28 INFO DAGScheduler: ResultStage 1
(foreachPartition at redisFunctions.scala:226) finished in 0.130 s
17/10/10 21:02:28 INFO DAGScheduler: Job 0 finished:
foreachPartition at redisFunctions.scala:226, took 2.675819 s
17/10/10 21:02:28 INFO SparkContext: Invoking stop() from shutdown
hook
17/10/10 21:02:28 INFO SparkUI: Stopped Spark web UI at
```

```
http://192.168.56.1:4040
17/10/10 21:02:28 INFO MapOutputTrackerMasterEndpoint:
MapOutputTrackerMasterEndpoint stopped!
17/10/10 21:02:28 INFO MemoryStore: MemoryStore cleared
17/10/10 21:02:28 INFO BlockManager: BlockManager stopped
17/10/10 21:02:28 INFO BlockManagerMaster: BlockManagerMaster
stopped
17/10/10 21:02:28 INFO
OutputCommitCoordinator$OutputCommitCoordinatorEndpoint:
OutputCommitCoordinator stopped!
17/10/10 21:02:28 INFO SparkContext: Successfully stopped
SparkContext
17/10/10 21:02:28 INFO ShutdownHookManager: Shutdown hook called
```

14. In `redis-cli`, we get the sum of the balances of all users:

```
127.0.0.1:6379> GET totalBalance
"492569.0"
```

How it works...

The code is quite self-explanatory. One thing you should notice is that due to the requirements of the Spark-Redis library, the `RDD[(String, String)]` is needed when you want to write the data to Redis as a simple key value pair. The first part of the `StringRDD` is the key you would like to set in Redis. So, in this example, before we set the data in Redis, we convert the result to `StringRDD` as a key called `totalBalance`. Different data types of Redis require different types of RDD in Spark-Redis.

There's more...

Apart from manipulating a single Redis Server, Spark-Redis supports connecting to multiple Redis Clusters or instances in your applications.

See also

- For more APIs provided by Spark-Redis, you can refer to `https://github.com/RedisLabs/spark-redis`

5
Replication

In this chapter, we will cover the following recipes:

- Setting up Redis replication
- Optimizing replication
- Troubleshooting replication

Introduction

So far, we have learned how to set up and connect to a single Redis Server. In a production environment, a single database instance is often subject to failures, such as system crashes, network partitions, or power outages. Like most other database systems, Redis also provides a replication mechanism, which enables data to be copied from one Redis Server (master) to one or more other Redis Servers (slaves).

Replication not only makes the entire system fault-tolerant, but can also be used to scale the system horizontally. In a read-heavy application, we can add multiple Redis read-only slaves to mitigate the pressure on the master server.

Redis replication is fundamental to the Redis Cluster, which provides high availability. In this chapter, we will first introduce how Redis replication works and how to set up a Redis master-slave replication environment. After that, we will show optimization guidelines and basic troubleshooting techniques concerning Redis replication.

Setting up Redis replication

In Chapter 1, *Getting Started with Redis*, we learned how to set up a Redis Server. A Redis Server runs in master mode by default. In this recipe, we will demonstrate how to set up a Redis slave server to replicate from the master server.

Getting ready...

You need to finish the installation of Redis Server as we described in the *Downloading and installing Redis* recipe in Chapter 1, *Getting Started with Redis*.

Prepare a configuration file for the Redis slave server. You can make a copy of redis.conf and rename it redis-slave.conf, then make the following changes:

```
port 6380
pidfile /var/run/redis_6380.pid
dir ./slave
slaveof 127.0.0.1 6379
```

Don't forget to create /redis/slave directory if it doesn't exist:

```
$mkdir -p /redis/slave
```

How to do it...

The steps for setting up Redis replication are as follows:

1. Start a Redis Server instance on port 6379 of localhost. You can skip this step if the server is already running. This is our master server:

   ```
   $cd /redis
   $bin/redis-server conf/redis.conf
   ```

2. Start another Redis Server instance with the configuration file redis-slave.conf. This is our slave server:

   ```
   $bin/redis-server conf/redis-slave.conf
   ```

3. Open two Terminals and connect to the master server at `127.0.0.1:6379` and `127.0.0.1:6380` using `redis-cli`:

```
$ bin/redis-cli -p 6379
127.0.0.1:6379>

$ bin/redis-cli -p 6380
127.0.0.1:6380>
```

4. Run `INFO REPLICATION` on both Terminals:

```
127.0.0.1:6379> INFO REPLICATION
# Replication
role:master
connected_slaves:1
slave0:ip=127.0.0.1,port=6380,state=online,offset=557,lag=1
master_replid:1fee079fc47716706a59225779c56b0e7033f3b1
master_replid2:0000000000000000000000000000000000000000
master_repl_offset:557
second_repl_offset:-1
repl_backlog_active:1
repl_backlog_size:1048576
repl_backlog_first_byte_offset:1
repl_backlog_histlen:557

127.0.0.1:6380> INFO REPLICATION
# Replication
role:slave
master_host:127.0.0.1
master_port:6379
master_link_status:up
master_last_io_seconds_ago:7
master_sync_in_progress:0
slave_repl_offset:557
slave_priority:100
slave_read_only:1
connected_slaves:0
master_replid:1fee079fc47716706a59225779c56b0e7033f3b1
master_replid2:0000000000000000000000000000000000000000
master_repl_offset:557
second_repl_offset:-1
repl_backlog_active:1
repl_backlog_size:1048576
repl_backlog_first_byte_offset:1
repl_backlog_histlen:557
```

5. On the master, create a new key:

```
127.0.0.1:6379> SET "new_key" "value"
OK
```

6. On the slave, try to get the value for the new key:

```
127.0.0.1:6380> GET "new_key"
"value"
```

7. On the slave, try to create a new key:

```
127.0.0.1:6380> SET "new_key_2" "value2"
(error) READONLY You can't write against a read only slave.
```

8. Shut down the slave instance:

```
127.0.0.1:6380> shutdown save
```

9. On the master, create another new key:

```
127.0.0.1:6379> SET "another_new_key" "another_value"
OK
```

10. Relaunch the slave instance:

```
$bin/redis-server bin/redis-slave.conf
```

11. Check `another_new_key` exists on slave:

```
127.0.0.1:6380> GET "another_new_key"
"another_value"
```

How it works...

In the *Getting ready* section, we updated the configuration file to instruct the slave server to run on port 6380 and use a different working directory to the master server. The new line slave of 127.0.0.1 6379 we added to redis-slave.conf indicates that the server that listens on port 6380 is a slave of 127.0.0.1:6379. In addition, SLAVEOF is a command that can be executed in redis-cli to make the current Redis Server a slave of another instance on-the-fly.

The INFO command prints out the current server's information. In step 4, we used INFO REPLICATION to check whether the replication link is established. Most replication information items are self-explanatory. The master_replid is a random string generated on the master server's startup. The master server is represented by master_replid for the purpose of replication. The master_repl_offset is a mark of the replication stream and increases with the data events on the master. A pair of (master_replid; master_repl_offset) can be used to identify a position on the replication stream of the master instance.

When master and slave instances are well connected and their replication link is established, the master forwards the write commands it receives to the slave the slave applies the commands in order to make its data synchronous with the master.

What happens when the slave is connecting to the master for the first time, or the slave is reconnecting to the master after a connection interruption? There are two resynchronization mechanisms in Redis replication: partial resynchronization and full resynchronization. When a Redis slave instance is started and connected to the master instance, it will always try to request a partial resynchronization by sending (master_replid; master_repl_offset), which indicates the last snapshot in sync with the master. If the master accepts the partial resynchronization, it will stream the incremental part of the commands starting with the last offset the slave stopped at. Otherwise, a full resynchronization is required. A full resynchronization is always needed the first time the slave connects to its master. Details about how the master decides whether to accept a partial resynchronization request will be discussed in the following *Optimizing replication* recipe. In order to copy all the data to the slave, the master needs to dump the data into a RDB file and then send the file to the slave. Once the slave receives the RDB file, it will flush all its data in memory and apply the data to the RDB file. The replication process on the master is purely asynchronous so it will not block the server from processing client requests at all.

Obviously, compared to full resynchronization, partial resynchronization does not require network transmission of a full data dump from the master. Also, dumping data to the RDB file will fork a background process and has memory overhead; we will explore this in the next chapter.

The process of partial resynchronization and full resynchronization is illustrated in the following diagram:

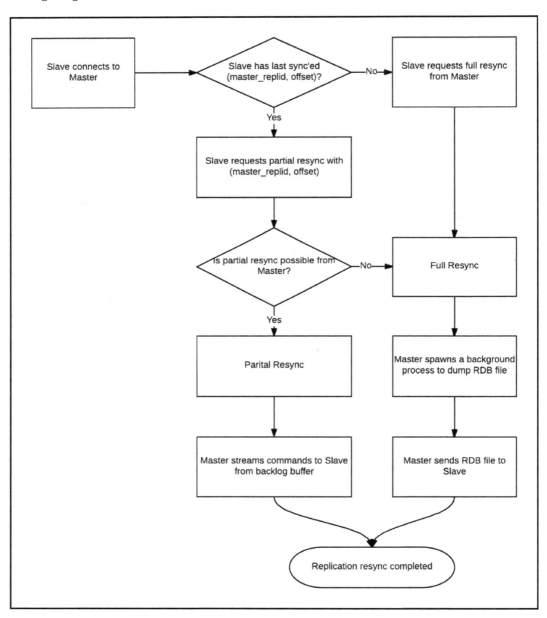

Let's take a look at the logs on the slave when it connects to the master for the first time. As we can see, the slave requested a full sync from the master because it has never connected to the master before and therefore does not have (`master_replid; master_repl_offset`):

```
15516:S 15 Oct 15:30:15.412 * Connecting to MASTER 127.0.0.1:6379
15516:S 15 Oct 15:30:15.412 * MASTER <-> SLAVE sync started
15516:S 15 Oct 15:30:15.412 * Non blocking connect for SYNC fired the
event.
15516:S 15 Oct 15:30:15.412 * Master replied to PING, replication can
continue...
15516:S 15 Oct 15:30:15.412 * Partial resynchronization not possible (no
cached master)
15516:S 15 Oct 15:30:15.421 * Full resync from master:
1fee079fc47716706a59225779c56b0e7033f3b1:0
15516:S 15 Oct 15:30:15.511 * MASTER <-> SLAVE sync: receiving 175 bytes
from master
15516:S 15 Oct 15:30:15.511 * MASTER <-> SLAVE sync: Flushing old data
15516:S 15 Oct 15:30:15.511 * MASTER <-> SLAVE sync: Loading DB in memory
15516:S 15 Oct 15:30:15.512 * MASTER <-> SLAVE sync: Finished with success
```

Here is the server log on the master:

```
15511:M 15 Oct 15:30:15.412 * Slave 127.0.0.1:6380 asks for synchronization
15511:M 15 Oct 15:30:15.412 * Full resync requested by slave 127.0.0.1:6380
15511:M 15 Oct 15:30:15.413 * Starting BGSAVE for SYNC with target: disk
15511:M 15 Oct 15:30:15.413 * Background saving started by pid 15520
15520:C 15 Oct 15:30:15.423 * DB saved on disk
15520:C 15 Oct 15:30:15.424 * RDB: 6 MB of memory used by copy-on-write
15511:M 15 Oct 15:30:15.511 * Background saving terminated with success
15511:M 15 Oct 15:30:15.511 * Synchronization with slave 127.0.0.1:6380
succeeded
```

The master received the full resynchronization request from the slave and started dumping the data on disk by forking a background process. After that, it sends the data dump to the slave.

Next, let's take a look at the server log of a partial resynchronization process. Specifically, we shut down the slave in step 8 and restarted it in step 10.

You can find the partial resynchronization server log on the slave:

```
15561:S 15 Oct 15:44:13.650 * Connecting to MASTER 127.0.0.1:6379
15561:S 15 Oct 15:44:13.650 * MASTER <-> SLAVE sync started
15561:S 15 Oct 15:44:13.650 * Non blocking connect for SYNC fired the
event.
15561:S 15 Oct 15:44:13.650 * Master replied to PING, replication can
```

```
continue...
15561:S 15 Oct 15:44:13.650 * Trying a partial resynchronization (request
1fee079fc47716706a59225779c56b0e7033f3b1:1126).
15561:S 15 Oct 15:44:13.650 * Successful partial resynchronization with
master.
15561:S 15 Oct 15:44:13.650 * MASTER <-> SLAVE sync: Master accepted a
Partial Resynchronization.
```

The partial resynchronization server log on the master shows:

```
15511:M 15 Oct 15:44:13.650 * Slave 127.0.0.1:6380 asks for synchronization
15511:M 15 Oct 15:44:13.650 * Partial resynchronization request from
127.0.0.1:6380 accepted. Sending 55 bytes of backlog starting from offset
1126.
```

From the preceding server log, we can see that the slave sent a partial resynchronization request with (master_replid; offset) pair (1fee079fc47716706a59225779c56b0e7033f3b1; 1126). The master accepted the request and started sending commands at offset 1126 from the backlog buffer. Please note, partial resynchronization after a slave restart was a new feature in Redis 4.0. In the implementation of Redis 4.0, master_replid and offset are stored in the RDB file. When the slave is shut down gracefully and restarted, master_replid and offset will be loaded with the RDB file, which makes partial resynchronization possible.

In step 7, we tried to create a new key on the slave but got an error message that the server is in read-only mode. This is because we set slave-read-only yes in configuration. In most cases, it is advisable to keep this configuration to avoid any data inconsistency between master and slaves.

There's more...

When a slave instance is promoted to a master instance, other slaves have to resync from the new master. Prior to Redis 4.0, this process is a full resynchronization because master_replid changed on the master. Since Redis 4.0, the new master remembers the master_replid and offset from the old master and therefore can accept partial resynchronization requests from other slaves, even if the master_replid in the requests is different. Specifically, when master failover happens, on the new master, (master_replid; master_repl_offset+1) will be copied to (master_replid2; second_repl_offset).

See also

- Please refer to the *Replication* topic from the official Redis documentation: `https://redis.io/topics/replication`
- Redis persistence and the RDB format will be explained in `Chapter 6`, *Persistence*

Optimizing replication

In the previous recipe, we talked about the basic workflow of Redis replication and learned how to set up a master-slave replication in Redis. While setting up replication is quite simple, there are many critical configuration parameters for Redis replication which deserve your special attention. Moreover, some default values of these parameters may even cause performance issues under certain circumstances. In the following two recipes of this chapter, we are going to discuss these configurations for the optimization and troubleshooting of Redis replication.

In this recipe, we will delve into a key parameter called `repl-backlog-size` to see how to tweak it in order to achieve a better performance for Redis replication by taking advantage of the partial resynchronization. In addition, some other parameters that may have an impact on the replication performance are also discussed.

Getting ready...

You need to finish the installation of the Redis Server as we described in the *Downloading and installing Redis* recipe in `Chapter 1`, *Getting Started with Redis*.

In this recipe, for illustration purposes, we will use iptables as a firewall to simulate a network isolation situation; root privileges are required for manipulating iptables.

How to do it...

The steps for optimizing replication are as follows:

1. Open a console and switch the current user to `root`. Then set some variables in the console for the basic information of a master and slave:

```
$ M_IP=127.0.0.1
$ M_PORT=6379
```

```
$ M_RDB_NAME=master.rdb
$ M_OUT=master.out
$ S1_IP=127.0.0.2
$ S1_PORT=6380
$ S1_OUT=slave_1.out
$ S1_RDB_NAME=slave_1.rdb
```

2. Start the two Redis instances:

```
$ nohup /redis/bin/redis-server --port $M_PORT --bind $M_IP --
dbfilename $M_RDB_NAME > $M_OUT &
$ nohup /redis/bin/redis-server --port $S1_PORT --bind $S1_IP --
dbfilename $S1_RDB_NAME  > $S1_OUT&
```

3. Sleep for a while to wait for the Redis instances to finish their startup. After the sleep, we set some sample data to one of the Redis instances:

```
$ sleep 10
$ echo set redis hello | nc $M_IP $M_PORT
$ echo lpush num 1 2 3 | nc $M_IP $M_PORT
```

4. Then set up the replication of these two Redis Servers by calling the SLAVEOF command. Sleep 10 seconds for the completion of the replication process:

```
$ echo slaveof 127.0.0.1 6379 | nc $S1_IP $S1_PORT
$ sleep 10
```

5. After finishing the data synchronization, we use iptables to cut down the network connection between the master and the slave:

```
$ echo "modify iptables"
$ iptables -I INPUT -s 127.0.0.1 -d 127.0.0.2 -j DROP
$ iptables -I OUTPUT -s 127.0.0.2 -d 127.0.0.1 -j DROP
```

6. During the networking isolation, we populate some sample data into the master server:

```
$ bash preparerepldata.sh 1000
$ du -sh repl.data
$ cat repl.data | /redis/bin/redis-cli --pipe -h $M_IP -p $M_PORT
```

7. Then we restore the networking connection between the master and slave by calling the `iptables` command. Before restoring the connection, we sleep for 70 seconds:

```
$ sleep 70
$ echo "restore iptables"
$ iptables -D INPUT -s 127.0.0.1 -d 127.0.0.2 -j DROP
$ iptables -D OUTPUT -s 127.0.0.2 -d 127.0.0.1 -j DROP
```

8. After reconnection, we sleep 10 seconds to resynchronize the data from the master and then shut down both the master and slave server:

```
$ sleep 10
$ echo "SHUTDOWN" | nc $M_IP $M_PORT
$ echo "SHUTDOWN" | nc $S1_IP $S1_PORT
```

9. Check the logs of the master and the slave. You can find the following replication-related messages:

```
# cat master.out
...
29086:M 15 Oct 20:25:49.020 # Connection with slave 127.0.0.2:6380
lost.
29086:M 15 Oct 20:26:04.037 * Slave 127.0.0.2:6380 asks for
synchronization
29086:M 15 Oct 20:26:04.037 * Partial resynchronization request
from 127.0.0.2:6380 accepted. Sending 139107 bytes of backlog
starting from offset 15.
...

# cat slave_1.out
...
29087:S 15 Oct 20:25:49.020 # MASTER timeout: no data nor PING
received...
29087:S 15 Oct 20:25:49.020 # Connection with master lost.
29087:S 15 Oct 20:25:49.020 * Caching the disconnected master
state.
29087:S 15 Oct 20:25:49.020 * Connecting to MASTER 127.0.0.1:6379
29087:S 15 Oct 20:25:49.020 * MASTER <-> SLAVE sync started
29087:S 15 Oct 20:26:04.037 * Non blocking connect for SYNC fired
the event.
29087:S 15 Oct 20:26:04.037 * Master replied to PING, replication
can continue...
29087:S 15 Oct 20:26:04.037 * Trying a partial resynchronization
(request e39b33ba4bb4bb0bf3623ad09d385a856f27463c:15).
29087:S 15 Oct 20:26:04.037 * Successful partial resynchronization
```

```
with master.
29087:S 15 Oct 20:26:04.037 * MASTER <-> SLAVE sync: Master
accepted a Partial Resynchronization.
...
```

10. Clean up all the logs and dump files. Repeat the previous steps. This time we
    increase the volume of data populated into the master during the disconnection
    of the network in step 6:

    ```
    $ bash preparerepldata.sh 11000
    ```

11. We check the logs of the master and the slave again:

    ```
    # cat master.out
    ...

    31156:M 15 Oct 20:31:01.747 # Disconnecting timedout slave:
    127.0.0.2:6380
    31156:M 15 Oct 20:31:01.747 # Connection with slave 127.0.0.2:6380
    lost.
    31156:M 15 Oct 20:31:32.809 * Slave 127.0.0.2:6380 asks for
    synchronization
    31156:M 15 Oct 20:31:32.809 * Unable to partial resync with slave
    127.0.0.2:6380 for lack of backlog (Slave request was: 15).
    31156:M 15 Oct 20:31:32.809 * Starting BGSAVE for SYNC with target:
    disk
    31156:M 15 Oct 20:31:32.810 * Background saving started by pid
    21293
    21293:C 15 Oct 20:31:32.864 * DB saved on disk
    21293:C 15 Oct 20:31:32.864 * RDB: 8 MB of memory used by copy-on-
    write
    31156:M 15 Oct 20:31:32.898 * Background saving terminated with
    success
    31156:M 15 Oct 20:31:32.898 * Synchronization with slave
    127.0.0.2:6380 succeeded
    ...

    # cat slave_1.out
    ...
    31157:S 15 Oct 20:31:01.746 # MASTER timeout: no data nor PING
    received...
    31157:S 15 Oct 20:31:01.746 # Connection with master lost.
    31157:S 15 Oct 20:31:01.746 * Caching the disconnected master
    state.
    31157:S 15 Oct 20:31:01.746 * Connecting to MASTER 127.0.0.1:6379
    31157:S 15 Oct 20:31:01.746 * MASTER <-> SLAVE sync started
    31157:S 15 Oct 20:31:32.809 * Non blocking connect for SYNC fired
    ```

```
the event.
31157:S 15 Oct 20:31:32.809 * Master replied to PING, replication
can continue...
31157:S 15 Oct 20:31:32.809 * Trying a partial resynchronization
(request a866cd909b0ceb7bbed690f73f633f97a471fd3d:15).
31157:S 15 Oct 20:31:32.810 * Full resync from master:
a866cd909b0ceb7bbed690f73f633f97a471fd3d:1529121
31157:S 15 Oct 20:31:32.810 * Discarding previously cached master
state.
31157:S 15 Oct 20:31:32.898 * MASTER <-> SLAVE sync: receiving
957221 bytes from master
31157:S 15 Oct 20:31:32.899 * MASTER <-> SLAVE sync: Flushing old
data
31157:S 15 Oct 20:31:32.899 * MASTER <-> SLAVE sync: Loading DB in
memory
31157:S 15 Oct 20:31:32.914 * MASTER <-> SLAVE sync: Finished with
success
..
```

How it works...

In the previous section, we started two Redis Servers and set up the replication between them. By checking the logs of the master and slave, we can tell that the first replication is a full data synchronization, which is not surprising since this is the first time the master and the slave have synchronized their data:

```
# cat master.out
...
31156:M 15 Oct 20:29:40.618 * Ready to accept connections
31156:M 15 Oct 20:29:51.637 * Slave 127.0.0.2:6380 asks for synchronization
31156:M 15 Oct 20:29:51.637 * Partial resynchronization not accepted:
Replication ID mismatch (Slave asked for
'709e798b196d833e4b6ff34f1e1cf1a392aa81c4', my replication IDs are
'9dd60b163d9aad07426704bd00c8fcdc5e509bd8' and
'0000000000000000000000000000000000000000')
31156:M 15 Oct 20:29:51.638 * Starting BGSAVE for SYNC with target: disk
31156:M 15 Oct 20:29:51.638 * Background saving started by pid 31175
31175:C 15 Oct 20:29:51.661 * DB saved on disk
31175:C 15 Oct 20:29:51.661 * RDB: 6 MB of memory used by copy-on-write
31156:M 15 Oct 20:29:51.736 * Background saving terminated with success
31156:M 15 Oct 20:29:51.736 * Synchronization with slave 127.0.0.2:6380
succeeded
```

We then cut off the networking connection by utilizing iptables. During the disconnection of the network, we generated some sample data and imported it into the master Redis instance. After that, we made the connection available again and checked the logs of these two Redis Servers.

The interesting part is that the different size of the sample data populated led to different types of Redis data resynchronization. The reason why this happened is that during the period the master loses the connection with the slave, a piece of memory, which is a ring buffer on the Redis master, keeps track of all recent `write` commands. This buffer is actually a fixed-length list.

In Redis, we call this buffer a **replication backlog**. Redis uses this backlog buffer to decide whether to start a full or partial data resynchronization. More specifically, after issuing the `SLAVEOF` command, the slave sends a partial resynchronization request to the master with the last replication offset and the ID of the last master (`master_replid`). When the connection between the master and slave is established, the master will first check if the `master_replid` in the request matches its own `master_replid`. Then, it will check if the `offset` in the request is retrievable from its backlog buffer. If the `offset` is in the range of the backlog, all the `write` commands during disconnection could be obtained from it, which indicates that a partial resynchronization can be done. Otherwise, if the volume of the `write` commands the master instance received during disconnection is more than the backlog buffer can store, the request for a partial resynchronization will be denied. Instead, a full data resynchronization will be started. That is to say, the default size of the replication backlog, which is 1 MB, is enough to store the `write` commands only if a small amount of data is written into the master during replication disconnection.

For the first time of testing, we generated around 96 KB data to import. Thus when the slave connected to the master again and asked for a partial resynchronization, the master managed to fetch the `write` command during the disconnection from the backlog buffer and sent it to the slave. Finally, the slave caught up with the master by partial replication. The benefit of partial resynchronization has been described in the previous *Setting up Redis replication* recipe.

In the second testing scenario, we generated 1.1 MB data for importing to the master during network disconnection. The size of the imported data is bigger than the default backlog size, so there is no doubt that a full resynchronization after the reconnection had to be performed.

From the previous discussion, we can conclude that the default size of the backlog is not enough to warrant a high writing traffic situation when a network disconnection happens between master and slave. In most cases, we should tweak this parameter to a higher value to meet our needs. By calculating the delta value of the `master_repl_offset` from the `INFO` command during peak hours, we can estimate an appropriate size for the replication backlog:

```
t*(master_repl_offset2- master_repl_offset1)/(t2-t1)
t is how long the disconnection may last in seconds.
```

We can also use this formula to estimate network traffic between the master and slave Redis instances.

Generally speaking, it doesn't make sense to set a value bigger than the size of the RDB snapshot. Doing so will not take advantage of the benefits of partial resynchronization because the size of data transferred in partial resynchronization and full resynchronization is almost the same.

There's more...

Another parameter for the replication backlog is `repl-backlog-ttl`, which indicates, if all slaves get disconnected from the master, how long the master Redis instance will wait to release the memory of the backlog. The default value of this parameter is 3600s, which is generally not a problem since the backlog buffer is quite small compared to the Redis instance memory.

Apart from the backlog size, there are some other configurations you can tweak in order to get better replication performance in some cases. From the point of view of network transmission, you can use less bandwidth by tuning the parameter `repl-disable-tcp-nodelay` to `yes`. If set to `yes`, Redis will try to combine several small packets into one packet. This is useful when the location of a master server is far from the slave server. Extra attention should be paid to the fact that this can lead to around 40 ms replication delay.

From the point of view of I/O and memory on the master, you can send the RDB content directly to the slaves without creating an RDB file on the disk by using diskless replication. The Redis master forks a new process to perform the RDB transmission. This mechanism can save a lot of disk I/O and some memory during RDB snapshotting. If you have a slow disk or high memory usage in your Redis host while the network bandwidth is sufficient, you can consider this option and give it a try. You can switch the replication mechanism from disk-backed (default) to diskless by setting `repl-diskless-sync` to `yes`. However, this feature is experimental currently, so be careful when using diskless replication in your production environment.

See also

- To design a partial sync in Redis, please refer to: `http://antirez.com/news/31`
- To design a diskless sync of Redis, please refer to: `http://antirez.com/news/81`
- For details of Redis replication, please refer to the *Setting up Redis replication* recipe in this chapter
- You can also find the meaning behind the configurations mentioned in this recipe at: `http://download.redis.io/redis-stable/redis.conf`
- If you are not familiar with the command `iptables`, refer to its man page at: `http://ipset.netfilter.org/iptables.man.html`

Troubleshooting replication

In a real production environment, you may run into many issues and get into trouble when using Redis replication. Many factors, such as disk I/O, network connectivity, the size of datasets, and long blocking operations, may become the root cause of replication failures.

In this recipe, we will take a look at a few replication failure cases and solutions to see what we can do if replication is not working as expected.

Getting ready...

You need to finish the installation of the Redis Server as we described in the *Downloading and installing Redis* recipe in `Chapter 1`, *Getting Started with Redis*. You should also finish setting up replication, as described in the *Setting up Redis replication* recipe in this chapter.

To generate a large amount of sample data, we use `fake2db` mentioned in the *Managing keys* recipe in `Chapter 2`, *Data Types* to populate some fake data to Redis. Due to differing hardware performance, it may take you several hours to finish the data population:

```
# fake2db --rows 3000000 --db redis
```

In addition, for testing purposes, we introduce another Redis testing data generator `redis-random-data-generator` to write sample data to Redis in real time. You can install it as follows:

```
$ sudo apt-get install npm
$ npm i redis-random-data-generator
$ wget
https://raw.githubusercontent.com/SaminOz/redis-random-data-generator/master/generator.js
```

How to do it...

To show how to perform the trouble shot of replication issue, take the following steps:

1. Open a console and get replication information for the `master` and `slave` Redis instance using `redis-cli`:

```
$ bin/redis-cli -p 6379 info Replication
# Replication
role:master
connected_slaves:1
slave0:ip=127.0.0.1,port=6380,state=online,offset=1288,lag=1
master_replid:8f7b9821477006200651baef11d6af7451dede3d
master_replid2:0000000000000000000000000000000000000000
master_repl_offset:1288
second_repl_offset:-1
repl_backlog_active:1
repl_backlog_size:1048576
repl_backlog_first_byte_offset:1
repl_backlog_histlen:1288

$ bin/redis-cli -p 6380 info Replication
# Replication
role:slave
master_host:127.0.0.1
master_port:6379
master_link_status:up
master_last_io_seconds_ago:1
master_sync_in_progress:0
```

```
slave_repl_offset:1302
slave_priority:100
slave_read_only:1
connected_slaves:0
master_replid:8f7b9821477006200651baef11d6af7451dede3d
master_replid2:0000000000000000000000000000000000000000
master_repl_offset:1302
second_repl_offset:-1
repl_backlog_active:1
repl_backlog_size:1048576
repl_backlog_first_byte_offset:1
repl_backlog_histlen:1302
```

2. After checking the status of replication, we try to block the master server for 80 seconds using the `debug sleep` command of Redis:

```
$ date;bin/redis-cli -p 6379 debug sleep 80; date
Tue Oct 17 16:15:54 CST 2017
OK
Tue Oct 17 16:17:14 CST 2017
```

3. We check the logs of the `Slave` and `Master` in Redis:

```
Slave log:
21894:S 17 Oct 16:16:52.823 # MASTER timeout: no data nor PING
received...
21894:S 17 Oct 16:16:52.823 # Connection with master lost.
21894:S 17 Oct 16:16:52.823 * Caching the disconnected master
state.
21894:S 17 Oct 16:16:52.823 * Connecting to MASTER 127.0.0.1:6379
21894:S 17 Oct 16:16:52.823 * MASTER <-> SLAVE sync started
21894:S 17 Oct 16:16:52.823 * Non blocking connect for SYNC fired
the event.
21894:S 17 Oct 16:17:14.353 * Master replied to PING, replication
can continue...
21894:S 17 Oct 16:17:14.353 * Trying a partial resynchronization
(request 8f7b9821477006200651baef11d6af7451dede3d:565381621).
21894:S 17 Oct 16:17:14.353 * Successful partial resynchronization
with master.
21894:S 17 Oct 16:17:14.353 * MASTER <-> SLAVE sync: Master
accepted a Partial Resynchronization.

Master log:
22024:M 17 Oct 16:17:14.353 # Connection with slave 127.0.0.1:6380
lost.
22024:M 17 Oct 16:17:14.353 * Slave 127.0.0.1:6380 asks for
synchronization
```

```
22024:M 17 Oct 16:17:14.353 * Partial resynchronization request
from 127.0.0.1:6380 accepted. Sending 0 bytes of backlog starting
from offset 565381621.
```

4. We hang the slave as soon as the resynchronization is finished this time:

```
$ date;bin/redis-cli -p 6380 debug sleep 80; date
Tue Oct 17 20:46:43 CST 2017
OK
Tue Oct 17 20:48:03 CST 2017
```

5. Check the Master and Slave logs:

```
Master:
22024:M 17 Oct 20:47:43.709 # Disconnecting timedout slave:
127.0.0.1:6380
22024:M 17 Oct 20:47:43.709 # Connection with slave 127.0.0.1:6380
lost.
22024:M 17 Oct 20:48:04.603 * Slave 127.0.0.1:6380 asks for
synchronization
22024:M 17 Oct 20:48:04.603 * Partial resynchronization request
from 127.0.0.1:6380 accepted. Sending 0 bytes of backlog starting
from offset 565403937.

Slave:
21894:S 17 Oct 20:48:03.697 # Connection with master lost.
21894:S 17 Oct 20:48:03.697 * Caching the disconnected master
state.
21894:S 17 Oct 20:48:04.602 * Connecting to MASTER 127.0.0.1:6379
21894:S 17 Oct 20:48:04.602 * MASTER <-> SLAVE sync started
21894:S 17 Oct 20:48:04.603 * Non blocking connect for SYNC fired
the event.
21894:S 17 Oct 20:48:04.603 * Master replied to PING, replication
can continue...
21894:S 17 Oct 20:48:04.603 * Trying a partial resynchronization
(request 8f7b9821477006200651baef11d6af7451dede3d:565403937).
21894:S 17 Oct 20:48:04.603 * Successful partial resynchronization
with master.
21894:S 17 Oct 20:48:04.603 * MASTER <-> SLAVE sync: Master
accepted a Partial Resynchronization.
```

6. To prepare the second scenario, we reset the replication of the Redis slave and flush all the data in the slave instance. Then we set up the replication again:

```
127.0.0.1:6380> SLAVEOF NO ONE
127.0.0.1:6380> FLUSHALL
127.0.0.1:6380> SLAVEOF 127.0.0.1 6379
```

7. During the establishment of replication, we populate a large amount of data:

```
for i in `seq 5`
do
nohup node generator.js hash 1000000 session &
done
```

8. Wait for a while and check the Master and Slave logs again:

```
Master:
16027:M 18 Oct 14:20:40.767 * Slave 127.0.0.1:6380 asks for
synchronization
16027:M 18 Oct 14:20:40.767 * Partial resynchronization not
accepted: Replication ID mismatch (Slave asked for
'40f921547ba9b599dff22d8d1fe2d7b03f284361', my replication IDs are
'774fce0f0ffe5afad272937699d714949cdfd9e8' and
'0000000000000000000000000000000000000000')
16027:M 18 Oct 14:20:40.767 * Starting BGSAVE for SYNC with target:
disk
16027:M 18 Oct 14:20:40.826 * Background saving started by pid
22756
16027:M 18 Oct 14:21:04.240 # Client id=51 addr=127.0.0.1:41853
fd=7 name= age=24 idle=24 flags=S db=0 sub=0 psub=0 multi=-1 qbuf=0
qbuf-free=0 obl=16384 oll=16362 omem=268435458 events=r cmd=psync
scheduled to be closed ASAP for overcoming of output buffer limits.
16027:M 18 Oct 14:21:04.256 # Connection with slave 127.0.0.1:6380
lost.
16027:M 18 Oct 14:22:04.896 * Slave 127.0.0.1:6380 asks for
synchronization
16027:M 18 Oct 14:22:04.896 * Full resync requested by slave
127.0.0.1:6380
16027:M 18 Oct 14:22:04.896 * Can't attach the slave to the current
BGSAVE. Waiting for next BGSAVE for SYNC
22756:C 18 Oct 14:22:13.932 * DB saved on disk
22756:C 18 Oct 14:22:13.949 * RDB: 5091 MB of memory used by copy-
on-write
16027:M 18 Oct 14:22:14.049 * Background saving terminated with
success
16027:M 18 Oct 14:22:14.049 * Starting BGSAVE for SYNC with target:
disk
16027:M 18 Oct 14:22:14.111 * Background saving started by pid
22845
22845:C 18 Oct 14:23:46.883 * DB saved on disk
22845:C 18 Oct 14:23:46.912 * RDB: 22 MB of memory used by copy-on-
write
16027:M 18 Oct 14:23:47.031 * Background saving terminated with
success
```

```
16027:M 18 Oct 14:24:40.644 * Synchronization with slave
127.0.0.1:6380 succeeded

Slave:
16022:S 18 Oct 14:20:40.765 * Connecting to MASTER 127.0.0.1:6379
16022:S 18 Oct 14:20:40.765 * MASTER <-> SLAVE sync started
16022:S 18 Oct 14:20:40.765 * Non blocking connect for SYNC fired
the event.
16022:S 18 Oct 14:20:40.767 * Master replied to PING, replication
can continue...
16022:S 18 Oct 14:20:40.767 * Trying a partial resynchronization
(request 40f921547ba9b599dff22d8d1fe2d7b03f284361:607439042).
16022:S 18 Oct 14:20:40.826 * Full resync from master:
774fce0f0ffe5afad272937699d714949cdfd9e8:3644738860
```
16022:S 18 Oct 14:20:40.827 * Discarding previously cached master state.
16022:S 18 Oct 14:22:04.896 # Timeout receiving bulk data from MASTER... If the problem persists try to set the 'repl-timeout' parameter in redis.conf to a larger value.
```
16022:S 18 Oct 14:22:04.896 * Connecting to MASTER 127.0.0.1:6379
16022:S 18 Oct 14:22:04.896 * MASTER <-> SLAVE sync started
16022:S 18 Oct 14:22:04.896 * Non blocking connect for SYNC fired
the event.
16022:S 18 Oct 14:22:04.896 * Master replied to PING, replication
can continue...
16022:S 18 Oct 14:22:04.896 * Partial resynchronization not
possible (no cached master)
16022:S 18 Oct 14:22:14.111 * Full resync from master:
774fce0f0ffe5afad272937699d714949cdfd9e8:5669698739
16022:S 18 Oct 14:23:47.031 * MASTER <-> SLAVE sync: receiving
6503393438 bytes from master
16022:S 18 Oct 14:24:40.656 * MASTER <-> SLAVE sync: Flushing old
data
16022:S 18 Oct 14:24:40.656 * MASTER <-> SLAVE sync: Loading DB in
memory
16022:S 18 Oct 14:26:08.477 * MASTER <-> SLAVE sync: Finished with
success
```

How it works...

In the *Setting up Redis replication* recipe, we learned that after processing write commands, the master will then send them to its slaves in order to have them synchronized with the master. From the master's point of view, to tell whether slaves are still alive, the master sends a PING at a predefined interval. You can adjust this interval by setting the configuration repl-ping-slave-period in the configuration file or from redis-cli. The default value of the ping interval is 10 s. From the slave's point of view, one slave sends REPLCONF ACK {offset} every second to report its replication offset. For both PING and REPLCONF ACK, there is a timeout specified by repl-timeout. The default value of the replication timeout is 60 s. If the interval between two PING or REPLCONF ACK is longer than the timeout, or there is no data traffic between master and slaves within repl-timeout, the replication connection will be cut off. The slave will have to initiate another replication request.

In our first test, at 16:15:54 we blocked the master for 80 s, which is longer than the timeout. The slave found that there was no data or ping from the master when the timeout was reached, so it dropped the connection with the master at 16:16:52.823. After that, the slave tried to reestablish the connection with the master until 16:17:14.353, then the master instance got back from sleeping and gave the slave a response. Then the replication could continue. After hanging the master, we then made the slave hang for 80 s. Similar logs could be obtained. The different part is that the master cut off the replication connection this time when the timeout was reached. After the slave awoke, it found that the connection with the master had been lost, so it gave the connection another try.

The second testing scenario is another common production issue. As we described in the *Setting up Redis replication* recipe, when establishing replication, a master instance first dumps its memory in the form of an RDB file and sends it to the slaves. When a slave finishes receiving the RDB file, it loads the RDB file into its memory. During these steps, all the write commands to the master instance will be buffered in a special client buffer called Slave client buffer. After loading RDB, the master will send the content of this buffer to a slave.

There is a limitation to the size of the buffer, which if exceeded will cause replication to start from the beginning. The default size limit of a replication buffer is slave 256 MB 64 MB 60. The word slave indicates this is the buffer size for slaves. The value 256 MB is a hard limit. Once this buffer size limit is reached, the master will close the connection immediately. The value 64 MB and 60 as a whole are soft limits. It means the master will close the connection once the buffer size is larger than 64 MB for a continuous period of 60 seconds.

By calling CLIENT LIST during data synchronization, you can catch the data replication client whose cmd is sysc or psysc (cmd=sysc/psysc) and the flag is S (flag=S). Then you can get the amount of memory used by the replication client buffer from the omem metric:

```
127.0.0.1:6379> CLIENT LIST
id=115 addr=127.0.0.1:46731 fd=11 name= age=41 idle=38 flags=S db=0 sub=0
psub=0 multi=-1 qbuf=0 qbuf-free=0 obl=16382 oll=123 omem=2009753 events=r
cmd=psync
```

In the previous test, after starting the synchronization, we pushed a large amount of sample data, which definitely exceeded the limit of the client buffer. The master detected this situation and logged the client metrics. The master instance cut off the connection soon afterwards:

```
16027:M 18 Oct 14:21:04.240 # Client id=51 addr=127.0.0.1:41853 fd=7 name=
age=24 idle=24 flags=S db=0 sub=0 psub=0 multi=-1 qbuf=0 qbuf-free=0
obl=16384 oll=16362 omem=268435458 events=r cmd=psync scheduled to be
closed ASAP for overcoming of output buffer limits.
16027:M 18 Oct 14:21:04.256 # Connection with slave 127.0.0.1:6380 lost.
```

After 60 seconds, which is the default value for replication timeout, the slave noticed there was no data obtained from the master server, so it restarted the replication automatically:

```
16022:S 18 Oct 14:22:04.896 # Timeout receiving bulk data from MASTER... If
the problem persists try to set the 'repl-timeout' parameter in redis.conf
to a larger value.
16022:S 18 Oct 14:22:04.896 * Connecting to MASTER 127.0.0.1:6379
```

There's more...

In real production environment, the value of repl-ping-slave-period must be smaller than the value of repl-timeout. Otherwise, replication timeout will be reached every time there is low traffic between master and slave. Usually, a blocking operation may cause replication timeout since the command processing engine of the Redis Server is single-threaded. To prevent the replication timeout from happening, you should try your best to avoid the use of long blocking commands. The default value of repl-timeout is enough for most cases.

Special attention must be paid in our second scenario. The time it took for the master to dump the memory was longer than 60 seconds, which won't cause replication timeout. The same holds true if the process of transferring an RDB file lasts longer than the replication timeout. Replication will also not be interrupted in this case. In the following example, it shows that the data transfer lasted around 23 minutes and the replication finished successfully:

```
16022:S 18 Oct 21:13:56.517 * MASTER <-> SLAVE sync: receiving 3983178656
bytes from master
16022:S 18 Oct 21:36:35.325 * MASTER <-> SLAVE sync: Flushing old data
16022:S 18 Oct 21:36:35.325 * MASTER <-> SLAVE sync: Loading DB in memory
16022:S 18 Oct 21:37:09.933 * MASTER <-> SLAVE sync: Finished with success
```

In the examples in this recipe, you can easily reproduce this scenario using the `tc` Linux command to set the delay of your loopback with a root account:

```
# tc qdisc add dev eth0 root netem delay 200ms
```

In addition, loading the RDB file slowly in the slave won't block the slave and it won't cause replication timeout as the following example shows:

```
13760:S 16 Oct 23:12:52.414 * MASTER <-> SLAVE sync: receiving 5289155794
bytes from master
13760:S 16 Oct 23:13:37.637 * MASTER <-> SLAVE sync: Flushing old data
13760:S 16 Oct 23:13:37.637 * MASTER <-> SLAVE sync: Loading DB in memory
13760:S 16 Oct 23:23:20.231 * MASTER <-> SLAVE sync: Finished with success
```

All in all, we can learn from the source code of Redis that the replication timeout will be fired only if no data is transferred between a master and slave when doing the resynchronization or the master/slave instance couldn't receive PING/REPLCONF ACK within the timeout period.

As a suggestion for the size of the replication client buffer, you can set a larger size by calling the CONFIG SET command or modifying the configuration file and restarting the instance in the production environment with high writing traffic. Extreme caution must be taken when you set this value using CONFIG SET. Units such as MB or GB are not supported. Here is an example to set the hard limit and soft limit of this buffer size to 512 MB and 128 MB/120 s:

```
127.0.0.1:6379> config set client-output-buffer-limit 'slave 536870912
134217728 120'
```

The last thing we would like to mention is that Redis takes a master-driven policy for the expiration of keys. That is to say, when a master expires a key it sends a `DEL` command to all the slaves. The `DEL` command is also buffered in the replication client buffer during synchronization.

In addition, if you set slaves to writable, caution should be exercised because, before Redis 4.0, keys with a timeout on a Redis writable slave never expired. This issue has been fixed in Redis 4.0 RC3 onward.

See also

- You can also find the meanings of the configurations mentioned in this recipe at: `http://download.redis.io/redis-stable/redis.conf`

6
Persistence

In this chapter, we will cover the following recipes:

- Manipulating RDB
- Exploring RDB
- Manipulating AOF
- Exploring AOF
- Combining RDB and AOF

Introduction

Since Redis stores data in memory, all data is lost when the server reboots. In the previous chapter, we learned how to set up Redis slaves to replicate data from the master. From the perspective of data redundancy, Redis replication can be used as a way to back up the data.

In order to keep the data safe, Redis also provides mechanisms to persist data to disk. There are two data persistence options: RDB and AOF. RDB is a point-in-time snapshot of Redis data, which is perfect for backups and disaster recovery. AOF is a log of write operations that will be replayed at server startup.

In this chapter, we will introduce how to enable and configure RDB and AOF in Redis. We will also take a look at the file format of RDB and AOF, as well as important configuration parameters to tune when setting up Redis persistence. At the end of this chapter, we will talk about combining RDB and AOF in Redis.

Manipulating RDB

As we described in the previous recipe, for an in-memory data store such as Redis, enabling persistence features is the best defense against data loss. One obvious way to implement persistence is to take a snapshot against the memory where the data is stored from time to time. That is basically the way RDB works in Redis.

In this recipe, we will take a look at how to perform and configure the RDB persistence feature and learn more about the process of taking the snapshot.

Getting ready...

You need to finish the installation of the Redis Server, as we described in the *Downloading and installing Redis* recipe in Chapter 1, *Getting Started with Redis*.

For the purpose of demonstration, we flush all the data with the FLUSHALL command and then we populate some sample data into our Redis instance by utilizing the redis-random-data-generator tool introduced in the *Troubleshooting replication* recipe in Chapter 5, *Replication*:

```
for i in `seq 10`
do
nohup node generator.js hash 1000000 session &
done
```

How to do it...

The steps for manipulating RDB are as follows:

1. To enable RDB persistence for a running Redis instance, call the CONFIG SET command as follows:

```
127.0.0.1:6379> CONFIG SET save "900 1"
OK
127.0.0.1:6379> CONFIG SET save "900 1 300 10 60 10000"
OK
```

2. If we would like to enable RDB permanently, set the save configuration in the Redis configuration file:

```
$ cat conf/redis.conf |grep "^save"
save 900 1
save 300 10
save 60 10000
```

3. To disable the RDB persistence feature for a running Redis instance, add an empty string to the save option with redis-cli:

```
$ bin/redis-cli config set save ""
OK
```

4. To disable RDB persistence, just comment out or delete the save options in the Redis configuration file:

```
#save 900 1
#save 300 10
#save 60 10000
```

5. To check if an RDB feature is enabled, get the configuration of save in redis-cli. If there is an empty string in the save option, that indicates the RDS feature is disabled. Otherwise, the snapshotting trigger policy of RDB will be obtained:

```
$ bin/redis-cli CONFIG GET save
1) "save"
2) "900 1 300 10 60 10000"
```

6. We can check if the RDB file has been generated in the Redis data directory:

```
$ ls -l dump.rdb
-rw-rw-r-- 1 redis redis 286 Oct 23 22:11 dump.rdb
```

7. To perform an RDB snapshot manually, call the SAVE command in redis-cli. The redis-cli is blocked for a while and then the Command Prompt returns the following:

```
127.0.0.1:6379> SAVE
OK
(23.25s)
127.0.0.1:6379>
```

8. Alternatively, we can call BGSAVE to perform a non-blocking RDB dumping:

```
127.0.0.1:6379> BGSAVE
Background saving started
```

9. Check the pid of the dumping process using the ps -ef |grep redis command:

```
$ps -ef |grep redis
redis     10708 21158 91 21:21 ?        00:00:06 redis-rdb-bgsave
0.0.0.0:6379
redis     21158     1  5 17:35 ?        00:12:46 bin/redis-server
0.0.0.0:6379
```

10. Quickly populate some sample data during RDB dumping:

```
$ node generator.js hash 100000
```

11. Check the log of the Redis Server:

```
$ cat log/redis.log
21158:M 21 Oct 21:21:41.408 * Background saving started by pid 777
777:C 21 Oct 21:22:04.316 * DB saved on disk
777:C 21 Oct 21:22:04.346 * RDB: 322 MB of memory used by copy-on-
write
21158:M 21 Oct 21:22:04.449 * Background saving terminated with
success
```

12. To fetch the metrics and status of persistence, issue INFO Persistence in redis-cli:

```
127.0.0.1:6379> INFO Persistence
# Persistence
loading:0
rdb_changes_since_last_save:0
rdb_bgsave_in_progress:1
rdb_last_save_time:1508590312
rdb_last_bgsave_status:ok
rdb_last_bgsave_time_sec:21
rdb_current_bgsave_time_sec:20
rdb_last_cow_size:2637824
```

How it works...

RDB works like a camera for the data memory of Redis. Once the trigger policy is reached, it will take a *photo* of the data in Redis by dumping all the data into a file on the local disk. Before introducing this process in detail, we'll first explain the value of the save option, which determines the trigger policy of RDB mentioned in the previous section. The pattern of the value is $x_1, y_1, x_2, y_2, ...$. That means, dumping the data in Redis after x seconds if at least y keys have been changed and no dumping process is in progress.

For the preceding example, 900 1 means that, once at least 1 key has changed within 900 seconds, an RDB snapshot will be taken. There can be more than one policy in the save option to control how frequently the RDB snapshot is taken.

We can manually start an RDB dumping process by issuing the SAVE or BGSAVE commands. The difference between these two commands is that the former starts a synchronous operation, which means the main thread of Redis does the dumping, while the latter performs the dumping in the background. You should never use SAVE in your production environment because it will block your Redis Server. Instead, with BGSAVE, the main thread of Redis continues to process the incoming commands while a child process is created by the fork() system call, and then it saves the dumping data file to a temp file named temp-<bgsave-pid>.rdb. When the dumping process is finished, this temp file is renamed to the name defined by setting dbfilename on the local directory specified by setting dir to replace the old dump. By the way, these two settings can be modified dynamically within redis-cli.

By listing the processes with the ps command, you can catch the child process with the name redis-rdb-bgsave, which is forked by the Redis Server to perform the BGSAVE. This child process saves all the data at the time the BGSAVE command is processed. Thanks to the **Copy-On-Write** (COW) mechanism, there is no need for the child process to use the same amount of memory as the Redis Server does.

During the process of dumping, we can use INFO Persistence to obtain the metrics of the ongoing persistence. In this example, the value of rdb_bgsave_in_progress is 1, indicating the dumping is in progress. The value of rdb_current_bgsave_time_sec is the time this ongoing BGSAVE lasts.

After the child finishes replacing the old dump file, it logs a message based on how much private data the child used as follows:

```
777:C 21 Oct 21:22:04.346 * RDB: 322 MB of memory used by copy-on-write
```

This basically counts how much modification the parent process performed compared to the child (including read buffers, write buffers, data modifications, and so on). In our example, we populated some sample data to Redis during dumping, so the memory used by COW (in the INFO command) is not very small (for 2 GB of data in Redis, if nothing is written in the process of dumping, 10 – 20 MB memory is usually used by COW). This metric is also saved in the rdb_last_cow_size metric obtained by the INFO command.

After the BGSAVE finishes, the status of the last BGSAVE is saved in the rdb_last_bgsave_status metric, and the Unix timestamp of the last successful save is saved in rdb_last_save_time:

```
127.0.0.1:6379> INFO Persistence
# Persistence
loading:0
rdb_changes_since_last_save:0
rdb_bgsave_in_progress:0
rdb_last_save_time:1508639640
rdb_last_bgsave_status:ok
rdb_last_bgsave_time_sec:20
rdb_current_bgsave_time_sec:-1
rdb_last_cow_size:15036416
```

There's more...

Here are some configuration options related to RDB persistence. It's recommended you leave the default value, which is yes for these options listed as follows:

- stop-writes-on-bgsave-error yes: When BGSAVE fails, as a protection mechanism, the Redis Server will stop accepting writes, if this option is set to yes.
- rdbcompression yes: Compression can reduce the size of the dump file dramatically, at the cost of more CPU usage for doing LZF compression.
- rdbchecksum yes: Creates a CRC64 checksum at the end of the snapshot file. The performance cost to pay during saving and loading the snapshot file is around 10%. Set to no for maximum performance, but less resistance to data corruption.

The dump generated by SAVE/BGSAVE can be used as a data backup file. You can utilize crontab in your operating system to periodically copy the RDB file to a local directory or remote distributed file system, such as Amazon S3/HDFS, for later restoration purposes:

```
cp /redis/data/dump.rdb /somewhere/safe/dump.$(date +%Y%m%d%H%M).rdb
```

To restore an RDB snapshot, you have to copy the file to the location specified by the `dir` option and set the read/write permission of this file to the user who starts the Redis instance. After that, you need to stop the instance by issuing the `SHUTDOWN NOSAVE` command and rename the new dump file to the name defined by `dbfilename`. With a restart, the dataset is loaded into Redis from the backup file.

See also

- You can find more discussions about RDB Persistence at: `https://redis.io/topics/persistence`
- You may have an interest in how COW works in an operating system; you can learn more details at: `https://en.wikipedia.org/wiki/Copy-on-write`

Exploring RDB

We have learned that, via persistence, Redis dumps its in-memory data to a file called `dump.rdb` by default. For beginners, it might be enough to understand the points mentioned in the previous recipe. For geeks who are eager to know more about how the RDB file works as a binary representation of Redis in-memory data, it's of great benefit to explore the RDB format. In this recipe, we will dig into the format of the RDB file to see what we can do with knowledge of the RDB format.

Getting ready...

You need to finish the installation of the Redis Server, as we described in the *Downloading and installing Redis* recipe in `Chapter 1`, *Getting Started with Redis*.

To inspect a binary file format, a binary editor is a must. In Ubuntu Linux, `bvi` is the most common binary editor. Install it as follows:

```
$ sudo apt-get install bvi
```

For macOS, you can download HexFriend at: `https://github.com/ridiculousfish/HexFiend/releases`

For the purpose of demonstration, flushing all the data with the `FLUSHALL` command is needed.

Because we will explore the RDB file in hex, an ASCII character should be looked up in an ASCII table. The website RapidTables (http://www.rapidtables.com/code/text/ascii-table.htm) is a great help for this.

How to do it...

The steps for exploring RDB are as follows:

1. Set a string key-value pair:

   ```
   127.0.0.1:6379> SET key value
   OK
   ```

2. Set a list key-value pair:

   ```
   127.0.0.1:6379> LPUSH listkey v1 v2
   (integer) 2
   ```

3. Set a hash key-value pair:

   ```
   127.0.0.1:6379> HSET hashkey k1 v1 k2 v2
   (integer) 2
   ```

4. Set a set key-value pair:

   ```
   127.0.0.1:6379> SADD setkey v1 v2
   (integer) 2
   ```

5. Set a sorted set key-value pair:

   ```
   127.0.0.1:6379> ZADD zset 1 v1 2 v2
   (integer) 2
   ```

6. To trigger RDB dumping, call the command SAVE in redis-cli:

   ```
   127.0.0.1:6379> SAVE
   OK
   ```

7. Open the dump.rdb file we just generated, with bvi editor:

   ```
   $ bvi dump.rdb
   ```

The content of `dump.rdb` is shown in the following screenshot:

```
00000000  52 45 44 49 53 30 30 30 38 FA 09 72 65 64 69 73  REDIS0008..redis
00000010  2D 76 65 72 05 34 2E 30 2E 31 FA 0A 72 65 64 69  -ver.4.0.1..redi
00000020  73 2D 62 69 74 73 C0 40 FA 05 63 74 69 6D 65 C2  s-bits.@..ctime.
00000030  7B F8 ED 59 FA 08 75 73 65 64 2D 6D 65 6D C2 98  {..Y..used-mem..
00000040  A1 0C 00 FA 0C 61 6F 66 2D 70 72 65 61 6D 62 6C  .....aof-preambl
00000050  65 C0 00 FA 07 72 65 70 6C 2D 69 64 28 65 30 61  e....repl-id(e0a
00000060  35 39 33 62 37 33 37 36 31 37 63 61 36 63 61 63  593b737617ca6cac
00000070  31 30 64 38 63 64 35 64 62 33 64 34 30 38 64 35  10d8cd5db3d408d5
00000080  61 30 30 33 65 FA 0B 72 65 70 6C 2D 6F 66 66 73  a003e..repl-offs
00000090  65 74 C1 CF 50 FE 00 FB 05 00 0D 07 68 61 73 68  et..P.......hash
000000A0  6B 65 79 1B 1B 00 00 00 16 00 00 00 04 00 00 02  key.............
000000B0  6B 31 04 02 76 31 04 02 6B 32 04 02 76 32 FF 0E  k1..v1..k2..v2..
000000C0  07 6C 69 73 74 6B 65 79 01 13 13 00 00 00 0E 00  .listkey........
000000D0  00 00 02 00 00 02 76 32 04 02 76 31 FF 02 06 73  ......v2..v1...s
000000E0  65 74 6B 65 79 02 02 76 31 02 76 32 00 03 6B 65  etkey..v1.v2..ke
000000F0  79 05 76 61 6C 75 65 0C 04 7A 73 65 74 17 17 00  y.value..zset...
00000100  00 00 14 00 00 00 04 00 00 02 76 31 04 F2 02 02  ..........v1....
00000110  76 32 04 F3 FF FF 4E CB 90 01 E1 BA 21 35        v2....N.....!5
```

How it works...

In the preceding example, some simple testing data was populated into the Redis instance. After that, an RDB dump was created via the `SAVE` command.

We then take a closer look at what the RDB has unearthed with the binary editor `bvi` in Linux. All the content of the RDB file has been converted into hex by `bvi`. By looking up the first five hex numbers (52 45 44 49 53) one by one in an ASCII table at RapidTables (`https://www.rapidtables.com/code/text/ascii-table.html`), we can tell that the first characters are `REDIS`:

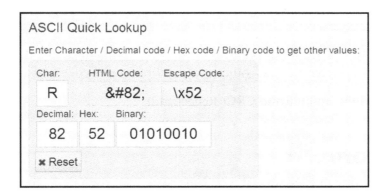

The following four characters behind the magic string are 30 30 30 38, which indicate that the RDB format version is 0008. REDIS0008 is a magic string of an RDB file.

After the magic string, there are eight kinds of metadata saved in the RDB file:

- redis-ver: The version of the Redis instance.
- redis-bits: The architecture of the host on which the Redis instance is running. 64 or 32 is a valid value for this metadata.
- ctime: The Unix timestamp of when this RDB was created.
- used-mem: The size of used memory at the time of dumping.
- repl_stream_db: The index of the database in a replication chain, exists only when a replication has been established.
- aof-preamble: Whether to put the RDB snapshot as a preamble of the AOF file.
- repl-id: The replication ID of the master.
- repl-offset: The replication offset of the master.

By the way, FA in the RDB file is an auxiliary operation code. There is always a key-value pair behind the auxiliary code.

After storing the metadata for each database in the Redis Server, the dumping process saves the database index (FE 00 in this example, indicating the index of database is 0), hash resize code, and database resize operation code, as well as expires the resize operation code. Then, an iteration is started to write every entry in Redis into the dump file. The format of a key-value pair in Redis is as follows:

```
| Expiration | Timestamp | Data Type | Key length | Key | Value Length | Value |
```

Due to the space limitations of this book, we won't go into the details of the preceding data format. If you are interested in this, you can refer to the source code files rdb.c and rdb.h.

The RDB file ends with an EOF and CRC64 checksum.

There's more...

With an understanding of RDB format, you can create your own Redis tools for memory analysis, data export/import, and multi Redis instance merging. If you search for the keywords Redis RDB on GitHub, you will learn more about the RDB format.

See also

- You can refer to
  `https://github.com/sripathikrishnan/redis-rdb-tools/wiki/Redis-RDB-Dump-File-Format` and
  `https://github.com/leonchen83/redis-replicator/wiki/RDB-dump-data-format` to learn more about the RDB format
- The author of Redis, Antirez, also described the design of RDB at:

  `https://redis.io/topics/rdd-2`

Manipulating AOF

In the previous two recipes, we learned about the RDB option for Redis data persistence. However, using RDB for data persistence does not provide very strong durability. As mentioned, an RDB data dump only contains a point-in-time data snapshot of Redis. Although Redis dumps data into the RDB file periodically, the data between two RDB dumps will be lost permanently when a Redis process crashes, or there is a hardware failure. AOF is an append-only log file that records the write commands of the Redis Server. The data durability of AOF is higher than RDB, because every write command is appended to the file. In this recipe, we will show you how to enable AOF in Redis and introduce some important configuration parameters of AOF.

Getting ready...

You need to finish the installation of the Redis Server, as we described in the *Downloading and installing Redis* recipe in `Chapter 1`, *Getting Started with Redis*.

How to do it...

The steps for manipulating AOF are as follows:

1. To enable AOF persistence for a running Redis instance, call the `CONFIG SET` command as follows:

   ```
   127.0.0.1:6379> CONFIG SET appendonly yes
   OK
   ```

2. If we would like to enable AOF permanently, add `appendonly yes` to the Redis configuration file and restart the server:

```
$ cat conf/redis.conf |grep "^appendonly"
appendonly yes
```

3. To disable the AOF persistence feature for a running Redis instance, set `appendonly` to no:

```
$ bin/redis-cli config set appendonly no
OK
```

4. To disable AOF persistence permanently, just set `appendonly no` in the configuration file and restart the server:

```
$ cat conf/redis.conf |grep "^appendonly"
appendonly no
```

5. To check if the AOF feature is enabled, we can use INFO PERSISTENCE and look for the AOF items:

```
127.0.0.1:6379> INFO PERSISTENCE
# Persistence
loading:0
...
aof_enabled:1
aof_rewrite_in_progress:0
```

6. Or we can check if the AOF file has been generated in the Redis data directory:

```
$ ls -l
-rw-r--r-- 1 root root  233 Oct 22 22:16 appendonly.aof
```

How it works...

When the AOF option is enabled, Redis will create the AOF file in the Redis data directory. The default AOF filename is `appendonly.aof`, which can be changed by setting the `appendfilename` parameter in the Redis configuration. Redis will also populate the AOF file with the current data in memory.

Whenever the Redis Server receives a write command that will result in an actual data change in memory, it will also append the command to the AOF file. However, if we take a deeper look at the file writing process, the operating system actually maintains a buffer to which the Redis commands will be written first. Data in the buffer has to be flushed to the disk to be saved permanently. This process is done by the Linux system call API `fsync()`, which is a blocking call until the disk device reports the data in the buffer is completed flushed.

We can tweak the frequency of calling `fsync()` when appending commands to the AOF file. This is done with the Redis configuration parameter `appendfsync`, and there are three options:

- `always`: `fsync()` will be called for every write command. This option ensures that only one command will be lost in the event of an unexpected server crash or hardware failure. However, since `fsync()` is a blocking call, the performance of Redis will be bounded by the write performance of the physical disk. It is not advisable to set `appendfsync` to `always` because the Redis Server's performance will be degraded significantly.
- `everysec`: `fsync()` will be called by Redis once per second. With this option, only one second of data will be lost in any unexpected disastrous event. It is often recommended you use this option for the balance of data durability and performance.
- `no`: `fsync()` will never be called by Redis. This option leaves the operating system to decide when to flush the data from the buffer to disk. In most Linux systems, the frequency is every 30 seconds.

When the Redis Server is shutting down, `fsync()` will be called explicitly to make sure all the data in the write buffer is flushed to disk.

The AOF file will be used to restore the data when the Redis Server is starting. Redis just replays the file by reading the commands and applying them to memory one by one. The data will be reconstructed after all the commands are processed.

There's more...

While Redis keeps appending write commands to the AOF file, the file size may grow significantly. This will slow the replay process when Redis is starting. Redis provides a mechanism to compress the AOF file with an *AOF rewrite*. As you might have guessed, some of the Redis keys had been deleted or expired, so they can be cleaned up in the AOF file. The values for certain Redis keys were updated multiple times and only the latest value needs to be stored in the AOF file. This is the basic idea of data compaction in an AOF rewrite. We can use the BGREWRITEAOF command to initiate the rewrite process, or let Redis perform an AOF rewrite automatically. We will discuss AOF rewrites in the following recipe.

The AOF file could be corrupted or truncated at the end if the operating system crashes. Redis provides a tool, redis-check-aof, which can be used to fix the corrupted AOF file. To fix a AOF file, simply run:

```
$ bin/redis-check-aof --fix appendonly.aof
```

See also

- You can find the more discussion about AOF persistence at the following link:
  https://redis.io/topics/persistence
- A blog post written by the author of Redis to explain data persistence:
  http://oldblog.antirez.com/post/redis-persistence-demystified.html
- Regarding fsync():
  https://linux.die.net/man/2/fsync

Exploring AOF

In the previous recipe, we learned how to set up AOF persistence in Redis. In this recipe, we are going to take a look at the content of the AOF file and explain the AOF rewrite process.

Getting ready...

You need to finish the installation of the Redis Server, as we described in the *Downloading and installing Redis* recipe in Chapter 1, *Getting Started with Redis*.

For the purpose of demonstration, we need to disable AOF and flush all the data with the FLUSHALL command first.

How to do it...

The steps for exploring AOF are as follows:

1. Enable AOF persistence:

```
127.0.0.1:6379> CONFIG SET appendonly yes
OK
```

2. Since there is no data in Redis, we should have an empty AOF file:

```
$ ls -l
-rw-rw---- 1 redis redis    0 Oct 23 20:47 appendonly.aof
```

3. Run the following commands in redis-cli:

```
127.0.0.1:6379> SET k1 v1
OK
127.0.0.1:6379> INCR counter
(integer) 1
127.0.0.1:16379> INCR counter
(integer) 2
127.0.0.1:6379> SET k2 v2
OK
127.0.0.1:6379> DEL k1
(integer) 1
127.0.0.1:6379> DEL k3
(integer) 0
127.0.0.1:6379> HSET mykey f1 v1 f2 v2
(integer) 2
```

4. Open the AOF file using a text editor:

```
*2\r\n$6\r\nSELECT\r\n$1\r\n0\r\n
*3\r\n$3\r\nset\r\n$2\r\nk1\r\n$2\r\nv1\r\n
*2\r\n$4\r\nincr\r\n$7\r\ncounter\r\n
*2\r\n$4\r\nincr\r\n$7\r\ncounter\r\n
...
```

5. Execute the BGREWRITEAOF command in redis-cli:

```
>127.0.0.1:6379> BGREWRITEAOF
Background append only file rewriting started
```

6. Inspect the AOF file again with a text editor:

```
*2\r\n$6\r\nSELECT\r\n$1\r\n0\r\n
*3\r\n$3\r\nSET\r\n$7\r\ncounter\r\n$1\r\n2\r\n
*3\r\n$3\r\nSET\r\n$2\r\nk2\r\n$2\r\nv2\r\n
*6\r\n$5\r\nHMSET\r\n$5\r\nmykey\r\n$2\r\nf1\r\n$2\r\nv1\r\n$2\r\nf
2\r\n$2\r\nv2\r\n
```

How it works...

In the *Getting ready* section, we disabled AOF persistence and cleared all the data in Redis. Re-enabling AOF persistence after that created an empty AOF file. Please note, we have to disable AOF persistence first before flushing the data, otherwise the AOF file will not be empty unless we run AOF rewrite.

In step 3, we issued seven commands to manipulate Redis keys:

- SET k1 v1
- INCR counter
- INCR counter
- SET k2 v2
- DEL k1
- DEL k3
- HSET mykey f1 v1 f2 v2

When we opened the AOF file for inspection, we found that the file contents seemed to be the Redis commands we just executed, in the RESP format as we introduced in the *Understanding Redis protocol* recipe of chapter 1, *Getting Started with Redis*.

There are two exceptions:

- There is a command, SELECT 0 at the beginning, which means database 0 is selected. Redis does support multiple databases that can be specified by numbers from 0 to 15, the default database is 0.
- The command, DEL k3 is not included in the AOF file, because this command does not cause any data changes in the database (key k3 does not exist).

In step 5, we executed an AOF rewrite. After it's finished, we can see the AOF file was compacted with the following change:

- Two INCR commands are replaced with one SET command.
- Commands for k1 are gone, as it's been deleted. Redis has an algorithm to compact and rewrite the AOF file, other examples are: multiple SET commands are replaced with an MSET command, commands for expired keys are removed, and so on.

A child process will be forked from the Redis main process to perform an AOF rewrite. The child process will create a new AOF file to store the rewrite results, so that the old AOF file will not be impacted in case the rewrite operation fails. The parent process continues to serve traffic and dumps write commands to the old AOF file. The COW mechanism is used when forking the child process, so it does not take the same amount of memory as the parent. However, because of the COW mechanism, the child process is not able to access the new data after the fork. Redis solves this problem by letting the parent process push write commands that are received after the fork into a buffer called aof_rewrite_buf_blocks. Once the child process finishes rewriting the new AOF file, it will send a signal to the parent process. The parent process will flush commands from aof_rewrite_buf_blocks into the new AOF file, then replace the old AOF file with the new one.

There's more...

Besides manually triggering an AOF rewrite with the BGREWRITEAOF command, we can also configure Redis to execute an AOF rewrite automatically. The following two configuration parameters are for this purpose:

- auto-aof-rewrite-min-size: An AOF rewrite will not be triggered if the AOF file size is less than this value. The default value is 64 MB.
- auto-aof-rewrite-percentage: Redis will remember the AOF file size after the last AOF rewrite operation. If the current AOF file size has increased by this percentage value, another AOF rewrite will be triggered. Setting this value to 0 will disable *Automatic AOF Rewrite*. The default value is 100.

The INFO PERSISTENCE command provides a lot of information about an AOF rewrite. For example, aof_last_bgrewrite_status indicates the status of the last AOF rewrite operation, aof_base_size is the size of the last AOF file, aof_rewrite_buffer_length is the size of aof_rewrite_buf_blocks, as previously mentioned:

```
127.0.0.1:6379> INFO PERSISTENCE
...
aof_enabled:1
aof_rewrite_in_progress:0
aof_rewrite_scheduled:0
aof_last_rewrite_time_sec:0
aof_current_rewrite_time_sec:-1
aof_last_bgrewrite_status:ok
aof_last_write_status:ok
aof_last_cow_size:6393856
aof_current_size:143
aof_base_size:143
aof_pending_rewrite:0
aof_buffer_length:0
aof_rewrite_buffer_length:0
aof_pending_bio_fsync:0
aof_delayed_fsync:0
```

See also

- You can refer to https://redis.io/commands/info for explanations of other AOF persistence information items

Combining RDB and AOF

In the previous recipes of this chapter, we have described both RDB and AOF persistence options. When it comes to data persistence, there are always several factors you should take into consideration: data loss in case of an outage, performance cost when saving data, the size of the persisted file, and the speed of restoring data. For RDB, data written into Redis between two snapshots may get lost. The latency and memory cost of a system call fork() in RDB may become a problem when the writing traffic is high and the dataset is big. However, compared to AOF, an RDB dumping file takes less disk space, and restoring data from an RDB dump is faster. In fact, you can enable both features at the same time.

In this recipe, we will explore how to take the best of both persistence approaches.

Getting ready...

You need to finish the installation of the Redis Server, as we described in the *Downloading and installing Redis* recipe in `Chapter 1`, *Getting Started with Redis*. Basic knowledge of both RDB and AOF is required.

How to do it...

1. To enable both RDB and AOF persistence features, set the following configuration options in the configuration file of Redis:

```
$ cat conf/redis.conf |egrep "^save|^append"
save 900 1
save 300 10
save 60 10000
appendonly yes
appendfilename "appendonly.aof"
appendfsync everysec
```

2. Populate some sample data into the Redis Server with the DEBUG POPULATE command and perform data persistence operations for both RDB and AOF. After those operations, set a simple string key-value pair:

```
127.0.0.1:6379> DEBUG POPULATE 1000000
OK
(1.61s)
127.0.0.1:6379> SAVE
OK
127.0.0.1:6379> BGREWRITEAOF
Background append only file rewriting started

127.0.0.1:6379> SET FOO BAR
OK
```

3. Check the RDB dump and AOF append log:

```
$ ls -l dump.rdb appendonly.aof
-rw-rw-r-- 1 redis redis 48676857 Oct 25 10:25 appendonly.aof
-rw-rw-r-- 1 redis redis 24777946 Oct 25 10:24 dump.rdb
```

4. Check the file size of the RDB dump and AOF log:

```
$ du -sm dump.rdb appendonly.aof
24      dump.rdb
47      appendonly.aof
```

5. Check the first 20 lines of the AOF file with the Vim editor:

```
 1 *2
 2 $6
 3 SELECT
 4 $1
 5 0
 6 *3
 7 $3
 8 SET
 9 $10
10 key:199713
11 $12
12 value:199713
13 *3
14 $3
15 SET
16 $10
17 key:547158
18 $12
19 value:547158
20 *3
21 $3
22 SET
```

Then, we check the last 10 lines of the AOF file with the Vim editor, as follows:

```
7000001 SET
7000002 $10
7000003 key:562743
7000004 $12
7000005 value:562743
7000006 *2
7000007 $6
7000008 SELECT
7000009 $1
7000010 0
7000011 *3
7000012 $3
7000013 SET
7000014 $3
7000015 FOO
7000016 $3
7000017 BAR
```

6. Change the configuration `aof-use-rdb-preamble` to `yes` and issue `BGREWRITEAOF` again to trigger an AOF file rewrite:

```
127.0.0.1:6379> CONFIG SET aof-use-rdb-preamble yes
OK
127.0.0.1:6379> BGREWRITEAOF
Background append only file rewriting started
```

7. Check the file size of the RDB dump and AOF log:

```
$ du -sm dump.rdb appendonly.aof
24      dump.rdb
24      appendonly.aof
```

8. Check the first 20 lines of the AOF file in the Vim editor:

```
   1 REDIS0008    redis-ver^E4.0.1[33m    2 redis-bits[34m^Ectime±▯
[34m^Hused-mem▯[34m^D4m^Laof-preamble4m^A4m^^
     Grepl-id(e5da1042134a3e4fe84be1db46a6ea4849c5c5824m^Krepl-offs
     t4m^@4m^@4m~@^@^@OB@^@^@
   3 key:455483^Lvalue:455483^@
   4 key:570281^Lvalue:570281^@
   5 key:356462^Lvalue:356462^@        key:67227^Kvalue:67227^@
   6 key:147364^Lvalue:147364^@
   7 key:255808^Lvalue:255808^@
   8 key:252551^Lvalue:252551^@
   9 key:591381^Lvalue:591381^@
  10 key:748670^Lvalue:748670^@
  11 key:213878^Lvalue:213878^@
  12 key:834908^Lvalue:834908^@
  13 key:421798^Lvalue:421798^@
  14 key:697478^Lvalue:697478^@
  15 key:107675^Lvalue:107675^@        key:94876^Kvalue:94876^@
  16 key:779533^Lvalue:779533^@
  17 key:538367^Lvalue:538367^@
  18 key:561941^Lvalue:561941^@
  19 key:163971^Lvalue:163971^@
  20 key:501156^Lvalue:501156^@
```

Then, we check the last 10 lines of the AOF file with the Vim editor, as follows:

```
908999 key:412162^Lvalue:412162^@
909000 key:926399^Lvalue:926399^@
909001 key:902673^Lvalue:902673^@
909002 key:404168^Lvalue:40416834m^Q▯[34m^_^H*2^M
909003 $6^M
909004 SELECT^M
909005 $1^M
909006 0^M
909007 *3^M
909008 $3^M
909009 set^M
909010 $3^M
909011 foo^M
909012 $3^M
909013 bar^M
```

How it works...

In the preceding example, some simple testing data was populated into the Redis instance. After that, an RDB dump was created via the SAVE command and the AOF file was rewritten via the BGREWRITEAOF command.

By listing the files, we found that the data has been persisted in both the form of RDB and AOF in the data directory of Redis. Based on the description in previous recipes, it's not a surprise to find the size of the AOF file is bigger than the size of the RDB dump.

Then, we inspected the starting and ending segments of AOF with the Vim editor. The write commands have been saved in the AOF format described in the previous *Exploring AOF* recipe.

After enabling both RDB and AOF methods, we set the configuration option aof-use-rdb-preamble to yes to enable the new mix-format persistence feature, provided since Redis 4.x. Once this option is set to yes, when rewriting the AOF file, Redis dumps the dataset in memory in the format of RDB first as a preamble of AOF. After rewriting, Redis continues to log the write commands in the AOF file, using the traditional AOF format. This kind of mixed format can be verified clearly via exploring the head and the tail of the AOF file after a rewrite. The RDB format is used first, at the beginning of the AOF file, if mix format is enabled. Redis benefits from the mixed persistence format, as Redis can rewrite and load the data file more quickly due to the compacted format of RDB, while retaining the merits of AOF for better data consistency.

There's more...

For Redis, prior to the 4.x version, you could enable RDB and AOF at the same time to achieve the best data safety. It's advisable to enable AOF and the mixed format of persistence after Redis 4.x. Please note that it does not make any sense to turn on the mixed format with the AOF option disabled, in that nothing will be appended to the AOF file even if you manually create the AOF file by calling BGREWRITEAOF. If you can live with some possible data loss, using RDB alone can achieve a better performance. Moreover, according to *Antirez*, the author of Redis, using AOF alone is discouraged, to prevent data lost in the event of bugs in the AOF engine.

Lastly, Redis guarantees that RDB dumping and AOF rewrites will never run at the same time. When starting up, Redis will always load the AOF file first, if it exists, even when both persistence options are enabled and the RDB file also exists. That is because the AOF file is considered to provide more robust data consistency. When loading the AOF file, if a mixed format of persistence is enabled, Redis first checks the first five characters of AOF. If they are REDIS, which is the magic string of an RDB file, as described in the *Exploring RDB* recipe, this AOF file is mix formatted. The Redis Server will load the RDB part first, and then the AOF part.

7
Setting Up High Availability and Cluster

In this chapter, we will cover the following recipes:

- Setting up Sentinel
- Testing Sentinel
- Administrating Sentinel
- Setting up Redis Cluster
- Testing Redis Cluster
- Administrating Redis Cluster

Introduction

For the requirements of a production environment, one single Redis instance is far from enough to provide a stable and efficient key-value data service with data redundancy and **high availability (HA)**. Using the replication and persistence of Redis may solve the problem of data redundancy. However, without human intervention, the whole Redis service is not able to be recovered when the master instance is down. While various kinds of solution have been worked out for the HA of Redis, Redis Sentinel, natively supported in Redis since version 2.6, is the most widely used HA architecture. By taking advantage of Sentinel, you can easily build a fault-tolerant Redis service.

As the amounts of data stored in Redis grow rapidly, the processing power and memory capacity of a Redis instance with a large dataset (usually above 16 G) may become a bottleneck for the application. And there are more and more latency or other issues when performing persistence or replication, as the size of datasets in Redis grows. For this situation, horizontal scalability, or scaling by adding more nodes to a Redis service, is an immediate need. Redis Cluster, supported since version 3.0, is presented for this kind of problem. Redis Cluster is an out-of-the-box solution for partitioning the dataset into multiple Redis master-slave instances.

In this chapter, we will follow the pattern of *Setting up*, *Testing*, and *Administrating* to discuss separately how to construct a production-ready Redis service using Sentinel and Redis Cluster.

Lastly, it's worth mentioning that, as a convention, the word **Cluster** with the first letter capitalized refers specifically to the Redis Cluster technique. You may find various kinds of third-party systems to implement the clustering feature of Redis before version 3.0 of Redis was released. So, don't confuse the Redis Cluster we will talk about in this chapter with other data clustering systems using Redis.

Setting up Sentinel

Redis Sentinel, as the name implies, acts as a guard for the Redis master and slave instances. One Sentinel is obviously not enough to guarantee high availability because a single Sentinel itself is also subject to failure. Because the master failover decision is based on a quorum system, at least three Sentinel processes are required as a robust distributed system that keeps monitoring the status of the Redis master data server. If multiple Sentinel processes detect that the master is down, one of the Sentinel process will be elected to promote a slave to replace the old master. With proper configuration, the entire process is automatic without any human intervention. In this recipe, we will demonstrate how to set up a simple environment of one master and two slaves, which is monitored by three Sentinels.

Getting ready...

You need to set up one Redis master server and two slave servers. You can refer to the *Setting up Redis replication* section in Chapter 6, *Persistence* for instructions. In this example, we will deploy Redis Server and Sentinel instances on three different hosts, the role, IP address, and port, shown in the following table:

Role	IP address	Port
Master	192.168.0.31	6379
Slave-1	192.168.0.32	6379
Slave-2	192.168.0.33	6379
Sentinel-1	192.168.0.31	26379
Sentinal-2	192.168.0.32	26379
Sentinel-3	192.168.0.33	26379

The overall architecture can be seen in the following image:

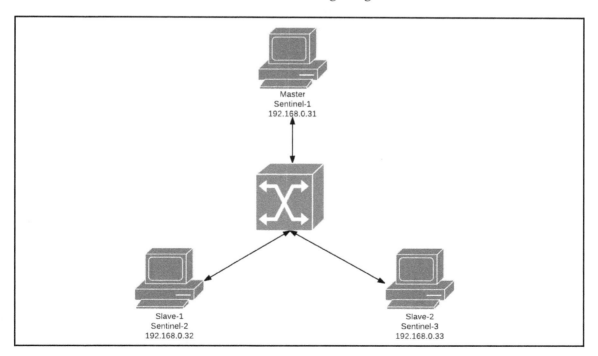

The three hosts must be able to communicate with each other. You need to set the binding IP correctly in the Redis configuration file, in order to let other hosts talk to the Redis instance. The default binding IP is `127.0.0.1`, which only enables access from the localhost. You can append the IP address as follows:

```
bind 127.0.0.1 192.168.0.31
```

Make sure all Redis data servers are up and running.

How to do it...

The steps for setting up Sentinel are as follows:

1. Prepare a configuration file, `sentinel.conf`, on each host. You can get a sample copy from the source code. Make sure the configuration file is writable by the user who runs the Sentinel process:

```
port 26379
dir /tmp
sentinel monitor mymaster 192.168.0.31 6379 2
sentinel down-after-milliseconds mymaster 30000
sentinel parallel-syncs mymaster 1
sentinel failover-timeout mymaster 180000
```

2. Start Sentinel processes on three hosts:

```
user@192.168.0.31:~$bin/redis-server conf/sentinel.conf --sentinel
user@192.168.0.32:~$bin/redis-server conf/sentinel.conf --sentinel
user@192.168.0.33:~$bin/redis-server conf/sentinel.conf --sentinel
```

3. Examine the logs on Sentinel-1:

```
21758:X 29 Oct 22:31:51.001 # Sentinel ID is
3ef95f7fd6420bfe22e38bfded1399382a63ce5b
21758:X 29 Oct 22:31:51.001 # +monitor master mymaster 192.168.0.31
6379 quorum 2
21758:X 29 Oct 22:31:51.001 * +slave slave 192.168.0.32:6379
192.168.0.32 6379 @ mymaster 192.168.0.31 6379
21758:X 29 Oct 22:31:51.003 * +slave slave 192.168.0.33:6379
192.168.0.33 6379 @ mymaster 192.168.0.31 6379
21758:X 29 Oct 22:31:52.021 * +sentinel sentinel
d24979c27871eafa62e797d1c8e51acc99bbda72 192.168.0.32 26379 @
mymaster 192.168.0.31 6379
21758:X 29 Oct 22:32:17.241 * +sentinel sentinel
a276b044b26100570bb1a4d83d5b3f9d66729f64 192.168.0.33 26379 @
```

```
mymaster 192.168.0.31 6379
```

4. Connect to Sentinel-1 using `redis-cli` and execute the `INFO SENTINEL` command. Please don't forget to specify the port, `26379`:

```
user@192.168.0.31:~$ bin/redis-cli -p 26379
127.0.0.1:26379> INFO SENTINEL
# Sentinel
sentinel_masters:1
sentinel_tilt:0
sentinel_running_scripts:0
sentinel_scripts_queue_length:0
sentinel_simulate_failure_flags:0
master0:name=mymaster,status=ok,address=192.168.0.31:6379,slaves=2,
sentinels=3
```

5. Examine the content of `sentinel.conf` on Sentinel-1:

```
user@192.168.0.31:~$ cat conf/sentinel.conf
...
# Generated by CONFIG REWRITE
sentinel known-slave mymaster 192.168.0.33 6379
sentinel known-slave mymaster 192.168.0.32 6379
sentinel known-sentinel mymaster 192.168.0.33 26379
a276b044b26100570bb1a4d83d5b3f9d66729f64
sentinel known-sentinel mymaster 192.168.0.32 26379
d24979c27871eafa62e797d1c8e51acc99bbda72
sentinel current-epoch 0
```

How it works...

In step 1, we prepared a configuration file for the Redis Sentinel processes. There is a sample `sentinel.conf` file in the Redis source code package, so in this example we just made changes on top of it. As mentioned, Redis Sentinel is a guard process for Redis data servers, therefore it has to listen to a different port than the data server's port. The default port for Redis Sentinel is `26379`. To add a new master server to the Sentinel for monitoring, we can add a line to the configuration file in the format of `sentinel monitor <master-name> <ip> <port> <quorum>`.

In this example, `sentinel monitor mymaster 192.168.0.31 6379 2` means the Sentinel is going to monitor the master server on `192.168.0.31:6379`, which is named `mymaster`. `<quorum>` means the minimum number of Sentinels that agree the master server is unreachable before a failover action can be taken. The down-after-milliseconds option means the maximum time in milliseconds that a Redis instance is allowed to be unreachable before the Sentinel marks it as down. The Sentinel will ping the data server every second to check if it is reachable.

In this example, if a server does not respond to the ping for more than 30 seconds, it will be deemed as down. When a master failover happens, one of the slaves will be elected as the new master, and other slaves will need to replicate from the new master. The `parallel-syncs` option denotes how many slaves can start the synchronization from the new master simultaneously.

A Sentinel process can be launched by `redis-server <sentinel.conf> --sentinel`. If you compile Redis from source code, you will find a `redis-sentinel` file, which is a symbolic link to `redis-server`. The Sentinel process can be also launched by `redis-sentinel <sentinel.conf>`.

From the Sentinel logs in step 3 and the last line of the `INFO SENTINEL` output in step 4, we can see that Sentinel-1 has successfully detected the slaves and other Sentinels (you will find the same result if you check the logs of Sentinel-2 and Sentinel-3).

You may be wondering how the Sentinel process is able to detect the slave servers and other Sentinels, as we only specified the master servers' information in the configuration file. You may think that, in order to get the slaves' information, the Sentinel can send the `INFO REPLICATION` command to the master. If there are multiple levels of slaves, they can be discovered in this way recursively. In fact, every 10 seconds, each Sentinel process sends `INFO REPLICATION` to all the data nodes (including masters and detected slaves) it is monitoring, to pull the latest information of the entire replication topology.

To detect and communicate with other Sentinel processes, every two seconds each Sentinel publishes a message about its status and its view of the master status to a channel named `__sentinel__:hello`. Therefore, other Sentinels' information can be discovered by subscribing to this channel.

Messages in the channel can be viewed by connecting to any of the data servers and subscribing to the channel:

```
user@redis-master:/redis$ bin/redis-cli -h 192.168.0.31
192.168.0.31:6379> SUBSCRIBE __sentinel__:hello
Reading messages... (press Ctrl-C to quit)
1) "subscribe"
2) "__sentinel__:hello"
3) (integer) 1
1) "message"
2) "__sentinel__:hello"
3)
"192.168.0.31,26379,3ef95f7fd6420bfe22e38bfded1399382a63ce5b,0,mymaster,192
.1
68.0.31,6379,0"
1) "message"
2) "__sentinel__:hello"
...
"192.168.0.31,26379,3ef95f7fd6420bfe22e38bfded1399382a63ce5b,0,mymaster,192
.1
68.0.31,6379,0"
```

The configuration files for Redis Sentinel will also be updated to reflect the information about slaves and other Sentinels. That's why the configuration file must be writable by the Sentinel process.

There's more...

It is worth mentioning that client-side support is needed to utilize Redis Sentinel. When we introduced Redis Java/Python clients in `Chapter 4`, *Developing with Redis*, we passed the master server's address to the API. However, with Redis Sentinel enabled, the master server's address will change when master failover happens. To get the latest master information, the client needs to query from the Sentinel. This can be done by the command `sentinel get-master-addr-by-name <master-name>`. The actual process is more complicated and we are not going to cover it here. Fortunately, both the Jedis and `redis-py` libraries have Sentinel support.

See also

- Official documentation for Redis Sentinel: `https://redis.io/topics/sentinel`

Testing Sentinel

We have demonstrated in the previous recipe how to set up an environment of one Redis master and two slaves, which is monitored by three Sentinels. In this recipe, we will do a couple of experiments in this environment and verify the Sentinels are doing their jobs correctly. We will also explain the master failover process in detail.

Getting ready...

You must finish the setup in the *Setting up Sentinel* section of this chapter. Additionally, you can refer to the table shown in the *Getting ready* section of the previous recipe, *Setting up Sentinel*.

How to do it...

To test the Redis Sentinel set up in the previous recipe, take the following steps:

1. Triggering a master failover manually:
    1. Connect to one of the Sentinels using `redis-cli`; here we are connecting to Sentinel-2 (`192.168.0.32`):

       ```
       192.168.0.32:26379> SENTINEL FAILOVER MYMASTER
       OK
       ```

    2. Verify the old master `192.168.0.31` has been failed over and is now a slave:

       ```
       192.168.0.31:26379> INFO REPLICATION
       # Replication
       role:slave
       master_host:192.168.0.33
       master_port:6379
       master_link_status:up
       ...
       ```

3. Examine the logs of Sentinel-2:

```
2283:X 12 Nov 15:35:14.782 # Executing user requested
FAILOVER of 'mymaster'
2283:X 12 Nov 15:35:14.782 # +new-epoch 1
2283:X 12 Nov 15:35:14.782 # +try-failover master mymaster
192.168.0.31 6379
2283:X 12 Nov 15:35:14.789 # +vote-for-leader
d24979c27871eafa62e797d1c8e51acc99bbda72 1
2283:X 12 Nov 15:35:14.789 # +elected-leader master
mymaster 192.168.0.31 6379
2283:X 12 Nov 15:35:14.789 # +failover-state-select-slave
master mymaster 192.168.0.31 6379
2283:X 12 Nov 15:35:14.872 # +selected-slave slave
192.168.0.33:6379 192.168.0.33 6379 @ mymaster 192.168.0.31
6379
2283:X 12 Nov 15:35:14.872 * +failover-state-send-slaveof-
noone slave 192.168.0.33:6379 192.168.0.33 6379 @ mymaster
192.168.0.31 6379
2283:X 12 Nov 15:35:14.949 * +failover-state-wait-promotion
slave 192.168.0.33:6379 192.168.0.33 6379 @ mymaster
192.168.0.31 6379
2283:X 12 Nov 15:35:15.799 # +promoted-slave slave
192.168.0.33:6379 192.168.0.33 6379 @ mymaster 192.168.0.31
6379
2283:X 12 Nov 15:35:15.800 # +failover-state-reconf-slaves
master mymaster 192.168.0.31 6379
2283:X 12 Nov 15:35:15.852 * +slave-reconf-sent slave
192.168.0.32:6379 192.168.0.32 6379 @ mymaster 192.168.0.31
6379
2283:X 12 Nov 15:35:16.503 * +slave-reconf-inprog slave
192.168.0.32:6379 192.168.0.32 6379 @ mymaster 192.168.0.31
6379
2283:X 12 Nov 15:35:16.503 * +slave-reconf-done slave
192.168.0.32:6379 192.168.0.32 6379 @ mymaster 192.168.0.31
6379
2283:X 12 Nov 15:35:16.580 # +failover-end master mymaster
192.168.0.31 6379
2283:X 12 Nov 15:35:16.580 # +switch-master mymaster
192.168.0.31 6379 192.168.0.33 6379
2283:X 12 Nov 15:35:16.580 * +slave slave 192.168.0.32:6379
192.168.0.32 6379 @ mymaster 192.168.0.33 6379
2283:X 12 Nov 15:35:16.581 * +slave slave 192.168.0.31:6379
192.168.0.31 6379 @ mymaster 192.168.0.33 6379
```

4. Examine the logs of `redis-server` on `192.168.0.33` (new master):

```
2274:M 12 Nov 15:35:14.953 # Setting secondary replication
ID to 8a005b14ac7166dfc913846060bee4a980f97785, valid up to
offset: 92256. New replication ID is
a897d63fb211d7ebf6c1269998dab1779d14f8a4
2274:M 12 Nov 15:35:14.953 # Connection with master lost.
2274:M 12 Nov 15:35:14.953 * Caching the disconnected
master state.
2274:M 12 Nov 15:35:14.953 * Discarding previously cached
master state.
2274:M 12 Nov 15:35:14.953 * MASTER MODE enabled (user
request from 'id=3 addr=192.168.0.32:60540 fd=9
name=sentinel-d24979c2-cmd age=356 idle=0 flags=x db=0
sub=0 psub=0 multi=3 qbuf=0 qbuf-free=32768 obl=36 oll=0
omem=0 events=r cmd=exec')
2274:M 12 Nov 15:35:14.954 # CONFIG REWRITE executed with
success.
2274:M 12 Nov 15:35:16.452 * Slave 192.168.0.32:6379 asks
for synchronization
2274:M 12 Nov 15:35:16.452 * Partial resynchronization not
accepted: Requested offset for second ID was 92534, but I
can reply up to 92256
. . .
2274:M 12 Nov 15:35:16.462 * Synchronization with slave
192.168.0.32:6379 succeeded
2274:M 12 Nov 15:35:26.839 * Slave 192.168.0.31:6379 asks
for synchronization
. . .
2274:M 12 Nov 15:35:26.936 * Background saving terminated
with success
2274:M 12 Nov 15:35:26.937 * Synchronization with slave
192.168.0.31:6379 succeeded
```

5. Examine the content of `sentinel.conf` on Sentinel-1:

```
user@192.168.0.31:~$ cat conf/sentinel.conf
port 26379
dir "/tmp"
sentinel myid d24979c27871eafa62e797d1c8e51acc99bbda72
sentinel monitor mymaster 192.168.0.33 6379 2
. . .
```

2. Simulating a master down:

Our master at this time is 192.168.0.33. Let's shut down the Redis Server on this host and see what the Sentinels will do:

1. Connect to the Redis Server on 192.168.0.33 via redis-cli and shut down the server:

```
192.168.0.33:6379> SHUTDOWN
not connected>
```

2. Check the status on 192.168.0.31 and 192.168.0.32:

```
192.168.0.31:6379> INFO REPLICATION
# Replication
role:master
connected_slaves:1
slave0:ip=192.168.0.32,port=6379,state=online,offset=349140
,lag=1
192.168.0.32:6379> INFO REPLICATION
# Replication
role:slave
master_host:192.168.0.31
master_port:6379
master_link_status:up
```

We can see that 192.168.0.31 has been promoted to the new master.

3. Examine the logs on the three Sentinels:

```
Sentinel-1 (3ef95f7fd6420bfe22e38bfded1399382a63ce5b):
2931:X 12 Nov 17:05:02.446 # +sdown master mymaster
192.168.0.33 6379
2931:X 12 Nov 17:05:03.570 # +odown master mymaster
192.168.0.33 6379 #quorum 2/2
2931:X 12 Nov 17:05:03.570 # +new-epoch 2
2931:X 12 Nov 17:05:03.570 # +try-failover master mymaster
192.168.0.33 6379
2931:X 12 Nov 17:05:03.573 # +vote-for-leader
3ef95f7fd6420bfe22e38bfded1399382a63ce5b 2
2931:X 12 Nov 17:05:03.573 #
a276b044b26100570bb1a4d83d5b3f9d66729f64 voted for
d24979c27871eafa62e797d1c8e51acc99bbda72 2
2931:X 12 Nov 17:05:04.224 # +config-update-from sentinel
d24979c27871eafa62e797d1c8e51acc99bbda72 192.168.0.32 26379
@ mymaster 192.168.0.33 6379
```

```
2931:X 12 Nov 17:05:04.224 # +switch-master mymaster
192.168.0.33 6379 192.168.0.31 6379
...
2931:X 12 Nov 17:05:34.283 # +sdown slave 192.168.0.33:6379
192.168.0.33 6379 @ mymaster 192.168.0.31 6379
Sentinel-2 (d24979c27871eafa62e797d1c8e51acc99bbda72):
3055:X 12 Nov 17:05:02.394 # +sdown master mymaster
192.168.0.33 6379
3055:X 12 Nov 17:05:03.505 # +odown master mymaster
192.168.0.33 6379 #quorum 2/2
3055:X 12 Nov 17:05:03.505 # +new-epoch 2
3055:X 12 Nov 17:05:03.505 # +try-failover master mymaster
192.168.0.33 6379
3055:X 12 Nov 17:05:03.507 # +vote-for-leader
d24979c27871eafa62e797d1c8e51acc99bbda72 2
3055:X 12 Nov 17:05:03.516 #
a276b044b26100570bb1a4d83d5b3f9d66729f64 voted for
d24979c27871eafa62e797d1c8e51acc99bbda72 2
3055:X 12 Nov 17:05:03.584 # +elected-leader master
mymaster 192.168.0.33 6379
3055:X 12 Nov 17:05:03.584 # +failover-state-select-slave
master mymaster 192.168.0.33 6379
3055:X 12 Nov 17:05:03.668 # +selected-slave slave
192.168.0.31:6379 192.168.0.31 6379 @ mymaster 192.168.0.33
6379
3055:X 12 Nov 17:05:03.668 * +failover-state-send-slaveof-
noone slave 192.168.0.31:6379 192.168.0.31 6379 @ mymaster
192.168.0.33 6379
3055:X 12 Nov 17:05:03.758 * +failover-state-wait-promotion
slave 192.168.0.31:6379 192.168.0.31 6379 @ mymaster
192.168.0.33 6379
3055:X 12 Nov 17:05:04.135 # +promoted-slave slave
192.168.0.31:6379 192.168.0.31 6379 @ mymaster 192.168.0.33
6379
3055:X 12 Nov 17:05:04.135 # +failover-state-reconf-slaves
master mymaster 192.168.0.33 6379
3055:X 12 Nov 17:05:04.224 * +slave-reconf-sent slave
192.168.0.32:6379 192.168.0.32 6379 @ mymaster 192.168.0.33
6379
3055:X 12 Nov 17:05:04.609 # -odown master mymaster
192.168.0.33 6379
3055:X 12 Nov 17:05:05.147 * +slave-reconf-inprog slave
192.168.0.32:6379 192.168.0.32 6379 @ mymaster 192.168.0.33
6379
3055:X 12 Nov 17:05:05.147 * +slave-reconf-done slave
192.168.0.32:6379 192.168.0.32 6379 @ mymaster 192.168.0.33
6379
3055:X 12 Nov 17:05:05.201 # +failover-end master mymaster
```

```
192.168.0.33 6379
3055:X 12 Nov 17:05:05.201 # +switch-master mymaster
192.168.0.33 6379 192.168.0.31 6379
3055:X 12 Nov 17:05:05.201 * +slave slave 192.168.0.32:6379
192.168.0.32 6379 @ mymaster 192.168.0.31 6379
3055:X 12 Nov 17:05:05.201 * +slave slave 192.168.0.33:6379
192.168.0.33 6379 @ mymaster 192.168.0.31 6379
3055:X 12 Nov 17:05:35.282 # +sdown slave 192.168.0.33:6379
192.168.0.33 6379 @ mymaster 192.168.0.31 6379
Sentinel-3 (a276b044b26100570bb1a4d83d5b3f9d66729f64):
2810:X 12 Nov 17:05:02.519 # +sdown master mymaster
192.168.0.33 6379
2810:X 12 Nov 17:05:03.512 # +new-epoch 2
2810:X 12 Nov 17:05:03.517 # +vote-for-leader
d24979c27871eafa62e797d1c8e51acc99bbda72 2
2810:X 12 Nov 17:05:04.225 # +config-update-from sentinel
d24979c27871eafa62e797d1c8e51acc99bbda72 192.168.0.32 26379
@ mymaster 192.168.0.33 6379
2810:X 12 Nov 17:05:04.225 # +switch-master mymaster
192.168.0.33 6379 192.168.0.31 6379
2810:X 12 Nov 17:05:04.225 * +slave slave 192.168.0.32:6379
192.168.0.32 6379 @ mymaster 192.168.0.31 6379
2810:X 12 Nov 17:05:04.225 * +slave slave 192.168.0.33:6379
192.168.0.33 6379 @ mymaster 192.168.0.31 6379
2810:X 12 Nov 17:05:34.277 # +sdown slave 192.168.0.33:6379
192.168.0.33 6379 @ mymaster 192.168.0.31 6379
```

3. Simulating two slaves down:

   As we have shut down the Redis Server on 192.168.0.33, currently there are one master (192.168.0.31) and one slave (192.168.0.32) running:

   1. Set min-slaves-to-write to 1 on the master:

      ```
      192.168.0.31:6379> CONFIG SET MIN-SLAVES-TO-WRITE 1
      OK
      ```

   2. Shut down the only slave 192.168.0.32:

      ```
      192.168.0.32:6379> SHUTDOWN
      ```

   3. Try to write to the master:

      ```
      127.0.0.1:6379> SET test_key 12345
      (error) NOREPLICAS Not enough good slaves to write.
      ```

4. Simulating one Sentinel down:

    1. Before doing this experiment, let's bring back the Redis Servers on
       `192.168.0.32` and `192.168.0.33`:

       ```
       user@192.168.0.32:/redis$ bin/redis-server conf/redis.conf
       user@192.168.0.33:/redis$ bin/redis-server conf/redis.conf
       ```

    2. Stop Sentinel-1:

       ```
       192.168.0.31:26379> SHUTDOWN
       ```

    3. Shut down the master `192.168.0.31` and verify whether the failover
       happens:

       ```
       192.168.0.31:6379> SHUTDOWN
       192.168.0.32:6379> info replication
       # Replication
       role:master
       connected_slaves:1
       slave0:ip=192.168.0.33,port=6379,state=online,offset=782227
       ,lag=0
       192.168.0.33:6379> info replication
       # Replication
       role:slave
       master_host:192.168.0.32
       master_port:6379
       master_link_status:up
       ```

5. Simulating two Sentinels down:

    1. Bring up the Redis Server on `192.168.0.31`. The current master is
       `192.168.0.32`.

       ```
       user@192.168.0.31:/redis$ bin/redis-server conf/redis.conf
       ```

    2. Stop Sentinel-2 and shut down the master, `192.168.0.32`

       ```
       192.168.0.32:6379> SHUTDOWN
       ```

    3. Examine the logs of Sentinel-3:

       ```
       . . .
       2810:X 12 Nov 18:22:41.171 # +sdown master mymaster
       192.168.0.32 6379
       ```

       Master failover did not happen.

How it works...

We'll explain what happened case by case in the previous section.

Triggering a master failover manually

In this experiment, we manually forced the Sentinel to failover the Redis master and promote a slave. This was done by issuing the command `sentinel failover <master-name>` to Sentinel-2. As we can see, `192.168.0.33` was promoted to the new master and the old master became a slave.

Now, let's take a look at the process in detail from the log of Sentinel-2; there are multiple Sentinel events (+vote-for-leader, +elected-leader, +selected-slave, and so on). Most of them are self-explanatory by name, but you can find a table of all Sentinel events in the *There's more* section.

1. Since this failover was triggered manually, the Sentinel does not need to seek agreements from other Sentinels before performing the failover operation. It was elected as the leader directly without any consensus.
2. Next, the Sentinel picked up a slave to promote, which is `192.168.0.33` in this experiment.
3. The Sentinel sent the command `slaveof no one` to `192.168.0.33`, so it became a master. If we check the server log of `192.168.0.33`, we will find that the server received the command from Sentinel-2, stopped replicating from the old master `192.168.0.31`, and was promoted to a master itself.
4. The Sentinel reconfigured the old master `192.168.0.31` and an other slave `192.168.0.32` to let them replicate from the new master.
5. In the last step, the Sentinel updated the information of the new master and propagated this information to other Sentinels via the channel `__sentinel__:hello`, so that clients would get the new master information.

The configuration files `redis.conf` and `sentinel.conf` were also updated accordingly to match the new host roles.

Simulating a master down

In this experiment, we simulated a failure on the Redis master server `192.168.0.33` by shutting it down manually. The Sentinels promoted `192.168.0.31` as the new master and finished the failover.

Let's see how the entire process happened:

1. On Sentinel-1, at `17:05:02.446`, it found the master server was unreachable. As we mentioned in the previous recipe, each Sentinel will ping the Redis master, slaves, and other Sentinels regularly. If a ping times out, the server will be regarded as down by the Sentinel. However, this is only a subjective view of one Sentinel, namely subjectively down (+sdown in Sentinel events). In this example, Sentinel-1 marked the master as +sdown.

2. To prevent false alarms, the Sentinel that marked the master as +sdown will send requests to other Sentinels to ask for their view of the master instance. Actions will be taken only when more than the number of <quorum> Sentinels view the master as down, which is called objectively down (+odown). In this example, Sentinel-1 got the response from other Sentinels at `17:05:03.570` and marked the master as +odown.

3. Next, Sentinel-1 attempted to perform the failover but did not get elected as the leader.

4. Almost at the same time, Sentinel-2 also marked the master as +sdown and +odown, and it was elected as the leader to perform the failover. The rest of the process is the same as in the step triggering a master failover manually.

How was the leader elected? The vote starts after +down on one of the Sentinels; the Sentinel will start soliciting votes for itself from other Sentinels. Each Sentinel has one vote only. Once another Sentinel receives the solicitation, if it hasn't voted before, it will accept the solicitation and reply to the solicitor. Otherwise, it will reject the solicitation and reply with the other leader it just voted. If a Sentinel has received greater than or equal to max (quorum, number of sentinels / 2 + 1) votes (including itself; the Sentinel will vote for itself before soliciting votes from others), it will become the leader. If a leader was not elected, the process will repeat.

Back to the Sentinel logs. Sentinel-1 sent out the solicitation at `17:05:03.573`, but got a response from Sentinel-3 (id: a276b044b26100570bb1a4d83d5b3f9d66729f64) that it had voted for Sentinel-2 (id: d24979c27871eafa62e797d1c8e51acc99bbda72). Sentinel-2 sent out the solicitation earlier at `17:05:03.507` and got the response from Sentinel-3 that it agreed to vote for Sentinel-2. Therefore, Sentinel-2 received two votes and became the leader.

Simulating two slaves down

In this experiment, we set `min-slaves-to-write` to 1 and shut down 2 slaves, leaving the master running only. The option `min-slaves-to-write` means *the minimum slaves required to accept the write request*. As there were no slaves, the write request was rejected by the master.

Simulating one Sentinel down

Stopping one Sentinel did not affect the failover process in this experiment, because the quorum could still be met for *objectively down* and the leader election.

Simulating two Sentinels down

Leaving one Sentinel running alone could not trigger *objectively down* as well as the leader election, therefore the Sentinel only marked `+sdown` for the master, and the failover never happened.

There's more...

There are many types of event in Redis Sentinel. Due to space limitations, we won't go through every type of event. You can refer to the Redis Sentinel documentation for more details: `https://redis.io/topics/sentinel`.

Administrating Sentinel

We learned how to set up and test Redis Sentinel in the previous two recipes. Besides monitoring the status of Redis masters and slaves, Redis Sentinel also provides convenient features such as executing scripts on Sentinel events, or on failover. In this recipe, we will first introduce a few Sentinel commands which are frequently used, then we will see how to utilize the scripts execution feature to automate some common operation.

Getting ready...

You must finish the setup in the *Setting up Sentinel* section of this chapter, and have Redis data servers and Sentinels up and running.

How to do it...

The operations for administrating Redis Sentinel are as follows:

1. Exploring Sentinel commands:
    1. Connect to one of the Sentinels using `redis-cli`:

       ```
       user@192.168.0.33:~$bin/redis-cli -h 192.168.0.33 -p 26379
       192.168.0.33:26379>
       ```

    2. To get current master data server information, use SENTINEL GET-MASTER-ADDR-BY-NAME <master-name>:

       ```
       192.168.0.33:26379> SENTINEL GET-MASTER-ADDR-BY-NAME
       mymaster
       1) "192.168.0.31"
       2) "6379"
       ```

    3. To get the state of all masters that are being monitored, use SENTINEL MASTERS:

       ```
       192.168.0.33:26379> SENTINEL MASTERS
       1) 1) "name"
       2) "mymaster"
       3) "ip"
       4) "192.168.0.31"
       5) "port"
       . . .
       17) "last-ok-ping-reply"
       18) "364"
       . . .
       ```

    4. Similarly, to get slaves' information for a monitored master node, use SENTINEL SLAVES <master-name>:

       ```
       192.168.0.33:26379> SENTINEL SLAVES mymaster
       1) 1) "name"
       2) "192.168.0.33:6379"
       3) "ip"
       4) "192.168.0.33"
       5) "port"
       6) "6379"
       7) "runid"
       8) "23b3730d1b32fde674c5ea07b9440c08cee9fabe"
       . . .
       ```

5. To update Sentinel configurations, use `SENTINEL SET`:

```
192.168.0.33:26379> SENTINEL SET MYMASTER DOWN-AFTER-
MILLISECONDS 1000
OK
```

2. Executing scripts on Sentinel events:
    1. We would like emails to be sent whenever there's a Sentinel event (for example, `+sdown`, `+odown`). Here we are using a Python script. This is just an example; you need to set the correct SMTP server and login credentials in a real environment. You can find this Python script from the source code package with this book.
    2. Update the configuration of the notification script on one of the Sentinels using the `SENTINEL SET` command. For example, we enabled this feature on Sentinel-3 (`192.168.0.33`):

```
192.168.0.33:26379> SENTINEL SET mymaster notification-
script mymaster /redis/scripts/sentinel_events_notify.py
OK
```

The `/redis/scripts/sentinel_events_notify.py` script should be triggered on every Sentinel event.

3. Executing scripts on failover:

Redis Sentinel can be configured to automatically run a script on failover. This feature is very useful when the configuration is different between the Redis master server and slaves. For example, we would like to disable the RDB persistence option on the master server but keep it enabled on slaves. When the master failover happens, one of the slaves is going to be promoted to master, but its configuration will not be updated by Sentinels, therefore the RDB persistence option will still be enabled on the new master unless we manually turn it off. With this feature, we can set up a script to automatically update the configuration when the role of the instance has changed.

    1. Disable RDB persistence on the master (`192.168.0.31`):

```
127.0.0.1:6379> CONFIG SET SAVE ""
OK
```

2. Prepare a script that updates the RDB configuration on failover according to the current role. You can find this Bash shell script in the source code package with this book.

3. Update the configuration on all Sentinels:

```
192.168.0.31:26379> sentinel set mymaster client-reconfig-
script /redis/scripts/rdb_control.bash
OK
192.168.0.32:26379> sentinel set mymaster client-reconfig-
script /redis/scripts/rdb_control.bash
OK
192.168.0.33:26379> sentinel set mymaster client-reconfig-
script /redis/scripts/rdb_control.bash
OK
```

4. Trigger a failover:

```
192.168.0.32:26379> SENTINEL FAILOVER mymaster
OK
```

5. Verify the RDB persistence option is disabled on the new master (192.168.0.33) and enabled on the old master (192.168.0.31):

```
192.168.0.33:6379> INFO REPLICATION
# Replication
role:master
connected_slaves:2
...
192.168.0.33:6379> CONFIG GET save
1) "save"
2) ""
192.168.0.31:6379> CONFIG GET save
1) "save"
2) "900 1 300 10 60 10000"
```

How it works...

In the example of executing scripts on Sentinel events, we set up a Python script to automatically send out notification emails whenever there is a new Sentinel event. This is called notification-script in Sentinel configuration. The arguments that are passed to the script are <event_type> and <event_description>. This feature is often used to notify the administrator or system ops of any critical events. You might want to add filters or set notification levels in the script so only specified events will be notified.

In the example of executing scripts on failover, we set up a shell script to automatically update the RDB persistence configuration whenever failover happens. This is called `client-reconfig-script` in Sentinel configuration.

The arguments that are passed to the script are `<master-name>` `<role>` `<state>` `<from-ip>` `<from-port>` `<to-ip>` `<to-port>`, where `<state>` is always `failover`, `<role>` is the role of the current Sentinel (`leader` or `observer`), `<from-ip>` and `<from-port>` are the IP address and port of the old master, and `<to-ip>` and `<to-port>` are the IP address and port of the new master.

In the script, we first check the role of the current instance by its IP address. Please note this is the new role after the failover. Then, according to the role, we update the configuration by calling `redis-cli`, to either enable (if the role is slave) or disable (if the role is master) the RDB persistence option.

There's more...

Both the `notification-script` and `client-config-script` will be executed on all Sentinels that have the option enabled in the configuration. For our email notification use case, we just need to enable `notification-script` on one of the Sentinels, because usually the events we are interested will appear on all Sentinels and only one email should be sent out.

The script should return `0` if the execution is successful. It will be retried up to 10 times if the return value is `1`. If a script does not finish in 60 seconds, it will be terminated with a `SIGKILL` and will be retried up to 10 times. The script will not be retried if returning a value higher than `1`.

Setting up Redis Cluster

In the previous recipes, we have learned how to set up, test, and maintain a high-availability architecture with Redis Sentinel. As we described in the *Introduction* to this chapter, the data in Redis has to be partitioned as it grows dramatically. For this scenario, without question, it's Redis Cluster, supported since 3.0 version, that comes into play. From this recipe on, we will follow the *setup-test-administration* pattern to show you how to use Redis Cluster to achieve automatic data sharding and high availability in Redis. In this recipe, we will first explore how to set up a Redis Cluster, and discuss how a Redis Cluster works.

Getting ready...

You need to finish the installation of the Redis Server as we described in the *Downloading and installing Redis* recipe in `Chapter 1`, *Getting Started with Redis*.

Basic knowledge of Redis replication, which is the subject of `Chapter 5`, *Replication*, is required for a better understanding of how the Redis Cluster works.

To prepare for the environment, you should also copy the `redis-trib.rb` script from the `src/` directory of the source code to the `script` folder.

How to do it...

In this section, we will set up a Redis Cluster with three master Redis nodes, each with a single Redis slave-instance node. The topology of this Cluster is shown here:

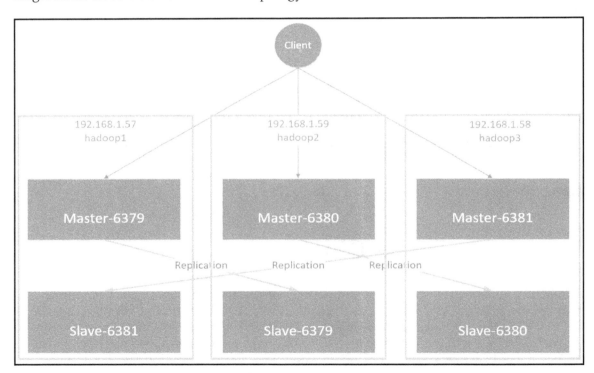

1. Each Redis instance has its own configuration file (`redis.conf`). To enable the Cluster feature, prepare a configuration file for every Redis instance and then change the IP, listening port, and `log` file path correspondingly (due to space limitations in this book, we only show you the configuration file of one instance on the first host; you can download all the configuration files from the source code provided along with this book):

```
redis@192.168.1.57:~> cat conf/redis-6379.conf
daemonize yes
pidfile "/redis/run/redis-6379.pid"
port 6379
bind 192.168.1.57
logfile "/redis/log/redis-6379.log"
dbfilename "dump-6379.rdb"
dir "/redis/data"
. . .
cluster-enabled yes
cluster-config-file nodes-6379.conf
cluster-node-timeout 10000
```

 When a Redis Cluster is running, each node has two TCP sockets open. The first is the standard Redis protocol for client connection. The second port is calculated from the sum of the first port plus 10,000 and used as a communication bus for node-to-node information exchange. This value 10,000 is hardcoded. Therefore, you can't start a Redis Cluster node with a listening port greater than `55536`.

2. Before moving on, we check if all the configuration files of each host have been well-prepared:

```
redis@192.168.1.57:~> ls conf/
redis-6379.conf redis-6381.conf
. . .
redis@192.168.1.58:~> ls conf/
redis-6380.conf redis-6381.conf
```

3. Clean the `data` directory and start each Redis instance on every host:

```
redis@192.168.1.57:~> rm -rf data/*
redis@192.168.1.57:~> bin/redis-server conf/redis-6379.conf
redis@192.168.1.57:~> bin/redis-server conf/redis-6381.conf
...
redis@192.168.1.58:~> rm -rf data/*
redis@192.168.1.58:~> bin/redis-server conf/redis-6380.conf
redis@192.168.1.58:~> bin/redis-server conf/redis-6381.conf
```

4. The node configuration files will be generated after the Redis instance has started. They can be found in the `data` directory. Check one of them to see what's in it:

```
redis@192.168.1.57:~> cat data/nodes-6379.conf
58285fa03c19f6e6f633fb5c58c6a314bf25503f :0@0 myself,master - 0 0 0
connected
vars currentEpoch 0 lastVoteEpoch 0
```

5. Before we set up the Cluster, we fetch the Redis Cluster running information by issuing the `INFO CLUSTER` command, and list the processes of Redis using the OS command `ps` (for brevity, only the host `192.168.1.57` is shown):

```
redis@192.168.1.57:~> bin/redis-cli -h 192.168.1.57 -p 6379 INFO
CLUSTER
# Cluster
cluster_enabled:1
redis@192.168.1.57:~> ps -ef |grep redis-server
redis 119911 1 0 16:22 ? 00:00:00 bin/redis-server
192.168.1.57:6379 [cluster]
redis 119942 1 0 16:22 ? 00:00:00 bin/redis-server
192.168.1.57:6381 [cluster]
```

6. Check the instance log:

```
redis@192.168.1.57:~> vim log/redis-6379.log
...
26569:C 05 Nov 16:50:33.832 # oO0oo00oo00Oo Redis is starting
oO0oo00oo00Oo
26569:C 05 Nov 16:50:33.832 # Redis version=4.0.1, bits=64,
commit=00000000, modified=0, pid=26569, just started
26569:C 05 Nov 16:50:33.832 # Configuration loaded
26570:M 05 Nov 16:50:33.835 * No cluster configuration found, I'm
58285fa03c19f6e6f633fb5c58c6a314bf25503f
26570:M 05 Nov 16:50:33.839 * Running mode=cluster, port=6379.
...
```

7. Let each Redis instance meet each other by issuing the CLUSTER MEET command with redis-cli. You can do this only on one host (the host 192.168.1.57 in this example):

```
redis@192.168.1.58:~> bin/redis-cli -h 192.168.1.57 -p 6379 CLUSTER
MEET 192.168.1.57 6379
OK
...
redis@192.168.1.58:~> bin/redis-cli -h 192.168.1.57 -p 6379 CLUSTER
MEET 192.168.1.58 6380
OK
redis@192.168.1.58:~> bin/redis-cli -h 192.168.1.57 -p 6379 CLUSTER
MEET 192.168.1.58 6381
OK
```

If you use hostname as the address of the node in Cluster, the following error will occur even if your hostname can be mapped to the IP correctly:
redis@192.168.1.58:~> bin/redis-cli -h 192.168.1.57 -p
6379 CLUSTER MEET 192.168.1.58 6381
(error) ERR Invalid node address specified:
192.168.1.58:6381

8. Next, make the data slots allocation. You can perform this step using redis-cli on a single host, by specifying the host and port:

```
redis@192.168.1.57:~> for i in {0..5400}; do redis-cli -h
192.168.1.57 -p 6379 CLUSTER ADDSLOTS $i; done
OK
...
OK
redis@192.168.1.57:~> for i in {5401..11000}; do redis-cli -h
192.168.1.59 -p 6380 CLUSTER ADDSLOTS $i; done
OK
...
OK
redis@192.168.1.57:~> for i in {11001..16383}; do redis-cli -h
192.168.1.58 -p 6381 CLUSTER ADDSLOTS $i; done
OK
...
OK
```

If you allocate a slot that has been already allocated before, you will get the following error:
```
redis@192.168.1.57:~> bin/redis-cli -h 192.168.1.58 -p
6381 CLUSTER ADDSLOTS 11111
(error) ERR Slot 11111 is already busy
```
If the ID of the slot you specified is beyond the scope of 0-16383, you will get the following error:
```
redis@192.168.1.57:~> bin/redis-cli -h 192.168.1.58 -p
6381 CLUSTER ADDSLOTS 22222
(error) ERR Invalid or out of range slot
```

9. Now, we have added all the nodes into a Cluster and allocated all the 16384 hash slots. We can list the nodes by sending the command CLUSTER NODES to any one of the nodes in the cluster:

```
redis@192.168.1.57:~> bin/redis-cli -h 192.168.1.57 -p 6379 CLUSTER
NODES
eeeabcab810d500db1d190c592fecbe89036f24f 192.168.1.58:6381@16381
master - 0 1509885956764 0 connected 11001-16383
549b5b261c765a97b74a374fec49f2ccf30f2acd 192.168.1.58:6380@16380
master - 0 1509885957000 3 connected
58285fa03c19f6e6f633fb5c58c6a314bf25503f 192.168.1.57:6379@16379
myself,master - 0 1509885955000 2 connected 0-5400
2ff47eb511f0d251eff1d5621e9285191a83ce9f 192.168.1.59:6380@16380
master - 0 1509885957767 1 connected 5401-11000
bc7b4a0c4596759058291f1b8f8de10966b5a1d1 192.168.1.59:6379@16379
master - 0 1509885957000 4 connected
7e06908bd0c7c3b23aaa17f84d96ad4c18016b1a 192.168.1.57:6381@16381
master - 0 1509885957066 0 connected
```

10. To implement data replication, set a node as a slave of one master node. We pick three nodes as slaves because we would like to have three master nodes in this cluster:

```
redis@192.168.1.57:~> bin/redis-cli -h 192.168.1.59 -p 6379 CLUSTER
REPLICATE 58285fa03c19f6e6f633fb5c58c6a314bf25503f
OK
redis@192.168.1.57:~> bin/redis-cli -h 192.168.1.58 -p 6380 CLUSTER
REPLICATE 2ff47eb511f0d251eff1d5621e9285191a83ce9f
OK
redis@192.168.1.57:~> bin/redis-cli -h 192.168.1.57 -p 6381 CLUSTER
REPLICATE eeeabcab810d500db1d190c592fecbe89036f24f
OK
```

11. Check the replication using the CLUSTER NODES command again, and then issue CLUSTER INFO to get more information about the Cluster:

```
192.168.1.57:6379> CLUSTER NODES
eeeabcab810d500db1d190c592fecbe89036f24f 192.168.1.58:6381@16381
master - 0 1510536168000 0 connected 11001-16383
549b5b261c765a97b74a374fec49f2ccf30f2acd 192.168.1.58:6380@16380
slave 2ff47eb511f0d251eff1d5621e9285191a83ce9f 0 1510536170545 3
connected
58285fa03c19f6e6f633fb5c58c6a314bf25503f 192.168.1.57:6379@16379
myself,master - 0 1510536168000 2 connected 0-5400
2ff47eb511f0d251eff1d5621e9285191a83ce9f 192.168.1.59:6380@16380
master - 0 1510536169541 1 connected 5401-11000
bc7b4a0c4596759058291f1b8f8de10966b5a1d1 192.168.1.59:6379@16379
slave 58285fa03c19f6e6f633fb5c58c6a314bf25503f 0 1510536167000 4
connected
7e06908bd0c7c3b23aaa17f84d96ad4c18016b1a 192.168.1.57:6381@16381
slave eeeabcab810d500db1d190c592fecbe89036f24f 0 1510536169000 5
connected
192.168.1.57:6379> CLUSTER INFO
cluster_state:ok
cluster_slots_assigned:16384
cluster_slots_ok:16384
cluster_slots_pfail:0
cluster_slots_fail:0
...
cluster_stats_messages_meet_received:2
cluster_stats_messages_received:1483481
```

12. By now, we have successfully set up a Redis Cluster. We can test it by setting and getting a simple string key-value pair:

```
redis@192.168.1.57:~> bin/redis-cli -h 192.168.1.57 -p 6379 -c
192.168.1.57:6379> set foo bar
-> Redirected to slot [12182] located at 192.168.1.58:6381
OK
192.168.1.58:6381> get foo
"bar"
```

How it works...

In the preceding example, we have guided you step by step through the process of setting up a Redis Cluster. The first step we took is to prepare the configuration file for each Redis instance:

```
cluster-enabled yes
cluster-config-file nodes-6381.conf
cluster-node-timeout 10000
```

After specifying a different listening port and data path for each instance separately, we enabled the Cluster feature by setting the `cluster-enabled` option to `yes`. Moreover, for each Redis instance, there is a Cluster node configuration file which will be generated during the setup of Redis Cluster, and can be modified every time some Cluster information should be persisted. The `cluster-config-file` option sets the name of this configuration file.

The Cluster node configuration file should not be changed manually.

Briefly speaking, the meaning of node timeout is: if the amount of time specified has elapsed, a failover will be fired to promote a slave to the master role. In the next recipe, we'll talk in detail about how this option affects the behavior of the Cluster.

After checking the configuration file of each instance and performing some necessary cleaning, we started all the Redis instances.

To check if the node is running in Cluster mode, we can issue the `CLUSTER INFO` command within `redis-cli` or search for `Running mode` in the Redis instance log. The Cluster node ID, which is an identifier for a Redis instance in a Redis Cluster, is recorded in the log. You can also tell if a Redis instance is running in the Cluster mode by using the OS command `ps`.

Now that we have configured and started all the Cluster nodes, it's time to create a Redis Cluster. Nodes in the Redis Cluster use the Redis Cluster protocol to talk to each other in the form of a mesh network topology. So, the first step we take is to let each node meet each other so that they can be working correctly in a Cluster. The command `CLUSTER MEET` is used for this purpose.

Although it is required that all nodes in a Redis Cluster know each other, there is no need to send this command to every node. That's because one node will propagate the information of its known nodes once it meets another node (that is the meaning of the exchange-of-gossip information in heartbeat packets mentioned in Redis Cluster documents). To avoid confusion, we can let one node meet all the other nodes. This way, all the nodes in a Cluster can communicate with each other.

In Redis Cluster, data is distributed into 16384 hash slots by the algorithm shown next:

```
HASH_SLOT = CRC16(key) mod 16384
```

Each master node is assigned a sub-range of hash slots to store a portion of the whole dataset. So, the second step we take is to allocate the slots among the master nodes using the command CLUSTER ADDSLOTS. After finishing the slot allocation, we check the Cluster by sending the CLUSTER NODES command. The output of the command is shown as follows:

```
eeeabcab810d500db1d190c592fecbe89036f24f 192.168.1.58:6381@16381 master - 0
1510536168000 0 connected 11001-16383
```

Each row is in the following format:

```
[Node-ID] [Instance-IP:Client-Port@Cluster-Bus-Port][Master\Slave\Myself]
[-\Node-ID] [Ping-Sent timestamp] [Pong-Recv timestamp] [Config-epoch]
[Connection status] [Slots allocated]
```

To provide data redundancy, we assign a slave to each master separately by sending CLUSTER REPLICATE node-id to the node you would like to make a slave. After setting up the replication, we can communicate the master-slave relationship by inspecting the output of the CLUSTER NODES command. For this example, we can easily tell that the instance running at 192.168.1.59:6379, whose ID is bc7b4a0c4596759058291f1b8f8de10966b5a1d1, is the slave of the instance with node ID 58285fa03c19f6e6f633fb5c58c6a314bf25503f, which is the instance running at 192.168.1.57:6379.

By now, we have successfully created a Redis Cluster. By sending CLUSTER INFO, you can obtain the status and metrics of the whole Cluster.

To test if the Cluster works as expected, we connect to the Cluster using redis-cli with the -c option to specify the Cluster mode. We set and then fetch a simple string key-value pair for testing. The node we connected is able to redirect the redis-cli tool to the right node in the Cluster.

There's more...

You may feel there are too many steps required for one to create a Redis Cluster. It's much easier to use the script `redis-trib.rb` shipped along with the Redis source code to perform the creation and administration of a Redis Cluster. You can refer to the Redis Cluster tutorial to find out more details.

For this example, we can check the Cluster status using the following command:

```
redis@192.168.1.57:~> ./script/redis-trib.rb check 192.168.1.57:6379
>>> Performing Cluster Check (using node 192.168.1.57:6379)
M: 58285fa03c19f6e6f633fb5c58c6a314bf25503f 192.168.1.57:6379
slots:0-5400 (5401 slots) master
...
slots: (0 slots) slave
replicates 58285fa03c19f6e6f633fb5c58c6a314bf25503f
S: 7e06908bd0c7c3b23aaa17f84d96ad4c18016b1a 192.168.1.57:6381
slots: (0 slots) slave
replicates eeeabcab810d500db1d190c592fecbe89036f24f
[OK] All nodes agree about slots configuration.
>>> Check for open slots...
>>> Check slots coverage...
[OK] All 16384 slots covered.
```

> For quick proof-of-concept testing, you can get a 6-node Redis Cluster with three masters and three slaves on a single host using the `create-cluster` script located in the `redis/utils/create-cluster` of the Redis source code package.

See also

- For a document on how to create a Redis Cluster, there is an official tutorial for your reference: https://redis.io/topics/cluster-tutorial
- You can find the details of the command CLUSTER NODES at: https://redis.io/commands/cluster-nodes
- You can also find the details of the command CLUSTER INFO at: https://redis.io/commands/cluster-info

Testing Redis Cluster

After setting up a Redis Cluster, it's necessary to simulate various kinds of failures to see how the Cluster behaves in the case of any unexpected outage or planned administration. In this recipe, we will test the Redis Cluster built in the previous recipe via a number of failure scenarios. Afterwards, the failover details will also be discussed.

Getting ready...

You need to have finished the *Setting up Redis Cluster* recipe in this chapter, and you need a host with `redis-cli` installed as a Redis client to the Cluster. As a summary of the previous recipe, the information of the Cluster is listed in the following table:

Instance name	IP address	Port	ID	Slots
I_A	192.168.1.57	6379	58285fa03c19f6e6f633fb5c58c6a314bf25503f	0-5400
I_A1	192.168.1.59	6379	bc7b4a0c4596759058291f1b8f8de10966b5a1d1	--
I_B	192.168.1.59	6380	2ff47eb511f0d251eff1d5621e9285191a83ce9f	5401-11000
I_B1	192.168.1.58	6380	549b5b261c765a97b74a374fec49f2ccf30f2acd	--
I_C	192.168.1.58	6381	eeeabcab810d500db1d190c592fecbe89036f24f	11001-16383
I_C1	192.168.1.57	6381	7e06908bd0c7c3b23aaa17f84d96ad4c18016b1a	--

Moreover, for testing purposes, we will introduce a test suite offered by the author of Redis, Antirez. You can follow the steps below to install it:

1. Install the Redis module of Ruby:

```
~$ gem install redis
~$ su - redis
~$ cd coding/
```

2. Download the test suite:

```
~$ mkdir coding
~$ cd coding
~/coding$ git clone https://github.com/antirez/redis-rb-cluster.git
~/coding$ cd redis-rb-cluster/
```

How to do it...

To test the Redis Cluster set up in the previous recipe, we will first start the testing program as a Redis client by the following command:

```
~$ ruby coding/redis-rb-cluster/consistency-test.rb 192.168.1.59 6380
1441 R (0 err) | 1441 W (0 err) |
4104 R (0 err) | 4104 W (0 err) |
25727 R (0 err) | 25727 W (0 err) |
. . .
```

1. Simulating a master down:
    1. Make the instance I_A crash using the Redis DEBUG SEGFAULT command:

        ```
        redis@192.168.1.57:~> bin/redis-cli -h 192.168.1.57 -p 6379
        -c DEBUG SEGFAULT
        Error: Server closed the connection
        ```

    2. Check the log of the I_A instance:

        ```
        96013:M 15 Nov 14:49:40.224 # Redis 4.0.1 crashed by
        signal: 11
        ```

    3. Check the output of the testing program:

        ```
        190927 R (0 err) | 190927 W (0 err) |
        201012 R (0 err) | 201012 W (0 err) |
        Reading: Connection lost (ECONNRESET)
        Writing: Too many Cluster redirections? (last error: MOVED
        183 192.168.1.57:6379)
        235022 R (2 err) | 235022 W (2 err) |
        Reading: Too many Cluster redirections? (last error: MOVED
        994 192.168.1.57:6379)
        Writing: Too many Cluster redirections? (last error: MOVED
        994 192.168.1.57:6379)
        . . . .
        261178 R (1310 err) | 261179 W (1309 err) |
        ```

    4. Check the log of the I_A1 instance:

        ```
        35623:S 15 Nov 14:49:40.355 # Connection with master lost.
        35623:S 15 Nov 14:49:40.356 * Caching the disconnected
        master state.
        35623:S 15 Nov 14:49:40.410 * Connecting to MASTER
        192.168.1.57:6379
        ```

```
35623:S 15 Nov 14:49:40.410 * MASTER <-> SLAVE sync started
35623:S 15 Nov 14:49:40.410 # Error condition on socket for
SYNC: Connection refused
...
35623:S 15 Nov 14:49:50.452 * Connecting to MASTER
192.168.1.57:6379
35623:S 15 Nov 14:49:50.452 * MASTER <-> SLAVE sync started
35623:S 15 Nov 14:49:50.452 # Error condition on socket for
SYNC: Connection refused
35623:S 15 Nov 14:49:50.970 * FAIL message received from
2ff47eb511f0d251eff1d5621e9285191a83ce9f about
58285fa03c19f6e6f633fb5c58c6a314bf25503f
35623:S 15 Nov 14:49:50.970 # Cluster state changed: fail
35623:S 15 Nov 14:49:51.053 # Start of election delayed for
888 milliseconds (rank #0, offset 5084834).
35623:S 15 Nov 14:49:51.455 * Connecting to MASTER
192.168.1.57:6379
35623:S 15 Nov 14:49:51.455 * MASTER <-> SLAVE sync started
35623:S 15 Nov 14:49:51.455 # Error condition on socket for
SYNC: Connection refused
35623:S 15 Nov 14:49:51.957 # Starting a failover election
for epoch 8.
35623:S 15 Nov 14:49:51.959 # Failover election won: I'm
the new master.
35623:S 15 Nov 14:49:51.959 # configEpoch set to 8 after
successful failover
35623:M 15 Nov 14:49:51.959 # Setting secondary replication
ID to 744a9fb2c14c245888b8e91edd212ae533dd33e3, valid up to
offset: 5084835. New replication ID is
b8fc14c9af26e00c40e964e8c70a8b6001602be1
35623:M 15 Nov 14:49:51.959 * Discarding previously cached
master state.
35623:M 15 Nov 14:49:51.960 # Cluster state changed: ok
```

5. Check the log of every other node:

```
=========I_B=========
35634:M 15 Nov 14:49:50.969 * Marking node
58285fa03c19f6e6f633fb5c58c6a314bf25503f as failing (quorum
reached).
35634:M 15 Nov 14:49:50.969 # Cluster state changed: fail
35634:M 15 Nov 14:49:51.959 # Failover auth granted to
bc7b4a0c4596759058291f1b8f8de10966b5a1d1 for epoch 8
35634:M 15 Nov 14:49:51.999 # Cluster state changed: ok
=========I_C=========
41354:M 15 Nov 14:50:49.154 * Marking node
58285fa03c19f6e6f633fb5c58c6a314bf25503f as failing (quorum
reached).
```

```
41354:M 15 Nov 14:50:49.154 # Cluster state changed: fail
41354:M 15 Nov 14:50:50.143 # Failover auth granted to
bc7b4a0c4596759058291f1b8f8de10966b5a1d1 for epoch 8
41354:M 15 Nov 14:50:50.145 # Cluster state changed: ok
=========I_B1==========
41646:S 15 Nov 14:50:49.154 * FAIL message received from
2ff47eb511f0d251eff1d5621e9285191a83ce9f about
58285fa03c19f6e6f633fb5c58c6a314bf25503f
41646:S 15 Nov 14:50:49.154 # Cluster state changed: fail
41646:S 15 Nov 14:50:50.146 # Cluster state changed: ok
=========I_C1==========
27576:S 15 Nov 14:49:50.968 * FAIL message received from
2ff47eb511f0d251eff1d5621e9285191a83ce9f about
58285fa03c19f6e6f633fb5c58c6a314bf25503f
27576:S 15 Nov 14:49:50.968 # Cluster state changed: fail
27576:S 15 Nov 14:49:51.959 # Cluster state changed: ok
```

6. Get the current status of the Cluster:

```
redis@192.168.1.57:~> ./script/redis-trib.rb check
192.168.1.57:6381
>>> Performing Cluster Check (using node 192.168.1.57:6381)
. . .
M: bc7b4a0c4596759058291f1b8f8de10966b5a1d1
192.168.1.59:6379
slots:0-5400 (5401 slots) master
0 additional replica(s)
. . .
[OK] All 16384 slots covered.
```

2. Recovering the crashed node:

   1. Bring back the I_A Redis instance:

      ```
      redis@192.168.1.57:~> bin/redis-server conf/redis-6379.conf
      ```

   2. Check the log of the I_A1 instance:

      ```
      35623:M 15 Nov 15:00:40.610 * Clear FAIL state for node
      58285fa03c19f6e6f633fb5c58c6a314bf25503f: master without
      slots is reachable again.
      35623:M 15 Nov 15:00:41.552 * Slave 192.168.1.57:6379 asks
      for synchronization
      35623:M 15 Nov 15:00:41.552 * Partial resynchronization not
      accepted: Replication ID mismatch (Slave asked for
      '9d2a374586d38080595d4ced9720eeef1c72e1d7', my replication
      IDs are 'b8fc14c9af26e00c40e964e8c70a8b6001602be1' and
      '744a9fb2c14c245888b8e91edd212ae533dd33e3')
      ```

```
35623:M 15 Nov 15:00:41.553 * Starting BGSAVE for SYNC with
target: disk
35623:M 15 Nov 15:00:41.553 * Background saving started by
pid 113122
113122:C 15 Nov 15:00:41.572 * DB saved on disk
113122:C 15 Nov 15:00:41.572 * RDB: 6 MB of memory used by
copy-on-write
35623:M 15 Nov 15:00:41.611 * Background saving terminated
with success
35623:M 15 Nov 15:00:41.614 * Synchronization with slave
192.168.1.57:6379 succeeded
```

3. Check the status of the Cluster:

```
redis@192.168.1.57:~/script> ./redis-trib.rb check
192.168.1.57:6381
>>> Performing Cluster Check (using node 192.168.1.57:6381)
S: 7e06908bd0c7c3b23aaa17f84d96ad4c18016b1a
192.168.1.57:6381
slots: (0 slots) slave
replicates eeeabcab810d500db1d190c592fecbe89036f24f
M: eeeabcab810d500db1d190c592fecbe89036f24f
192.168.1.58:6381
slots:11001-16383 (5383 slots) master
1 additional replica(s)
M: 2ff47eb511f0d251eff1d5621e9285191a83ce9f
192.168.1.59:6380
slots:5401-11000 (5600 slots) master
1 additional replica(s)
M: bc7b4a0c4596759058291f1b8f8de10966b5a1d1
192.168.1.59:6379
slots:0-5400 (5401 slots) master
1 additional replica(s)
S: 58285fa03c19f6e6f633fb5c58c6a314bf25503f
192.168.1.57:6379
slots: (0 slots) slave
replicates bc7b4a0c4596759058291f1b8f8de10966b5a1d1
S: 549b5b261c765a97b74a374fec49f2ccf30f2acd
192.168.1.58:6380
slots: (0 slots) slave
replicates 2ff47eb511f0d251eff1d5621e9285191a83ce9f
[OK] All nodes agree about slots configuration.
>>> Check for open slots...
>>> Check slots coverage...
[OK] All 16384 slots covered.
```

3. Simulating the slave down:
    1. Make I_C1 crash using the Redis DEBUG SEGFAULT command:

    ```
    redis@192.168.1.57:~> bin/redis-cli -h 192.168.1.57 -p 6381
    -c DEBUG SEGFAULT
    Error: Server closed the connection
    ```

    2. Check the log of I_C:

    ```
    41354:M 15 Nov 15:13:03.564 # Connection with slave
    192.168.1.57:6381 lost.
    41354:M 15 Nov 15:13:13.750 * FAIL message received from
    bc7b4a0c4596759058291f1b8f8de10966b5a1d1 about
    7e06908bd0c7c3b23aaa17f84d96ad4c18016b1a
    ```

    3. Check the log of I_A:

    ```
    112615:S 15 Nov 15:12:15.528 * FAIL message received from
    bc7b4a0c4596759058291f1b8f8de10966b5a1d1 about
    7e06908bd0c7c3b23aaa17f84d96ad4c18016b1a
    ```

    4. Check the status of the Cluster:

    ```
    redis@192.168.1.57:~> ./script/redis-trib.rb check
    192.168.1.57:6379
    >>> Performing Cluster Check (using node 192.168.1.57:6379)
    . . .
    M: eeeabcab810d500db1d190c592fecbe89036f24f
    192.168.1.58:6381
    slots:11001-16383 (5383 slots) master
    0 additional replica(s)
    . . .
    [OK] All 16384 slots covered.
    ```

4. Simulate both master and slave with one shard down:
    1. Since we have crashed I_C1, we will bring down the I_C instance now:

    ```
    redis@192.168.1.57:~> bin/redis-cli -h 192.168.1.58 -p 6381
    -c DEBUG SEGFAULT
    Error: Server closed the connection
    ```

2. Check the log of `I_A1`:

```
35623:M 15 Nov 15:47:29.855 # Cluster state changed: fail
```

3. Check the status of the Cluster:

```
redis@192.168.1.57:~> ./script/redis-trib.rb check
192.168.1.57:6379
>>> Performing Cluster Check (using node 192.168.1.57:6379)
S: 58285fa03c19f6e6f633fb5c58c6a314bf25503f
192.168.1.57:6379
slots: (0 slots) slave
replicates bc7b4a0c4596759058291f1b8f8de10966b5a1d1
M: 2ff47eb511f0d251eff1d5621e9285191a83ce9f
192.168.1.59:6380
slots:5401-11000 (5600 slots) master
1 additional replica(s)
M: bc7b4a0c4596759058291f1b8f8de10966b5a1d1
192.168.1.59:6379
slots:0-5400 (5401 slots) master
1 additional replica(s)
S: 549b5b261c765a97b74a374fec49f2ccf30f2acd
192.168.1.58:6380
slots: (0 slots) slave
replicates 2ff47eb511f0d251eff1d5621e9285191a83ce9f
[OK] All nodes agree about slots configuration.
>>> Check for open slots...
>>> Check slots coverage...
[ERR] Not all 16384 slots are covered by nodes.
```

4. Check the output of the testing program:

```
~$ ruby coding/redis-rb-cluster/consistency-test.rb
192.168.1.57 6379
0 R (6261 err) | 0 W (6261 err) |
. . .
Reading: CLUSTERDOWN The cluster is down
Writing: CLUSTERDOWN The cluster is down
0 R (7727 err) | 0 W (7727 err) |
```

How it works...

By running the testing script `consistency-test.rb`, we can write to and read from a Redis Cluster periodically. The number of writes, reads, and as well as errors is logged while the script is running. Any data inconsistency can also be captured.

The first testing we performed is to bring a master instance down. We used the DEBUG SEGFAULT command to crash the I_A instance with the node ID 58285fa03c19f6e6f633fb5c58c6a314bf25503f. This command resulted in a segmentation fault of a Redis instance. As a result, the instance exited, as shown in the log of I_A. From the output of the testing program, it can be seen clearly that some write and read requests failed for a while. Later, the Cluster resumed handling the requests. In fact, the period when the Cluster didn't work relates to the process of the I_A1 failover. Let's dive into the log of I_A1 to learn more about the failover.

First, the slave instance found that the connection to its master got lost at 14:49:40. It tried to reconnect to its master instance for around 10 seconds, which is the amount of time specified by the option cluster-node-timeout. Later, at 14:49:50, the failure of the I_A instance was confirmed by the received FAIL message, and the state of the Cluster was considered to be a failure. I_A1 got voted by the two alive masters, and then it was turned in the new master at 14:49:51. Finally, the state of the Cluster was changed to OK again. From the timeline shown in the logs of other masters and slaves, we can tell that I_B, whose node ID is 2ff47eb511f0d251eff1d5621e9285191a83ce9f, first marked the I_A as FAIL and broadcasted this message to all the slaves.

Although all the slots were covered and the state of the Cluster was OK, by checking the Cluster, we found that the new master serving the slots 0-5400 had no replica.

The second testing we performed was to recover the crashed node in the previous testing. By starting the I_A instance again, we found it became a slave of the I_A1 instance, which is now a master node after failover. The FAIL state of I_A was removed and a resynchronization was started. Finally, the new master instance I_A1 serving the slots 0-5400 had one replica provided by I_A.

The third testing we performed was to crash a slave. The node we picked was I_C1. After bringing I_C1 down, we found the state of the Cluster was not changed because the instance that crashed was a slave that didn't serve the slots.

The last testing we performed was to bring down both master and slave of one shard. Because not all the slots were covered, the state of the Cluster was turned into FAIL. So, the testing program got the error CLUSTERDOWN The cluster is down.

There's more...

Actually, before the FAIL message, there is a PFAIL (possible failure) state propagated among the nodes in the cluster. The state PFAIL means that a node, no matter if it's a master or a slave, can flag another node as PFAIL if another node is unreachable. It then propagates this information through the heartbeat. Node A first sets node B as PFAIL. Then, when A receives PFAIL or FAIL of B from the majority of masters within NODE_TIMEOUT * 2, it will modify PFAIL to FAIL and broadcast the message to other nodes.

So, in our example, if we crashed two masters almost at the same time, the Cluster won't do the failover even if the two masters have their slaves separately. That is because the majority of masters are down. As a result, no PFAIL can be set to FAIL. Therefore, no failover will take place. For this reason, as a production practice, you should never deploy a majority of masters on the same host.

See also

- You can refer to *Redis Cluster Specification* to find out more details about Redis Cluster: https://redis.io/topics/cluster-spec
- For the command DEBUG SEGFAULT, you may learn more about it at: https://redis.io/commands/debug-segfault
- You can also dive into the source code of Redis Cluster to learn more details: http://download.redis.io/redis-stable/src/cluster.c
- There is also a presentation from the author, Antirez, talking about Redis Cluster: https://redis.io/presentation/Redis_Cluster.pdf

Administrating Redis Cluster

Due to its full-mesh topology and failover mechanism, Redis Cluster is more complicated than a single master-slave Redis architecture. It's of great importance for those who do the administration to learn how to obtain the running topology and status of the Cluster. Moreover, one of the great benefits of using Redis Cluster is its flexibility to add or remove nodes easily. These operations are quite common when you use Redis Cluster.

In this recipe, we will guide you on how to perform common administration operations in Redis Cluster.

Getting ready...

You need to finish the *Setting up Redis Cluster* recipe in this chapter. You also need a host with `redis-cli` installed as a Redis client to the Cluster. For the demonstration environment, you can refer to the table provided in the *Getting ready* section of the *Testing Redis Cluster* recipe.

How to do it...

The operations for administrating Redis Cluster are as follows:

1. Fetch the state of the Cluster:

   ```
   redis@192.168.1.57:~> bin/redis-cli -h 192.168.1.57 -p 6381 -c
   CLUSTER INFO
   cluster_state:ok
   cluster_slots_assigned:16384
   cluster_slots_ok:16384
   . . .
   cluster_stats_messages_pong_received:113
   cluster_stats_messages_fail_received:2
   cluster_stats_messages_auth-req_received:2
   cluster_stats_messages_received:233
   ```

2. Check the status of the nodes in the Cluster:

   ```
   redis@192.168.1.57:~> bin/redis-cli -h 192.168.1.57 -p 6381 -c
   CLUSTER NODES
   eeeabcab810d500db1d190c592fecbe89036f24f 192.168.1.58:6381@16381
   master - 0 1510818967000 0 connected 11001-16383
   . . .
   58285fa03c19f6e6f633fb5c58c6a314bf25503f 192.168.1.57:6379@16379
   slave bc7b4a0c4596759058291f1b8f8de10966b5a1d1 0 1510818968000 14
   connected
   2ff47eb511f0d251eff1d5621e9285191a83ce9f 192.168.1.59:6380@16380
   master - 0 1510818967067 1 connected 5401-11000
   ```

3. Trigger a manual failover to promote a slave to master:

   ```
   redis@192.168.1.57:~> bin/redis-cli -h 192.168.1.57 -p 6381 -c
   CLUSTER FAILOVER
   OK
   ```

4. Fetch the slave's information from a specified master:

```
redis@192.168.1.57:~> bin/redis-cli -h 192.168.1.57 -p 6381 -c
CLUSTER SLAVES 7e06908bd0c7c3b23aaa17f84d96ad4c18016b1a
1) "eeeabcab810d500db1d190c592fecbe89036f24f
192.168.1.58:6381@16381 slave
7e06908bd0c7c3b23aaa17f84d96ad4c18016b1a 0 1510819599257 17
connected"
```

5. Add a shard (both the master and its slave instances) to a running cluster.

1. Prepare the configuration file of the master and slave with the listening port 6382:

```
redis@192.168.1.57:~> cat conf/redis-6382.conf
daemonize yes
pidfile "/redis/run/redis-6382.pid"
port 6382
bind 192.168.1.57
logfile "/redis/log/redis-6382.log"
dbfilename "dump-6382.rdb"
dir "/redis/data"
...
cluster-enabled yes
cluster-config-file nodes-6382.conf
cluster-node-timeout 10000
```

2. Start the two instances separately on 192.168.1.57 and 192.168.1.59:

```
~> bin/redis-server conf/redis-6382.conf
```

3. Add both the master and slave instances:

```
redis@192.168.1.57:~> bin/redis-cli -h 192.168.1.57 -p 6379
-c CLUSTER MEET 192.168.1.57 6382
OK
redis@192.168.1.57:~> bin/redis-cli -h 192.168.1.57 -p 6379
-c CLUSTER MEET 192.168.1.59 6382
OK
```

If the following error occurs when you want to add a node, it indicates that the node is holding some data, or the node configuration file already exists :

```
[ERR] Node 192.168.145.128:6382 is not empty. Either the
node already knows other nodes (check with CLUSTER NODES)
or contains some key in database 0.
```

You can take the steps shown as follows to reset your node:

1. Enter the directory specified by the `dir` option and delete the node configuration file.
2. Connect to the node with `redis-cli` and issue the command `FLUSHDB`.
3. Delete all the RDB and AOF files.

4. List the IDs of two nodes:

```
redis@192.168.1.57:~> script/redis-trib.rb check
192.168.1.57:6381
>>> Performing Cluster Check (using node 192.168.1.57:6381)
M: 7e06908bd0c7c3b23aaa17f84d96ad4c18016b1a
192.168.1.57:6381
slots:11001-16383 (5383 slots) master
1 additional replica(s)
M: a693372f4fee1b1cf2bd4cb1f4881d2caa0d7a7c
192.168.1.57:6382
slots: (0 slots) master
0 additional replica(s)
...
M: 7abe13b549b66218990c9fc8e2d209803f03665d
192.168.1.59:6382
slots: (0 slots) master
0 additional replica(s)
[OK] All 16384 slots covered.
```

5. Set the replication of the two instances:

```
redis@192.168.1.57:~> bin/redis-cli -h 192.168.1.57 -p 6382
-c CLUSTER REPLICATE
7abe13b549b66218990c9fc8e2d209803f03665d
OK
```

6. Check the replication relationship:

```
redis@192.168.1.57:~> script/redis-trib.rb check
192.168.1.57:6381
>>> Performing Cluster Check (using node 192.168.1.57:6381)
...
S: a693372f4fee1b1cf2bd4cb1f4881d2caa0d7a7c
192.168.1.57:6382
slots: (0 slots) slave
replicates 7abe13b549b66218990c9fc8e2d209803f03665d
M: 7abe13b549b66218990c9fc8e2d209803f03665d
192.168.1.59:6382
slots: (0 slots) master
1 additional replica(s)
...
[OK] All 16384 slots covered.
```

7. Migrate the 500 slots from the I_A instance to the new, added instance:

```
redis@192.168.1.57:~> script/redis-trib.rb reshard --from
bc7b4a0c4596759058291f1b8f8de10966b5a1d1 --to
7abe13b549b66218990c9fc8e2d209803f03665d --slots 100 --yes
192.168.1.57:6379
>>> Performing Cluster Check (using node 192.168.1.57:6379)
...
M: 7abe13b549b66218990c9fc8e2d209803f03665d
192.168.1.59:6382
slots: (0 slots) master
0 additional replica(s)
...
S: a693372f4fee1b1cf2bd4cb1f4881d2caa0d7a7c
192.168.1.57:6382
slots: (0 slots) slave
replicates bc7b4a0c4596759058291f1b8f8de10966b5a1d1
...
[OK] All 16384 slots covered.
Ready to move 100 slots.
Source nodes:
M: bc7b4a0c4596759058291f1b8f8de10966b5a1d1
192.168.1.59:6379
slots:0-5400 (5401 slots) master
2 additional replica(s)
Destination node:
M: 7abe13b549b66218990c9fc8e2d209803f03665d
192.168.1.59:6382
slots: (0 slots) master
```

```
0 additional replica(s)
Resharding plan:
Moving slot 0 from bc7b4a0c4596759058291f1b8f8de10966b5a1d1
Moving slot 1 from bc7b4a0c4596759058291f1b8f8de10966b5a1d1
Moving slot 2 from bc7b4a0c4596759058291f1b8f8de10966b5a1d1
. . .
Moving slot 0 from 192.168.1.59:6379 to 192.168.1.59:6382:
. .
. . .
Moving slot 98 from 192.168.1.59:6379 to 192.168.1.59:6382:
. . .
Moving slot 99 from 192.168.1.59:6379 to 192.168.1.59:6382:
```

8. Check the Cluster again:

```
redis@192.168.1.57:~> script/redis-trib.rb check
192.168.1.57:6381
>>> Performing Cluster Check (using node 192.168.1.57:6381)
. . .
S: a693372f4fee1b1cf2bd4cb1f4881d2caa0d7a7c
192.168.1.57:6382
slots: (0 slots) slave
replicates bc7b4a0c4596759058291f1b8f8de10966b5a1d1
M: 7abe13b549b66218990c9fc8e2d209803f03665d
192.168.1.59:6382
slots:0-99 (100 slots) master
1 additional replica(s)
. . .
[OK] All 16384 slots covered.
```

6. Remove a shard (both the master and its slave instances) from a running Cluster:

1. Remove the slave node:

```
redis@192.168.1.57:~> script/redis-trib.rb del-node
192.168.1.57:6379 a693372f4fee1b1cf2bd4cb1f4881d2caa0d7a7c
>>> Removing node a693372f4fee1b1cf2bd4cb1f4881d2caa0d7a7c
from cluster 192.168.1.57:6379
>>> Sending CLUSTER FORGET messages to the cluster...
>>> SHUTDOWN the node.
```

2. Migrate the slots allocated in the master instance you will remove:

```
redis@192.168.1.57:~> script/redis-trib.rb reshard --to
bc7b4a0c4596759058291f1b8f8de10966b5a1d1 --from
7abe13b549b66218990c9fc8e2d209803f03665d --slots 100 --yes
192.168.1.57:6379
```

3. Remove the master node:

```
redis@192.168.1.57:~> script/redis-trib.rb del-node
192.168.1.57:6379 7abe13b549b66218990c9fc8e2d209803f03665d
>>> Removing node 7abe13b549b66218990c9fc8e2d209803f03665d
from cluster 192.168.1.57:6379
>>> Sending CLUSTER FORGET messages to the cluster...
>>> SHUTDOWN the node.
```

4. Check the status of the Cluster:

```
redis@192.168.1.57:~> script/redis-trib.rb check
192.168.1.57:6381
```

How it works...

The commands shown in the previous section are quite self-explanatory. One thing you should know is that, while the slots are being resharded from node to node, writing and reading requests to the Cluster won't be affected.

Due to the space limitations in this book, we didn't introduce slot commands such as CLUSTER ADDSLOTS, CLUSTER DELSLOTS, or CLUSTER SETSLOT. Actually, understanding how these commands work is very helpful when it comes to knowing how a Cluster performs slot resharding operations without interfering with request handling.

There's more...

In the *Data migration* recipe of Chapter 9, *Administrating Redis*, we will show you how to migrate data from a single Redis instance to a Redis Cluster.

See also

- For commands in Redis Cluster, you can refer to the official documents at: https://redis.io/commands#cluster

- You can also learn more about the redis-trib.rb script with the help option

8
Deploying to a Production Environment

In this chapter, we will cover the following recipes:

- Deploying Redis on Linux
- Securing Redis
- Setting client connection options
- Configuring memory policy
- Benchmarking
- Logging

Introduction

As we have shown in Chapter 1, *Getting Started with Redis*, setting up a Redis instance for testing is quick and easy. When it comes to deploying a Redis Server to the production environment, more things need to be taken into account. In this chapter, we will focus on Redis deployment to a Linux system. We will start with operating system level optimizations for running a production Redis Server. Then we will talk about server-side configurations for client connections and how to make Redis secure in a production environment. How to configure memory policy will also be discussed. Finally, we will introduce the logging options and the benchmarking tool of Redis.

Deploying Redis on Linux

Although you can install Redis on almost all modern **operating systems** (**OS**) by compiling its source code, Linux is the most common OS running Redis. Before you start the Redis instance, it is often necessary to set some Linux kernel and OS level parameters to proper values, in order to obtain the maximum performance in the production environment. In this recipe, we will introduce some vital kernel and OS parameters or settings for Redis.

Getting ready...

You need to finish the installation of the Redis Server, as we described in the *Downloading and installing Redis* recipe in `Chapter 1`, *Getting Started with Redis*.

How to do it...

The configurations for deploying Redis on Linux are as follows:

1. Set the following memory-related kernel parameters:

   ```
   ~$ sudo sysctl -w vm.overcommit_memory=1
   ~$ sudo sysctl -w vm.swappiness=0
   ```

   To persist these parameters add the following:

   ```
   echo vm.overcommit_memory=1" >> /etc/sysctl.confecho
   "vm.swappiness=0" >> /etc/sysctl.conf
   ```

   To check if these parameters have been set, add the following:

   ```
   ~$ sudo sysctl vm.overcommit_memory vm.swappiness
   vm.overcommit_memory = 1
   vm.swappiness = 0
   ```

2. Moreover, disable the transparent huge page feature:

   ```
   ~$ sudo su -
   ~# echo never > /sys/kernel/mm/transparent_hugepage/enabled
   ~$ echo never > /sys/kernel/mm/transparent_hugepage/defrag
   ```

To persist these settings, add the following:

```
~ # cat >> /etc/rc.local << EOF
echo never > /sys/kernel/mm/transparent_hugepage/enabled
echo never > /sys/kernel/mm/transparent_hugepage/defrag
EOF
```

For RedHat Linux, you can append echo never >
/sys/kernel/mm/redhat_transparent_hugepage/enabled into
/etc/rc.local.

To check if these parameters have been set, add the following:

```
~$ cat /sys/kernel/mm/transparent_hugepage/enabled
always madvise [never]
~$ cat /sys/kernel/mm/transparent_hugepage/defrag
always madvise [never]
```

3. For networking optimization, set the following network-related kernel parameters:

```
~$ sudo sysctl -w net.core.somaxconn=65535
~$ sudo sysctl -w net.ipv4.tcp_max_syn_backlog=65535
```

To persist these parameters, add the following:

```
echo "net.core.somaxconn=65535" >> /etc/sysctl.conf
echo "net.ipv4.tcp_max_syn_backlog=65535" >> /etc/sysctl.conf
```

To check if these parameters have been set, add the following:

```
~$ sudo sysctl net.core.somaxconn net.ipv4.tcp_max_syn_backlog
net.core.somaxconn = 65535
net.ipv4.tcp_max_syn_backlog = 65535
```

4. To set a higher value for maximum open files of one process, you should first switch to the user who will start the Redis process, and then issue the ulimit command:

```
~$ su - redis~$ ulimit -n 288000
```

You must set a value smaller than /proc/sys/fs/file-max to nofile.
So before setting, you need to check the value of /proc/sys/fs/file-max with the command cat.

To persist this parameter, add the following two lines to
`/etc/security/limits.conf`:

```
redis soft nofile 288000
redis hard nofile 288000
```

To check if these parameters have been set, add the following:

```
~$ ulimit -Hn -Sn
open files                           (-n) 288000
open files                           (-n) 288000
```

How it works...

We will go through each setting or parameter mentioned in the previous section. The first
setting we tweaked is `overcommit_memory`. As described in Chapter 6, *Persistence*, Redis
takes advantage of **copy-on-write** (**COW**) when starting a background save. That means
there is no need to have as much free RAM as the size of dataset in Redis. However, Linux,
by default, may have the chance to check if there is enough free RAM to duplicate all the
parent processes' memory pages. It may lead to the risk of getting a process OOM-killed. If
that happens, you will find the save failure in the Redis running log as follows:

```
[1524] 24 Sep 10:00:56.037 # Can't save in background: fork: Cannot
allocate memory
```

In fact, when you encounter such a failure, you will find the following logs, if you take a
close look at the running log of Redis:

```
5885:M 19 Nov 09:18:29.324 # WARNING overcommit_memory is set to 0!
Background save may fail under low memory condition. To fix this issue add
'vm.overcommit_memory = 1' to /etc/sysctl.conf and then reboot or run the
command 'sysctl vm.overcommit_memory=1' for this to take effect.
```

To solve the problem, you should set overcommit to `1`, that indicates, when a program calls
something such as `malloc()` to allocate a chunk of memory, it will always succeed even if
the system knows it does not have all the memory space that is being asked for. The second
memory-related setting is `vm.swappiness`. This parameter defines how much (and how
often) your Linux kernel will copy RAM contents to swap.

 The higher the value of the `swappiness` parameter, the more aggressively
your kernel will swap.

With swapping enabled, Redis may attempt to access memory pages that are on disk. This will cause the Redis process to be blocked by the disk I/O operation, which can be a slow process. We often try to make full use of the high-processing speed of Redis, therefore, slowing Redis when swapping is not desirable. It's always recommended to set vm.swappiness to 0. It's worth mentioning that setting this parameter to 0 has different meanings for the different kernel versions:

- For Linux 3.5 and newer, 0 for swappiness means to disable swapping entirely.
- For Linux 3.4 and older, it means to swap only to avoid an *out of memory* condition.
- For Redis, we first try our best to avoid swappiness. Moreover, when there is not much RAM the Redis instance can use, we would rather allow the Redis process to be killed than slow it down for swapping. The HA or Cluster mechanism will take care of the crash, if Redis is able to behave like a fail-fast service. So no matter what the Linux kernel version is, 0 for this parameter is always recommended.

The next tweak we made is disabling the transparent huge page feature provided by the Linux kernel. This feature may lead to a slow fork when persisting. So, it is recommended you disable this feature, otherwise, there is a warning message in the Redis running log when the instance is started:

```
3248:M 21 Oct 22:16:23.485 # WARNING you have Transparent Huge Pages (THP)
support enabled in your kernel. This will create latency and memory usage
issues with Redis. To fix this issue run the command 'echo never >
/sys/kernel/mm/transparent_hugepage/enabled' as root, and add it to your
/etc/rc.local in order to retain the setting after a reboot. Redis must be
restarted after THP is disabled.
```

For networking, we set the net.core.somaxconn and net.ipv4.tcp_max_syn_backlog to 65535, which is much higher than the default value of 128. The former kernel parameter sets an upper limit on the value of the backlog parameter passed to the listen function. The latter parameter sets the maximum queue length of pending connections. In Redis, there is an option, tcp-backlog, with the default value 511. Setting these values higher can optimize the TCP connections. If you don't set net.core.somaxconn to a value higher than 511, the following warning message will be shown in the Redis running log when the instance starts:

```
WARNING: The TCP backlog setting of 511 cannot be enforced because
/proc/sys/net/core/somaxconn is set to the lower value of 128.
```

Lastly, we also set the max number of files that a process is able to open. It's required to make sure that the value of this OS parameter is higher than the option `maxclients` in Redis. If that is not satisfied, you will see the following logs in the Redis running log:

```
# You requested maxclients of 10000 requiring at least 10032 max file
descriptors.
# Redis can't set maximum open files to 10032 because of OS error:
Operation not permitted
# Current maximum open files is 4096. maxclients has been reduced to 4064
to compensate for low ulimit. If you need higher maxclients increase
'ulimit -n'.
```

There's more...

In the *Setting client connection options* recipe of this chapter, we will show you how to set the `maxclients` and `tcp-backlog` options.

See also

- You can find more information at the Redis FAQ
  at: https://redis.io/topics/faq
- For more details on swappiness, you can refer to the related page on Wikipedia: https://en.wikipedia.org/wiki/Swappiness
- For more details on transparent huge pages, you can refer to the related documentation
  at: https://www.kernel.org/doc/Documentation/vm/transhuge.txt
- For more details on Redis deployment, you can refer to the related documentation at: https://redis.io/topics/admin

Securing Redis

Security is apparently one of the fundamental concerns in any production environment. However, Redis itself provides very limited features in terms of security, because it is designed to be deployed in an environment where all clients are trusted. The original design idea of Redis is more focused on the optimization of maximum performance and simplicity rather than the full authentication and access control support. Although most of Redis' security relies on the outside of Redis (OS, firewall), there is still something we can do to protect a Redis Server from unwanted access and attack. In this recipe, we will discuss some common practices to secure Redis in the production environment.

Getting ready...

You need to finish the installation of the Redis Server, as we described in the *Downloading and installing Redis* recipe in `Chapter 1`, *Getting Started with Redis*.

How to do it...

Let's discuss how to secure Redis with proper network configuration. It is never advisable to expose a Redis production server to the internet, where any untrusted client can access it. Therefore, it is imperative to configure Redis to bind to an IP address that is part of a trusted network:

1. To update the binding IP address and port, set `bind` and `port` in the configuration file:

   ```
   bind 127.0.0.1 192.168.0.31
   port 36379
   ```

2. Don't forget to update the corresponding settings in Replica and Sentinel's configuration:

   ```
   #Replica's configuration (redis.conf)
   slaveof 192.168.0.31 36379

   #Sentinel's configuration (sentinel.conf)
   sentinel monitor mymaster 192.168.0.31 36379
   ```

We can also configure Redis to stop listening to any network interface but listen to a Unix domain socket instead. In this way, only local clients who have permission on the socket can access Redis:

1. To configure Redis to listen to a Unix socket only, set the unixsocket and unixsocketperm directive in the configuration file, and set port to 0:

```
port 0
unixsocket /var/run/redis/redis.sock
unixsocketperm 766
```

2. To connect to a Redis Server listening on a Unix socket with redis-cli, use redis-cli -s <socket>:

```
~$ bin/redis-cli -s /var/run/redis/redis.sock
redis /var/run/redis/redis.sock>
```

It's always a good practice to secure Redis with password authentication. Redis provides a very simple authentication mechanism to prevent unauthorized access. A password can be set for the entire Redis Server, so that all clients need to be authenticated by the password before issuing commands:

1. To set the password for a Redis Server, add the password in plain text to the requirepass section of the configuration file:

```
requirepass foobared
```

2. To access the Redis Server with authentication enabled, use the AUTH command:

```
$ bin/redis-cli
127.0.0.1:6379> SET test 123
(error) NOAUTH Authentication required.
127.0.0.1:6379> AUTH foobared
OK
127.0.0.1:6379> SET test 123
OK
```

3. If the Redis Server has replicas, add the master's password to all of the slave's configuration:

```
masterauth foobared
```

Redis can also be configured to have specified commands renamed. If we rename certain dangerous commands such as CONFIG or FLUSHDB to names that are hard to guess, it is almost impossible for clients to execute those commands. Commands can also be completely disabled if higher security is required.

1. To rename a command, add rename-command directives in the Redis configuration file:

   ```
   rename-command CONFIG F3E9DD63CDDAD0EBBA50EC22D78A00F34F6B9CB1
   ```

2. To disable a command completely, just rename it to an empty string:

   ```
   rename-command CONFIG ""
   ```

How it works...

We introduced three configuration options to tune Redis in order to enhance its security. As mentioned, you are strongly advised not to expose Redis to the public network. If your Redis Server has to be accessed via the public network, using a binding port different from the default port of 6379 would somewhat alleviate the risk of port scanners, although it is not difficult to detect the server behind the port via Redis protocols.

The Redis authentication password resides in the configuration file as plain text. Hence, the access permissions of the Redis configuration file should be set strictly to prevent non-administrator access. Also, the password feature of Redis should be considered as the last line of defense, as the traffic between server and clients is unencrypted and so the password in the AUTH command may be eavesdropped on by sniffers.

The password option in a Redis master instance will not be inherited by slave instances, therefore you have to set the password for slaves separately. Renaming or disabling dangerous commands prevents high-risk operations, even if the server is compromised. However, as the renaming instruction is in the Redis configuration file, so it is again imperative to protect the configuration file with strict access permissions.

There's more...

Redis has a special mode called `protected mode`, which can be enabled by setting `protected-mode yes` in the configuration file. If `protected mode` is enabled, and at the same time the Redis Server is configured to listen to all interfaces (there is no `bind` directive specified in the configuration file), and password authentication is disabled, Redis will only reply to queries from loopback interfaces and Unix sockets. Queries from other interfaces will get a reply with the error.

The `protected mode` is enabled by default and should not be disabled unless Redis has to listen to all interfaces and the network environment is safe, even with password authentication disabled. Other precautions can be taken in the operating system to protect Redis. One is, do not run Redis with root, but with a dedicated user who has limited privileges. Also, the user should be disabled in SSH login. Another procedure is setting a whitelist in an OS firewall to allow access from trusted IP addresses.

See also

- The official topic of Redis Security: `https://redis.io/topics/security`
- A few things about Redis Security: `http://antirez.com/news/96`

Setting client connection options

For the clients of Redis, there are several important configuration parameters on the server side. In this recipe, we will introduce these parameters and also offer you the best practice of setting these client connection options.

Getting ready...

You need to finish the installation of the Redis Server, as we described in the *Downloading and installing Redis* recipe in Chapter 1, *Getting Started with Redis*.

How to do it...

The steps for configuring the clients are as follows:

1. To set the networking parameters for clients, add the following lines into the Redis configuration file, redis.conf:

   ```
   timeout 0
   tcp-backlog 511
   ```

2. To set the maximum number of clients and tcp-keepalive interval for a Redis instance and Redis Sentinel, add the following line into the Redis configuration file and Redis Sentinel configuration file:

   ```
   maxclients 10000
   tcp-keepalive 300
   ```

3. To set the client buffer parameters for clients, add the following lines in the Redis configuration file, redis.conf:

   ```
   client-output-buffer-limit normal 0 0 0
   client-output-buffer-limit slave 512mb 256mb 60
   client-output-buffer-limit pubsub 32mb 8mb 60
   ```

How it works...

We will go through each parameter mentioned in the previous section. The two parameters we first set for the Redis instance are both related to the networking between Redis and clients. The first option is timeout. This option means the Redis Server will close the connection after a client has been idle for N seconds. Actually, the timeout specified will be passed into setsockopt() to set the SO_SNDTIMEO option. You can refer to the man page of the socket for details.

The second option is tcp-backlog. This option sets the size of the pending socket request queue. In the *Deploying Redis on Linux* recipe, we introduced the kernel parameter somaxconn. You should ensure that the value of tcp-backlog is smaller than somaxconn. In a real production environment, we suggest setting a higher value than the default–10,000 is a proper value for most cases. The options, maxclients and tcp-keepalive can be applied to both the Redis instance and Sentinel.

We strongly recommend you ensure these two parameters are set for the Redis Server instance and Redis Sentinel services. The option `maxclients` limits the max number of connections from clients. Once the number of connections exceeds this limit, the incoming connections will receive an error message, as follows, and be closed immediately:

```
ERR max number of clients reached.
```

The next option is `tcp-keepalive`. If a non-zero value is set for this option, the server will send `TCP ACK` at the specified time interval to notify the network equipment, in between that the connection is still alive. If a client does not respond to TCP alive messages, the client is treated as dead and the connection is closed by the server. It's extremely useful when there is a hardware firewall between your clients and Redis Server.

For example, the firewall of Juniper will cut off the connection between client and itself, when the connection has been in an idle state for 1,800 seconds. However, both the client side and the server side won't get informed about the disconnection. So, from the server's point of view, the connection is still alive. If you disable this option, the server won't release the connection. On the other hand, from the client's point of view, it will reconnect to the Redis Server once it has found a disconnection. That causes the number of connections to continuously increase. So, keeping the default setting is preferable to prevent such connection issues from happening. By default, this option is set to `300`.

The last three parameters are all client output buffer related. Instead of sending the output of a command directly to the client, Redis will first populate the result into an output buffer for every connection and then send the content in one shot. Different kinds of clients (normal connection, pub/sub connection, slaves connection) have different output buffer sizes. The format of this configuration parameter is:

```
client-output-buffer-limit <class> <hard limit> <soft limit> <soft
seconds>
```

There are hard limits and soft limits for the output buffer size. We will introduce the meaning of hard limits and soft limits of the output buffer in the *Troubleshooting replication* recipe in Chapter 5, *Replication*.

See also

- You can learn more about Redis clients at:

  `https://redis.io/topics/clients`

- For more details on TCP Keepalive, you can refer to the related page at:

  `http://www.tldp.org/HOWTO/html_single/TCP-Keepalive-HOWTO/`

- For details on Linux sockets, you can refer to the related man pages at:

  `http://man7.org/linux/man-pages/man7/socket.7.html` and `http://man7.org/linux/man-pages/man2/setsockopt.2.html`

Configuring memory policy

As an in-memory data store, Redis uses more memory space than databases that always persist data to disk. Although nowadays the cost of memory is lower, it is still necessary to budget the memory space for Redis in the production environment. In addition, as Redis is often used as a cache, besides setting timeout values to make keys expire automatically, we also need to consider the conviction policy when the cache is full. In this recipe, we will introduce two important memory configuration options in Redis with examples.

Getting ready...

You need to finish the installation of the Redis Server, as we described in the *Downloading and installing Redis* recipe in `Chapter 1`, *Getting Started with Redis*.

How to do it...

The steps for configuring memory policies are as follows:

1. To get the current memory usage, use `INFO MEMORY`:

   ```
   127.0.0.1:6379> INFO MEMORY
   # Memory
   used_memory:836848
   used_memory_human:817.23K
   ```

```
used_memory_rss:10174464
used_memory_rss_human:9.70M
used_memory_peak:973056
used_memory_peak_human:950.25K
used_memory_peak_perc:86.00%
used_memory_overhead:816270
used_memory_startup:765632
used_memory_dataset:20578
used_memory_dataset_perc:28.90%
total_system_memory:8371417088
total_system_memory_human:7.80G
used_memory_lua:37888
used_memory_lua_human:37.00K
maxmemory:0
maxmemory_human:0B
maxmemory_policy:noeviction
mem_fragmentation_ratio:12.16
mem_allocator:jemalloc-4.0.3
active_defrag_running:0
lazyfree_pending_objects:0
```

2. For demonstration purposes, let us set the MAXMEMORY just a little bit before used_memory:

   ```
   127.0.0.1:6379> CONFIG SET MAXMEMORY 836900
   OK
   ```

3. Try to add a few new keys:

   ```
   127.0.0.1:6379> SET new_key 1234567890
   (error) OOM command not allowed when used memory > 'maxmemory'.
   ```

4. Change MAXMEMORY-POLICY to allkeys-lru:

   ```
   127.0.0.1:6379> CONFIG SET MAXMEMORY-POLICY allkeys-lru
   OK
   ```

5. Try to create a new key again:

   ```
   127.0.0.1:6379> SET new_key 1234567890
   OK
   ```

How it works...

INFO MEMORY prints all memory-related information in the current Redis instance. The items we are interested in are used_memory, maxmemory, and maxmemory_policy. The used_memory item means the memory space is currently allocated in bytes.

In this example, 836848 bytes were allocated. The maxmemory is the memory space limit for Redis, the default value is 0, which means there is no limit and Redis can use all possible memory space on the host (on 64-bit systems, the limit is 3GB on 32-bit systems). This value can be configured by the maxmemory directive. The maxmemory_policy is the eviction policy when the memory space limit is reached, and the default value is noeviction, which means no keys should be evicted by Redis. This value can be configured with the maxmemory-policy directive.

In step 2, we set maxmemory to a value (836900) just a little bit above the value of used_memory (836848). This means the maximum memory space that can be allocated for Redis is 836900 bytes (not including AOF buffer size and slave output buffer size). This limit was easily reached when we were trying to create new keys. When the maxmemory limit is reached (used_memory - AOF_buffer_size - slave_output_buffer_size >= maxmemory) and a request that will need more memory space is received, Redis will check maxmemory-policy and decide what to do. In this example, the policy was set to noeviction, so Redis just rejected the key creation request and returned an error.

The following table contains the options that can be set for the maxmemory-policy directive and the corresponding action, when the maxmemory limit is reached:

Option	Action
noeviction	Don't evict anything, just return an error on write operations (except DEL and other commands that do not require more memory space).
allkeys-lru	Evict any key using approximated **Least Recently Used (LRU)** algorithm.
volatile-lru	Evict using approximated LRU algorithm among the keys with a timeout set. Fall back to the noeviction policy if no such key can be found.
allkeys-lfu	Evict any key using approximated **Least Frequently Used (LFU)** algorithm.
volatile-lfu	Evict using approximated LFU among the keys with a timeout set. Fall back to the noeviction policy if no such key can be found.

`allkeys-random`	Evict a random key, could be any key.
`volatile-random`	Evict a random key among the ones with a timeout set. Fall back to the `noeviction` policy if no such key can be found.
`volatile-ttl`	Evict the key with the nearest expire time (minor TTL). Fall back to the `noeviction` policy if no such key can be found.

In step 4, we changed the `maxmemory-policy` to `allkeys-lru` to allow keys to be evicted when the `maxmemory` limit is reached. Therefore, creating a new key succeeded after that.

There's more...

It is advisable to set a `maxmemory` value on production Redis Servers, this is extremely useful and important when deploying multiple Redis instances on the same host. Each instance is isolated in terms of memory usage and will not be impacted by other instances.

It is worth mentioning that the memory space of client buffers is also counted in the `used_memory` value. Therefore, you should not expect all the memory space to be used by data objects. It's worth mentioning that when the limit of `maxmemory` is calculated, both the slave output client buffer and the AOF buffer size are not taken into account.

Also, it is not recommended to set the `maxmemory` value too close to the available system memory size, because memory space should be reserved for other processes, such as the Redis fork process to save RDB dumps.

If you are going to use Redis as a cache server, it is imperative to set the `maxmemory-policy` to a value other than `noeviction`. However, you should avoid having Redis evict keys too frequently, as the key eviction process significantly impacts server performance.

See also

- Both the LRU and LFU algorithms in Redis are approximated ones, because the exact implementations cost more memory. There are a few options that can be tuned for the algorithms. You can find out more at: `https://redis.io/topics/lru-cache`.

Benchmarking

As we described earlier, the processing speed of Redis depends on the following factors: the power of CPU, the network bandwidth, the size of dataset, the operation you perform, and so on. So it's essential to know how fast your Redis instance is after deploying to production. It's the performance benchmark that comes into play at this time. If the result of the benchmark cannot meet your requirements, you need to consider upgrading your hardware or adjusting the way you are going to use Redis. In this recipe, we will introduce the Redis benchmark tool, redis-benchmark and explain how to do a Redis benchmark with it.

Getting ready...

You need to finish the installation of the Redis Server, as we described in the *Downloading and installing Redis* recipe in Chapter 1, *Getting Started with Redis*.

How to do it...

The steps for benchmarking are as follows:

1. You can find the executable file of the Redis benchmark tool under the bin/ directory:

   ```
   $ ls bin/redis-benchmark
   bin/redis-benchmark
   ```

2. To obtain the help information of this tool, just run it with the --help option:

   ```
   $ bin/redis-benchmark  --help
   Usage: redis-benchmark [-h <host>] [-p <port>] [-c <clients>] [-n
   <requests>] [-k <boolean>]

    -h <hostname>        Server hostname (default 127.0.0.1)
    -p <port>            Server port (default 6379)
    -s <socket>          Server socket (overrides host and port)
   ...

                         names are the same as the ones produced as
   output.
    -I                   Idle mode. Just open N idle connections and
   wait.
   ```

3. Start benchmarking with the default configuration:

```
$ bin/redis-benchmark
====== PING_INLINE ======
  100000 requests completed in 0.52 seconds
  50 parallel clients
  3 bytes payload
  keep alive: 1

100.00% <= 0 milliseconds
190839.70 requests per second
. . .
====== MSET (10 keys) ======
  100000 requests completed in 0.71 seconds
  50 parallel clients
  3 bytes payload
  keep alive: 1

99.95% <= 1 milliseconds
100.00% <= 1 milliseconds
141043.72 requests per second
```

4. We can also run a benchmark test on one API only and specify the size of the value for this benchmarking:

```
$ bin/redis-benchmark -t SET -c 100 -n 10000000 -r 10000000 -d 256
====== SET ======
  10000000 requests completed in 73.63 seconds
  100 parallel clients
  256 bytes payload
  keep alive: 1

99.18% <= 1 milliseconds
. . .
100.00% <= 4901 milliseconds
100.00% <= 4902 milliseconds
100.00% <= 4909 milliseconds
100.00% <= 4910 milliseconds
100.00% <= 4910 milliseconds
135806.83 requests per second

redis@gnuhpc-desktop:~/bin$ ./redis-benchmark -n 100000 -q script
load "redis.call('set','foo','bar')"
script load redis.call('set','foo','bar'): 190476.20 requests per
second
```

5. To test how much performance improvement we will get by utilizing the pipeline feature, we can start benchmarking using the -P option:

```
$ bin/redis-benchmark -t SET -c 100 -n 10000000 -r 10000000 -d 256
-P 10000
====== SET ======
  10000000 requests completed in 36.21 seconds
  100 parallel clients
  256 bytes payload
  keep alive: 1

0.00% <= 9 milliseconds
0.70% <= 10 milliseconds
2.50% <= 11 milliseconds
...
99.80% <= 478 milliseconds
99.90% <= 725 milliseconds
100.00% <= 725 milliseconds
276189.69 requests per second
```

6. To perform Lua script benchmarking, we can use the `script load` option:

```
$ bin/redis-benchmark -n 100000 script load
"redis.call('set','foo','bar')"
====== script load redis.call('set','foo','bar') ======
  100000 requests completed in 0.56 seconds
  50 parallel clients
  3 bytes payload
  keep alive: 1

100.00% <= 0 milliseconds
179211.45 requests per second
```

How it works...

The usage of this benchmark tool is quite self-explanatory. The most important information you should obtain from the result of the benchmark is how many requests your Redis instance handled per second for a particular Redis operation. For example, from the first benchmarking in the previous section, you can tell that Redis processed 141,043.72 requests per second for the MSET operation.

There's more...

It is critical to note that the benchmarking result just gives you an extreme testing result for your Redis alone and you should never use it as a *stress test* for your whole application's performance. Moreover, if you want to simulate the real application environment, you should start the Redis benchmark tool on the same host that the applications get deployed.

In this way, the overhead of network hop is the same for both the benchmark tool and the applications. It can be a big help for you to get a more practical testing result. Lastly, if you want to do a benchmark of a Redis Cluster with N shards, the performance of the Cluster can be roughly estimated through the benchmarking result against one of the N shards multiplied by N.

See also

- You can learn more about Redis benchmark tools at: https://redis.io/topics/benchmarks
- There is a Redis Cluster benchmarking discussion in the issue section of the Redis project at: https://github.com/antirez/redis/issues/4041
- There is another Redis benchmark tool, memtier_benchmark from RedisLabs, you can give it a try at: https://github.com/RedisLabs/memtier_benchmark

Logging

Logging on a production system is important as it is a reflection of past status. When the system malfunctions, we may figure out the root cause of the problem by inspecting and analyzing the logs. In this recipe, we will introduce the logging options in Redis and show you how to interpret the logs of the Redis Server and Sentinels.

Getting ready...

You need to finish the installation of the Redis Server, as we described in the *Downloading and installing Redis* recipe in Chapter 1, *Getting Started with Redis*. If you would like to inspect the logs of the Redis slave server and Sentinel, you also need to set up an environment with sentinels as we described in the *Setting up Sentinel* recipe of Chapter 7, *Setting up High Availability and Cluster*.

How to do it...

The steps for logging options and how to interpret the log are as follows:

1. To update the log level of Redis, update the `loglevel` directive in the Redis configuration, here we are changing the log level to debug on a Redis master server:

   ```
   loglevel debug
   ```

2. To update the log file location, set the `logfile` directive in the Redis configuration:

   ```
   logfile "/var/log/redis/redis-server.log"
   ```

3. You can also update the `loglevel` and `logfile` location by using the command `CONFIG SET`. This is useful when you want to temporarily lower the log level to debug an issue:

   ```
   127.0.0.1:6379> CONFIG SET loglevel debug
   OK
   127.0.0.1:6379> CONFIG SET logfile "/var/log/redis/redis-
   server.log"
   OK
   ```

4. Do the same to one of the Sentinels, but specify a different log location:

   ```
   loglevel debug
   logfile "/var/log/redis/redis-sentinel.log"
   ```

5. Inspect the `log` file for the Redis master server:

   ```
   $ less /var/log/redis/redis-server.log
   1580:M 19 Nov 15:39:39.120 * Ready to accept connections
   1580:M 19 Nov 15:39:39.120 - DB 0: 8 keys (0 volatile) in 8 slots
   HT.
   1580:M 19 Nov 15:39:39.120 - 0 clients connected (0 slaves), 766144
   bytes in use
   ...
   1580:M 19 Nov 15:39:39.502 * Starting BGSAVE for SYNC with target:
   disk
   1580:M 19 Nov 15:39:39.503 * Background saving started by pid 1584
   1584:C 19 Nov 15:39:39.507 * DB saved on disk
   ...
   1580:M 19 Nov 15:40:06.829 # User requested shutdown...
   1580:M 19 Nov 15:40:06.829 * Saving the final RDB snapshot before
   ```

```
exiting.
1580:M 19 Nov 15:40:06.831 * DB saved on disk
. . .
```

6. Inspect the `log` file for the Redis slave server:

```
1645:S 19 Nov 15:46:22.916 * Connecting to MASTER 192.168.0.33:6379
1645:S 19 Nov 15:46:22.917 * MASTER <-> SLAVE sync started
1645:S 19 Nov 15:46:22.917 # Error condition on socket for SYNC:
Connection refused
1645:S 19 Nov 15:46:23.926 * Connecting to MASTER 192.168.0.33:6379
1645:S 19 Nov 15:46:23.926 * MASTER <-> SLAVE sync started
1645:S 19 Nov 15:46:23.926 * Non blocking connect for SYNC fired
the event.
1645:S 19 Nov 15:46:23.926 * Master replied to PING, replication
can continue...
```

7. Inspect the `log` file for the Redis Sentinel:

```
1710:X 19 Nov 15:48:18.014 # Sentinel ID is
3ef95f7fd6420bfe22e38bfded1399382a63ce5b
1710:X 19 Nov 15:48:18.014 # +monitor master mymaster 192.168.0.33
6379 quorum 2
1710:X 19 Nov 15:48:18.513 - Accepted 192.168.0.33:37898
. . .
```

How it works...

Redis has four log levels from low to high: debug, verbose, notice, and warning. Only messages whose level is equal to or above the configured log level will be appended to the log. For example, if `loglevel` is set to verbose, only verbose, notice, and warning messages will be found in the log. The lower log level we set, the more messages we see in the log.

In this example, we set the log level to debug on the master server and one of the Sentinels, although this is not necessary for the production environment because the debug level will print all log messages. The default log level notice is enough most of the time, unless you need more logs to debug. The `logfile` directive controls the output file location of the logs. If it is set to an empty string, Redis will print the logs to standard output. If a daemonized mode is enabled in Redis and the `logfile` is set to empty, all logs will be redirected to `/dev/null` and will be lost.

Therefore, it is necessary to set the `logfile` properly when Redis is running in daemonized mode. By viewing the `logfile`, we can see that each line in the Redis log follows the format as follows:

```
pid:role timestamp loglevel message
```

`pid` is the Redis Server or Sentinel process ID. `role` is the role of the Redis instance represented by a single character of the following value:

```
X Sentinel
C RDB/AOF writing child
S slave
M master
```

`timestamp` is the event timestamp. `loglevel` is the log message level represented by a single character of the following value:

```
. debug
- verbose
* notice
# warning
```

9
Administrating Redis

In this chapter, we will cover the following recipes:

- Managing Redis Server configurations
- Operating Redis using bin/redis-cli
- Backup and restore
- Monitoring memory
- Managing clients
- Data migration

Introduction

Routine Redis operation tasks are needed after you put your Redis service online. In this chapter, we will focus on administrating Redis Servers.

We will start by setting the configuration of the Redis Server. Then, we will introduce a number of useful features of `redis-cli`, which is the most widely used admin tool. After that, data backup and recovery will be discussed in detail. Later, we will show you how to monitor the memory of a Redis instance through various kinds of metrics. As another important part of Redis administration, how to manage clients, will also be discussed. Finally, some tools used for data migration between two Redis instances or a Redis instance and a Redis Cluster will be introduced.

Managing Redis Server configurations

We have already set or updated Redis Server configurations multiple times in previous recipes. In this recipe, we will revisit the ways to manage Redis Server configurations and introduce two commands related to Redis configuration.

Getting ready...

You need to finish the installation of Redis Server as we described in the *Downloading and installing Redis* recipe in `Chapter 1`, *Getting Started with Redis*.

How to do it...

The steps for managing Redis Server configurations are as follows:

1. To start a Redis Server with configurations loaded from a `config` file, append the config file path after `redis-server`:

   ```
   $ bin/redis-server conf/redis.conf
   ```

2. To include another config file, use the `include` directive in the Redis config file. For example, we can put common configurations into `/redis/conf/redis-common.conf` and include it in `redis.conf`:

   ```
   include /redis/conf/redis-common.conf
   ```

3. To override configuration parameters when starting Redis Server, append the configuration directives and values after `redis-server`:

   ```
   $ bin/redis-server conf/redis.conf --loglevel verbose --port 6666
   ```

4. To retrieve a server configuration parameter, use the `CONFIG GET` command:

   ```
   127.0.0.1:6379> CONFIG GET port
   1) "port"
   2) "6379"
   ```

5. To set or update a server configuration parameter, use the `CONFIG SET` command:

   ```
   127.0.0.1:6379> CONFIG SET loglevel debug
   ```

OK

6. To persist current server configurations to the config file, use CONFIG REWRITE:

```
127.0.0.1:6379> CONFIG SET loglevel debug
OK
127.0.0.1:6379> CONFIG REWRITE
OK
$ grep loglevel conf/redis.conf
loglevel debug
```

7. To reset the statistics reported by Redis using the INFO command, use CONFIG RESETSTAT:

```
127.0.0.1:6379> INFO STATS
# Stats
total_connections_received:1
total_commands_processed:11
...
127.0.0.1:6379> CONFIG RESETSTAT
OK
127.0.0.1:6379> INFO STATS
# Stats
total_connections_received:0
total_commands_processed:1
...
```

How it works...

In step 1, we launched a Redis Server with the configuration file conf/redis.conf. If we don't specify the configuration file, Redis is also able to start with the built-in default configurations. However, this should be used for test purposes only and should never be used in a production environment.

In step 2, we can see that another configuration file, redis-common.conf, is included in redis.conf. This feature is useful when multiple Redis instances are running on the same host. We can put into redis-common.conf configurations shared by all instances and include it in the configuration file of each instance.

CONFIG REWRITE will write current configurations into the configuration file. If you have made any changes using CONFIG SET, the new configuration will be saved in the configuration file. In step 6, we first changed the loglevel config and executed CONFIG REWRITE. After that, we can see that loglevel is also updated in redis.conf.

Please note that, if Redis is started without a configuration file, CONFIG REWRITE will report an error, because it doesn't know where to write configurations.

CONFIG RESETSTAT is like the reset button of your vehicle's trip odometer. It resets a couple of counters returned by the INFO STATS command. Specifically, the following counters will be reset to 0:

- Keyspace hits
- Keyspace misses
- Number of commands processed
- Number of connections received
- Number of expired keys
- Number of rejected connections
- Latest fork(2) time
- The aof_delayed_fsync counter

Operating Redis using bin/redis-cli

The command-line tool bin/redis-cli is extremely helpful for operating Redis instances. Several usages have been demonstrated in previous recipes. In this recipe, we will introduce other useful practical operations of bin/redis-cli.

Getting ready...

You need to finish the installation of Redis Server, as we described in the *Downloading and installing Redis* recipe in Chapter 1, *Getting Started with Redis*.

How to do it...

To show how to operate Redis using redis-cli, take the following steps:

1. To run a command using bin/redis-cli, just append the command you want to run after bin/redis-cli:

```
$ bin/redis-cli HMSET hashkeyA field1 value1 feild2 value2
OK
```

2. To get the raw format of a command output, use the option `--raw`:

```
$ bin/redis-cli --raw HGETALL hashkeyA
field1
value1
feild2
value2
```

Without the option `--raw`, you will obtain the output for better human readability by default:
```
$ bin/redis-cli hgetall hashkeyA
1) "field1"
2) "value1"
3) "feild2"
4) "value2"
```

3. To get the CSV format of a command output, use the option `--csv`:

```
$ bin/redis-cli LPUSH listkeyA value1 value2 value3
(integer) 3
$ bin/redis-cli --csv LRANGE listkeyA 0 -1
"value3","value2","value1"
```

4. The last argument of the `bin/redis-cli` command can also be taken from `stdin`:

```
$ echo -n "bar" | bin/redis-cli -x SET foo
OK
$ bin/redis-cli GET foo
"bar"
$ bin/redis-cli -x SET hosts < /etc/hosts
OK
$ bin/redis-cli --raw GET hosts
127.0.0.1 localhost
127.0.1.1 gnuhpc-desktop
# The following lines are desirable for IPv6 capable hosts
::1 ip6-localhost ip6-loopback
fe00::0 ip6-localnet
ff00::0 ip6-mcastprefix
ff02::1 ip6-allnodes
ff02::2 ip6-allrouters
```

5. If you want to execute a bunch of commands written in a file, you can simply redirect the file content to `bin/redis-cli` using pipeline:

```
$ cat commands
set key1 value1
set key2 value2
$ cat commands |bin/redis-cli
OK
OK
```

6. From the *Using pipeline* recipe, we have learned that the pipeline feature should be utilized for better performance if there are a large number of commands to execute in Redis. We can enable the pipeline feature of Redis in `bin/redis-cli` with the option `--pipe`:

```
$ unix2dos commands
unix2dos: converting file commands to DOS format ...
$ cat commands |bin/redis-cli --pipe
All data transferred. Waiting for the last reply...
Last reply received from server.
errors: 0, replies: 2
```

7. We can execute a command repeatedly in a specific interval with options `-r <count>` and `-i <delay>`:

```
$ bin/redis-cli -r 5 -i 1 INFO MEMORY | grep used_memory:
used_memory:209036072
used_memory:209036072
used_memory:209036072
used_memory:209036072
used_memory:209036072
```

8. To iterate the keys with a certain pattern, use the option `--pattern`:

```
$ bin/redis-cli --scan --pattern 'session:*7ab0'
session:e9788147-a4dd-470d-af6b-df1e2fae7ab0
session:ef04be00-b4f2-4778-8023-82994d237ab0
session:4764e56f-a73e-4e64-bc68-03e51e067ab0
session:b030fb27-b560-4c39-8892-c5f6989f7ab0
session:51588697-191f-4e71-9a69-6540ff397ab0
session:37f0259c-f7ea-4fde-9883-ec3298e77ab0
session:c45db486-bfb2-4240-91b3-fd9850ba7ab0
session:7226bb09-b03a-4393-b98d-5f3f59097ab0
```

How it works...

The preceding examples are quite self-explanatory. You can easily use the output of `bin/redis-cli` as the input of another script for further processing and vice versa.

One thing you should notice is that, with the `--pipe` option, you have to convert the command files to the DOS format. That's because `bin/redis-cli` can only accept the command in the format of raw Redis protocol when the pipeline feature is enabled. For the details of Redis protocol, you can refer to the *Understanding Redis protocol* recipe in `Chapter 1`, *Getting Started with Redis*.

There's more...

There are several performance related options in `bin/redis-cli`. We will introduce them in `Chapter 10`, *Troubleshooting Redis*.

See also

- For a complete reference of `bin/redis-cli`, you can refer to the official documentation at `https://redis.io/topics/rediscli`

Backup and restore

It is always important to have backup plans for production databases. Once things break, such as hard disk failure, accidental data deletion, or network intrusion, backing up the data can protect against data losses. In `Chapter 6`, *Persistence*, we have learned that Redis data can be persisted into the RDB file. In this recipe, we will revisit the RDB persistence option and show you the detailed steps you can take to back up and restore data for Redis.

Getting ready...

You need to finish the installation of Redis Server, as we described in the *Downloading and installing Redis* recipe in `Chapter 1`, *Getting Started with Redis*.

How to do it...

Let us see how to backup and restore Redis data.

Backing up Redis data

Firstly, to back up Redis data, take the following steps:

1. Execute the BGSAVE command on Redis Server:

    ```
    $ bin/redis-cli BGSAVE
    Background saving started
    ```

2. Copy the saved RDB file to a safe location:

    ```
    $ cp /var/lib/redis/dump.rdb /mnt/backup/redis/dump.$(date
    +%Y%m%d%H%M).rdb
    ```

Restoring Redis data from an RDB file

Next, take the following steps to restore Redis data from the RDB file created in the backing up section:

1. Check if AOF is enabled in Redis:

    ```
    $ bin/redis-cli CONFIG GET appendonly
    1) "appendonly"
    2) "yes"
    ```

2. If AOF is not enabled, skip this step and progress to step 3. Otherwise, disable AOF first:

    ```
    $ bin/redis-cli CONFIG SET appendonly no
    OK
    $ bin/redis-cli CONFIG REWRITE
    OK
    ```

3. Shut down Redis Server and delete or rename both AOF and RDB files in the data directory:

    ```
    $ bin/redis-cli SHUTDOWN
    $ rm *.aof *.rdb
    ```

4. Now, copy the snapshot RDB file to be restored into the Redis data directory and rename it `dump.rdb`: (make sure it matches `dbfilename` in configuration):

```
$ cp /mnt/backup/redis/dump.201712250100.rdb
/var/lib/redis/dump.rdb
```

5. Set the correct permission to `dump.rdb` and start Redis Server:

```
$ chown redis:redis dump.rdb
$ bin/redis-server conf/redis-server.conf
```

6. Re-enable AOF persistence, if needed:

```
$ bin/redis-cli CONFIG SET appendonly yes
OK
$ bin/redis-cli CONFIG REWRITE
OK
```

How it works...

The preceding steps are quite straightforward. The `BGSAVE` flushes all data into the `RDB` file, therefore backing up this file is enough. It is worth setting up a crontab job to do the backup regularly.

It is important to disable AOF before restoring data to Redis, because Redis will try to restore data from the AOF file if AOF is enabled. If the AOF file can not be found (we deleted/renamed it in step 3), Redis will be started with an empty dataset. In this case, once the RDB snapshot is triggered due to the key changes, the original RDB file will be rewritten.

Monitoring memory

Since Redis is an in-memory data service, it's of great essence to monitor the memory usage of Redis. In this recipe, we will learn the details of how to monitor the memory of Redis via the `INFO` command and `MEMORY` command.

Getting ready...

You need to finish the installation of Redis Server, as we described in the *Downloading and installing Redis* recipe in `Chapter 1`, *Getting Started with Redis*.

How to do it...

The operations to monitor memory of Redis are shown as following:

1. To obtain the overall memory-related metrics of Redis, issue `INFO MEMORY` with `bin/redis-cli`:

```
$ bin/redis-cli INFO MEMORY
# Memory
used_memory:211428088
used_memory_human:201.63M
used_memory_rss:251547648
used_memory_rss_human:239.89M
used_memory_peak:3865330064
used_memory_peak_human:3.60G
used_memory_peak_perc:5.47%
used_memory_overhead:49242362
used_memory_startup:765624
used_memory_dataset:162185726
used_memory_dataset_perc:76.99%
total_system_memory:67467202560
total_system_memory_human:62.83G
used_memory_lua:40960
used_memory_lua_human:40.00K
maxmemory:4000000000
maxmemory_human:3.73G
maxmemory_policy:noeviction
mem_fragmentation_ratio:1.19
mem_allocator:jemalloc-4.0.3
active_defrag_running:0
lazyfree_pending_objects:0
```

2. If you would like to estimate the memory usage of one key, you can issue the `MEMORY USAGE` command:

```
127.0.0.1:6379> set foo bar
OK
127.0.0.1:6379> MEMORY USAGE foo
(integer) 54
```

The command MEMORY USAGE does not calculate the length of the key itself and the key expiration memory assumption:

```
127.0.0.1:6379> set foo bar
OK
127.0.0.1:6379> MEMORY USAGE foo
(integer) 54
127.0.0.1:6379> set foooooooooooooooooooo bar
OK
127.0.0.1:6379> MEMORY USAGE foooooooooooooooooooo
(integer) 54
4) "value2"
127.0.0.1:6379> EXPIRE foo 600
(integer) 1
127.0.0.1:6379> MEMORY USAGE foo
(integer) 54
```

3. If you would like to inspect every part of the memory assumption in a Redis instance, you can use MEMORY STATS:

```
$ bin/redis-cli --csv MEMORY STATS
"peak.allocated",3865330064,"total.allocated",211428088,"startup.al
located",765624,"replication.backlog",0,"clients.slaves",0,"clients
.normal",83346,"aof.buffer",0,"db.0","overhead.hashtable.main",4839
3288,"overhead.hashtable.expires",32,"db.1","overhead.hashtable.mai
n",72,"overhead.hashtable.expires",0,"overhead.total",49242362,"key
s.count",1000118,"keys.bytes-per-
key",210,"dataset.bytes",162185726,"dataset.percentage","76.9884338
37890625","peak.percentage","5.4698591232299805","fragmentation","1
.1897543668746948"
```

4. Redis also provides a powerful diagnostic command for memory issues, MEMORY DOCTOR:

```
$ bin/redis-cli MEMORY DOCTOR

Sam, I detected a few issues in this Redis instance memory
implants:

* Peak memory: In the past this instance used more than 150% the
memory that is currently using. The allocator is normally not able
to release memory after a peak, so you can expect to see a big
fragmentation ratio, however this is actually harmless and is only
due to the memory peak, and if the Redis instance Resident Set Size
(RSS) is currently bigger than expected, the memory will be used as
soon as you fill the Redis instance with more data. If the memory
```

peak was only occasional and you want to try to reclaim memory, please try the MEMORY PURGE command, otherwise the only other option is to shutdown and restart the instance.

I'm here to keep you safe, Sam. I want to help you.

5. You can also use the `--bigkeys` option of `bin/redis-cli` to find out which are the biggest keys and the average sizes per key type:

```
$ bin/redis-cli --bigkeys
# Scanning the entire keyspace to find biggest keys as well as
# average sizes per key type. You can use -i 0.1 to sleep 0.1 sec
# per 100 SCAN commands (not usually needed).
[00.00%] Biggest hash found so far 'session:39b2276f-1474-4afe-
a619-2929b91d0430' with 7 fields
[00.00%] Biggest hash found so far
'session:bd9ff9f7-0e4f-42e3-9e08-0179120b0e22' with 10 fields
[00.30%] Biggest string found so far 'lru:31' with 5 bytes
[01.98%] Biggest string found so far 'key2' with 6 bytes
[26.47%] Biggest string found so far 'name' with 8 bytes
[27.31%] Biggest hash found so far 'user:0000004' with 1000 fields
[39.66%] Biggest string found so far 'hosts' with 351 bytes
[56.95%] Biggest hash found so far 'bighash' with 18593 fields
[87.13%] Biggest list found so far 'listkeyA' with 3 items
[99.99%] Sampled 1000000 keys so far
-------- summary -------
Sampled 1000116 keys in the keyspace!
Total key length in bytes is 44000724 (avg len 44.00)
Biggest string found 'hosts' has 351 bytes
Biggest list found 'listkeyA' has 3 items
Biggest hash found 'bighash' has 18593 fields
103 strings with 862 bytes (00.01% of keys, avg size 8.37)
1 lists with 3 items (00.00% of keys, avg size 3.00)
0 sets with 0 members (00.00% of keys, avg size 0.00)
1000012 hashs with 5528165 fields (99.99% of keys, avg size 5.53)
0 zsets with 0 members (00.00% of keys, avg size 0.00)
```

How it works...

INFO MEMORY is the most widely used command to obtain the memory usage of the whole Redis instance. Here is the meaning of each metric returned by this command:

- used_memory: Total number of bytes allocated by Redis using its allocator
- used_memory_human: Human readable representation of the previous value

- `used_memory_rss`: Number of bytes that Redis allocated, as seen by the operating system
- `used_memory_rss_human`: Human readable representation of previous value
- `used_memory_peak`: Peak memory consumed by Redis (in bytes)
- `used_memory_peak_human`: Human readable representation of previous value
- `used_memory_peak_perc`: (used_memory/used_memory_peak)*100%
- `used_memory_overhead`: All the memory overhead used by Redis internally to maintain the dataset, including all the client output buffer, query buffer, AOF rewrite buffer, and replication backlog
- `used_memory_startup`: Memory assumption when the Redis Server started
- `used_memory_dataset`: used_memory – used_memory_overhead
- `used_memory_dataset_perc`: 100% * (used_memory_dataset/(used_memory – used_memory_startup)
- `total_system_memory`: Total system memory capacity
- `total_system_memory_human`: Human readable representation of previous value
- `used_memory_lua`: Lua script stored memory assumption
- `used_memory_lua_human`: Human readable representation of previous value
- `maxmemory`: Max memory settings for the Redis instance
- `maxmemory_human`: Human readable representation of previous value
- `maxmemory_policy`: Eviction policy when max memory is reached
- `mem_fragmentation_ratio`: used_memory_rss/used_memory
- `mem_allocator`: Memory allocator
- `active_defrag_running`: 0 for none active defrag task is running. 1 for active defrag task is running
- `lazyfree_pending_objects`: 0 for none lazy free pending objects exist

The command MEMORY USAGE estimates the memory assumption of a key. It has an option to specify the number of sampling when performing the estimation. Under the hood, Redis utilizes the average of the samples from a collection data type (hash, list, and so on) to roughly estimate the memory usage of the key. As shown in the following code, the more samples there are, the more accurate the result is. As shown as follows, the more samples we take, the more accurate the result is. More samples and higher data accuracy also come at the cost of slower estimation process:

```
$ cat populatedata6.sh
#!/bin/bash
```

```
DATAFILE="hash.data"
echo -n "HMSET bighash " > $DATAFILE
for i in `seq -f "%010g" 1 30000`
do
echo -n "$[ $RANDOM % 30000] $[ $RANDOM % 30000] " >> $DATAFILE
done
unix2dos $DATAFILE
cat $DATAFILE | bin/redis-cli
$ bash populatedata6.sh
unix2dos: converting file hash.data to DOS format ...
OK
$ time bin/redis-cli MEMORY USAGE bighash SAMPLES 100
(integer) 1084090
real 0m0.002s
user 0m0.000s
sys 0m0.000s
$ time bin/redis-cli MEMORY USAGE bighash SAMPLES 15000
(integer) 1083861
real 0m0.003s
user 0m0.000s
sys 0m0.004s
$ time bin/redis-cli MEMORY USAGE bighash SAMPLES 20000
(integer) 1083868
real 0m0.004s
user 0m0.000s
sys 0m0.000s
```

The command MEMORY STATS shows every part of memory assumption in Redis. There are some metrics that overlap the output of MEMORY INFO. We will highlight the meaning of the rest metrics only returned by MEMORY STATS:

- replication.backlog: Replication backlog memory assumption (in bytes)
- clients.slaves: Slave client output buffer memory assumption (in bytes)
- clients.normal: Normal clients buffer memory assumption (in bytes)
- aof.buffer: AOF buffer memory assumption (in bytes)
- overhead.hashtable.main: Memory cost for maintaining the data in Redis
- overhead.hashtable.expires: Memory cost for storing the expiration information in Redis
- keys.count: Total number of keys (including all the databases of the Redis instance)
- keys.bytes-per-key: (total.allocated-startup.allocated)/keys.count

The command MEMORY DOCTOR provides some memory issue hints. The main logic of this command is as follows:

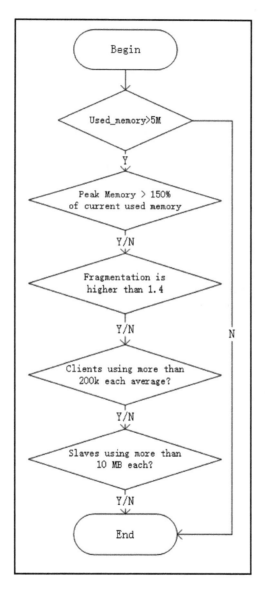

There is more...

In the *Troubleshooting memory issues* recipe in `Chapter 10`, *Troubleshooting Redis*, we will take advantage of the commands introduced in the previous section to troubleshoot the memory issues.

See also

- For a complete reference of the meanings of `INFO MEMORY`, you can refer to the documents at `https://redis.io/commands/INFO`
- For the new `MEMORY` command since version 4.0, you can refer to the release notes of 4.0 at `http://antirez.com/news/110`

Managing clients

Generally speaking, Redis is a TCP server using the client-server model. Thus, it's of great importance for the Redis administrators to manage the clients connected to Redis Server. In this recipe, we will start by introducing how to collect the global information of the Redis instance and, then, we will go through how to list and kill the Redis clients from server side. Some important configuration options will also be shown.

Getting ready...

You need to finish setting up the replication of Redis Server as we described in the *Setting up Redis replication* recipe in `Chapter 5`, *Replication*.

How to do it...

The operations for managing clients are as follows:

1. For demonstration purposes, start two `redis-benchmark` processes first:

```
bin$ nohup ./redis-benchmark -c 5 -n 100000 -r 1000 -d 1000 &
bin$ nohup ./redis-benchmark -c 5 -n 100000 -r 1000 -d 1000 &
```

2. In addition, issue the BLPOP command using bin/redis-cli, as follows:

```
$ bin/redis-cli BRPOP job_queue 0
```

3. To collect the overall client-related metrics of Redis, issue INFO CLIENTS and INFO STATS with bin/redis-cli:

```
$ bin/redis-cli INFO CLIENTS
# Clients
connected_clients:12
client_longest_output_list:28
client_biggest_input_buf:0
blocked_clients:1
$ bin/redis-cli INFO STATS |grep connection
total_connections_received:4921
rejected_connections:0
```

4. If you would like to learn the details of every client, issue a CLIENT LIST command with bin/redis-cli:

```
127.0.0.1:6379> CLIENT LIST
id=4827 addr=127.0.0.1:47838 fd=7 name= age=0 idle=0 flags=N db=0
sub=0 psub=0 multi=-1 qbuf=0 qbuf-free=32768 obl=4 oll=0 omem=0
events=r cmd=hset
...
id=4826 addr=127.0.0.1:47836 fd=18 name= age=1 idle=0 flags=N db=0
sub=0 psub=0 multi=-1 qbuf=0 qbuf-free=32768 obl=1009 oll=0 omem=0
events=r cmd=lpop
id=4 addr=127.0.0.1:34892 fd=8 name= age=352 idle=0 flags=S db=0
sub=0 psub=0 multi=-1 qbuf=0 qbuf-free=0 obl=3303 oll=0 omem=0
events=r cmd=replconf
id=4036 addr=127.0.0.1:46254 fd=29 name= age=228 idle=209 flags=b
db=0 sub=0 psub=0 multi=-1 qbuf=0 qbuf-free=0 obl=0 oll=0 omem=0
events=r cmd=brpop
id=5 addr=127.0.0.1:38192 fd=9 name= age=345 idle=0 flags=N db=0
sub=0 psub=0 multi=-1 qbuf=0 qbuf-free=32768 obl=0 oll=0 omem=0
events=r cmd=client
```

With the command CLIENT SETNAME name, you are able to identify a client by setting its name. By doing so, it's much easier to distinguish the incoming connection if more than one application connects to the same Redis instance:

```
127.0.0.1:6379> CLIENT SETNAME bin/redis-cli
OK
127.0.0.1:6379> CLIENT LIST
id=4902 addr=127.0.0.1:47990 fd=9
name=bin/redis-cli
age=8 idle=0 flags=N db=0 sub=0 psub=0 multi=-1 qbuf=0
qbuf-free=32768 obl=0 oll=0 omem=0 events=r cmd=client
```

5. You can kill the client connection by issuing CLIENT KILL client-host:client-port:

   ```
   127.0.0.1:6379> CLIENT KILL 127.0.0.1:46254
   OK
   ```

6. From the client side, you will find the disconnection immediately.

   ```
   $ bin/redis-cli BRPOP job_queue 0
   Error: Server closed the connection
   ```

   Instead of killing the connection, you can suspend all the Redis clients for the specified period of time with the CLIENT PAUSE command. For example, you can suspend the Redis connection for the 60s:

```
127.0.0.1:6379> CLIENT PAUSE 60000
OK
127.0.0.1:6379> DBSIZE
(integer) 3001
(57.13s)
```

During the pause, Redis Server stops processing all the commands coming from normal and pub/sub-clients. All the connected clients will be stuck during the pause, and the incoming connections will also be hanged. However, the replication will work continuously. Moreover, the dataset is guaranteed to be static. So, you can perform the data migration using replication mechanism during the pause.

How it works...

`INFO CLIENTS` returns four client-related metrics. Here is the meaning of each metric:

- `connected_clients`: Number of client connections. Please take note that this metric does not include the connections from slaves.
- `client_longest_output_list`: The longest output list among current client connections. We will discuss the output list later in this recipe.
- `client_biggest_input_buf`: The biggest input buffer among current client connections. We will discuss this metric later in this recipe.
- `blocked_clients`: Number of clients pending on a blocking operation, such as BLPOP, BRPOP, BRPOPLPUSH, and so on. Don't panic when this metric is not equal to 0. It only indicates the number of clients pending by the blocking command.

`INFO STATS` returns two client-related metrics. One is `total_connections_received`, which is the total number of connections since the Redis Server started. Another metric is `rejected_connections`. It means the number of connections rejected because of `maxclients` limit. You should pay special attention to this metric. Once this metric increases, it indicates the maxclients limit has reached and new connections will be denied.

The `CLIENT LIST` command shows the details of every connection. Here is the meaning of all fields for one connection:

- `id`: A unique 64-bit client ID
- `addr`: Address/port of the client
- `fd`: File descriptor corresponding to the socket
- `age`: Total duration of the connection in seconds
- `idle`: Idle time of the connection in seconds
- `flags`: The client state, for example, N stands for a normal client, S stands for a slave client, and so on
- `db`: Current database ID
- `sub`: Number of channel subscriptions
- `psub`: Number of pattern matching subscriptions
- `multi`: Number of commands in a MULTI/EXEC context
- `qbuf`: Query buffer length (0 means no query pending)

- `qbuf-free`: Free space of the query buffer (`0` means the buffer is full)
- `obl`: The space used by the output fixed buffer
- `oll`: Output list length (replies are queued in this list when the buffer is full)
- `omem`: Output buffer memory usage
- `events`: File descriptor events (`r` for readable socket and `w` for writable socket)
- `cmd`: Last command issued by this client

There are some new concepts in these preceding fields. The first one is **query buffer**. For every connection, Redis allocates a piece of memory as its query buffer. All the commands received from this connection will be saved in its query buffer before getting executed. Redis Server will fetch commands from the query buffer and execute them. This size of the query buffer is between 0 and 1 GB. Once the query buffer size exceeds 1 GB, the connection will be closed by Redis Server as soon as possible. The metrics `qbuf` and `qbuf-free` give you the query buffer size and free space of this buffer.

Another new concept is **output buffer**. It's not a completely new concept actually as we have introduced the Slave client buffer in the *Troubleshooting replication* recipe. In fact, every client including slave client has an output buffer. All the data to be returned from Redis Server will be saved first in this buffer and then be sent to the client. There are two parts of the client output buffer—fixed buffer (16 KB) and dynamic output list. The metric `obl` indicates the space used by the fixed buffer. The metric `oll` means the number of items in the dynamic output list. The metric `omem` shows the space (in bytes) used by the client output buffer of this connection.

Lastly, the metric age and idle can help you dig out the long idle connections. In most cases, the long idle connections may be a signal of a connection leak issue.

There's more...

Please consider that the memory allocated for query buffer and output buffer are calculated into `used_memory_overhead` returned by the `INFO MEMORY` command excluding the output buffer of the monitor client. Due to the fact that `used_memory` = `used_memory_overhead` + `used_memory_dataset`, these two kinds of buffer are also taken into account by the `used_memory` metric.

See also

- For a complete reference of the Redis client command, you can refer to the official documents and find out all the CLIENT commands
at https://redis.io/commands#server
- For important Redis client configuration options, you can refer to the *Setting client connection options* recipe in Chapter 8, *Deploying to a Production Environment*

Data migration

Date migration is required when you would like to move or copy the data stored in one Redis instance to another for some reason. In this recipe, we will show you several methods that can be used to perform data migration of Redis.

Getting ready...

You need to finish the installation of Redis Server as we described in the *Downloading and installing Redis* recipe in Chapter 1, *Getting Started with Redis*.

You also need to finish the *Setting up Redis Cluster* recipe in Chapter 7, *Setting Up High Availability and Cluster*, to learn the basic knowledge of Redis Cluster.

How to do it...

The first way to perform a single Redis instance to another single Redis instance migration works as follows:

1. First, let's start two Redis instances:

```
$ bin/redis-server conf/redis.conf
$ bin/redis-server conf/redis2.conf
$ ps -ef |grep redis-server
redis 361 32707 0 14:14 pts/5 00:00:00 grep redis-server
redis 21413 1 0 Dec10 ? 00:03:10 bin/redis-server 0.0.0.0:6379
redis 32762 1 0 14:13 ? 00:00:00 bin/redis-server 0.0.0.0:6380
127.0.0.1:6379> info Keyspace
# Keyspace
db0:keys=1000000,expires=0,avg_ttl=922042600
```

2. By acting as a slave of the source instance, we can replicate all the data from the source Redis:

```
127.0.0.1:6380> SLAVEOF 192.168.1.7 6379
OK
127.0.0.1:6380> info Keyspace
# Keyspace
db0:keys=1000000,expires=0,avg_ttl=922042600
```

3. When the synchronization is finished, we set the destination instance as a master by issuing the SLAVEOF NO ONE command:

```
127.0.0.1:6380> SLAVEOF NO ONE
OK
```

The second way to perform a single Redis instance to another single Redis instance migration works as follows:

1. Instead of setting up the master-slave relationship, we can use the AOF persistence file to do the data migration. For both the source and target Redis instance, you should enable AOF persistence and also set the configuration aof-use-rdb-preamble to yes. By doing this, you can benefit from the advantages of both RDB and AOF:

```
127.0.0.1:6379> CONFIG SET appendonly yes
OK
127.0.0.1:6379> CONFIG SET aof-use-rdb-preamble yes
OK
127.0.0.1:6380> CONFIG SET appendonly yes
OK
127.0.0.1:6380> CONFIG SET aof-use-rdb-preamble yes
OK
127.0.0.1:6380> CONFIG SET aof-use-rdb-preamble yes
OK
```

2. Issue the BGREWRITEAOF command at the source instance:

```
127.0.0.1:6379> BGREWRITEAOF
Background saving started
```

3. Stop the target instance:

```
$ bin/redis-cli -p 6380 shutdown
```

4. Copy the `append.aof` file to the data directory of the target instance and restart the target instance.

The third way to perform a single Redis instance to another single Redis instance migration is to move specific keys from one instance to another, using the `MIGRATE` command:

```
$ KEYS=`bin/redis-cli -p 6379 --scan --pattern user:* | awk
'{printf("%s ",$1)}'`
$ echo $KEYS
user:0000004 user:0000008 user:0000009 user:0000007 user:0000003
user:0000005 user:0000002 user:0000006 user:0000000 user:0000010
user:0000001
$ bin/redis-cli -p 6379 MIGRATE 127.0.0.1 6380 "" 0 5000 REPLACE
keys $KEYS
OK
$ bin/redis-cli -p 6380 --scan --pattern user:*
user:0000000
user:0000002
user:0000006
user:0000001
user:0000008
user:0000010
user:0000007
user:0000005
user:0000009
user:0000004
user:0000003
```

The first way to perform a single Redis instance to a Redis Cluster migration works as follows:

1. To migrate data from a Redis instance to a brand new Redis Cluster, the first thing you should do is set up a Redis Cluster that owns all the masters, but has no slaves for each master. For migration purposes, you have to move all the slots to one master. To learn how to set up a Redis Cluster, you can refer to the *Setting up Redis Cluster* recipe in `Chapter 7`, *Setting Up High Availability and Cluster*. The final status of the cluster looks as follows:

```
redis@192.168.1.65:~> bin/redis-cli -h 192.168.1.65 -p 6379 cluster
nodes e74f75b566fcfb21c3543cfb71ddc8c6df68b9d9
192.168.1.67:6381@16381 master - 0 1513216226912 6 connected
```

```
02f217d2fb77c068c462013851fa287de53d577c 192.168.1.66:6380@16380
master - 0 1513216226000 7 connected
610c014ce0478453ab478db6707839556bb05e13 192.168.1.65:6379@16379
myself,master - 0 1513216224000 8 connected 0-16383
```

2. Enable AOF persistence and also set the configuration of `aof-use-rdb-preamble` to `yes`:

```
127.0.0.1:6379> CONFIG SET appendonly yes
OK
127.0.0.1:6379> CONFIG SET aof-use-rdb-preamble yes
OK
```

3. Let's generate some sample data and then start rewriting AOF in the background. To check if the rewriting process has finished, issue `INFO` persistence within `bin/redis-cli`:

```
127.0.0.1:6379> DEBUG POPULATE 1000000
OK
127.0.0.1:6379> INFO KEYSPACE
# Keyspace
db0:keys=1000000,expires=0,avg_ttl=0
127.0.0.1:6379> BGREWRITEAOF
Background saving started
127.0.0.1:6379> INFO persistence
# Persistence
aof_rewrite_in_progress:0
```

4. Shut down the master with all the slots and copy the AOF persistence file to the data `dir` of this Redis instance:

```
redis@192.168.1.65:~> bin/redis-cli -h 192.168.1.65 -p 6379
SHUTDOWN
redis@192.168.1.65:~/data> scp
redis@192.168.1.7:/redis/appendonly.aof .
```

5. Start this Redis and check if the AOF file has been loaded:

```
redis@192.168.1.65:~> bin/redis-server conf/redis-6379.conf
redis@192.168.1.65:~> bin/redis-cli -h 192.168.1.65 -p 6379 INFO
Keyspace
# Keyspace
db0:keys=1000000,expires=0,avg_ttl=0
```

6. Reshard the dataset using the `redis-trib.rb` script:

```
redis@192.168.1.65:~> script/redis-trib.rb reshard --from
610c014ce0478453ab478db6707839556bb05e13 --to
e74f75b566fcfb21c3543cfb71ddc8c6df68b9d9 --slots 5000 --yes
192.168.1.65:6379
redis@192.168.1.65:~> script/redis-trib.rb reshard --from
610c014ce0478453ab478db6707839556bb05e13 --to
02f217d2fb77c068c462013851fa287de53d577c --slots 5000 --yes
192.168.1.65:6379
```

7. To check if all the slots have been sharded as we wish, issue the CLUSTER NODES command to a node in the cluster:

```
redis@192.168.1.65:~> bin/redis-cli -h 192.168.1.65 cluster nodes
02f217d2fb77c068c462013851fa287de53d577c 192.168.1.66:6380@16380
master - 0 1513158338408 7 connected 5000-9999
e74f75b566fcfb21c3543cfb71ddc8c6df68b9d9 192.168.1.67:6381@16381
master - 0 1513158339410 6 connected 0-4999
610c014ce0478453ab478db6707839556bb05e13 192.168.1.65:6379@16379
myself,master - 0 1513158338000 5 connected 10000-16383
```

8. We can also issue the DBSIZE command to every master node of the cluster. By summing up all the key count (*389,638 + 305,153 + 305,209 = 1,000,000*), we can conclude that all the data has already been migrated to the Redis Cluster:

```
redis@192.168.1.65:~> script/redis-trib.rb call 192.168.1.65:6379
dbsize
>>> Calling DBSIZE
192.168.1.65:6379: 389638
192.168.1.67:6381: 305209
192.168.1.66:6380: 305153
```

9. Lastly, as a necessary step, you should add the slave node to each master as a backup. You can refer to the *Setting up Redis Cluster* recipe in Chapter 7, *Setting Up High Availability and Cluster*, to learn how to achieve it.

The second way to perform a single Redis instance to a Redis Cluster migration works as follows:

1. First, we set up all the master nodes in the Redis Cluster and finish the slots allocation. The status of the cluster is shown as follows:

```
redis@192.168.1.65:~> bin/redis-cli -h 192.168.1.65 -p 6379 cluster
nodes
6033a29badec100591bf42dee02a76d5abc66131 192.168.1.66:6380@16380
master - 0 1513222558953 0 connected 5401-11000
1de11e3729e66ff694820fa3e3d5de5e3e73f4d8 192.168.1.65:6379@16379
myself,master - 0 1513222557000 1 connected 0-5400
3e87c418b9a685bb47e08ce7eaec631a9f58c282 192.168.1.67:6381@16381
master - 0 1513222559956 2 connected 11001-16383
```

2. Shut down one node of the cluster and copy the AOF persistence data file to the data directory of the node. After that, restart the node:

```
redis@192.168.1.65:~> bin/redis-cli -h 192.168.1.65 -p 6379
shutdown
redis@192.168.1.65:~> cd data
redis@192.168.1.65:~/data> scp
redis@192.168.1.7:/redis/appendonly.aof .
redis@192.168.1.65:~> bin/redis-server conf/redis-6379.conf
```

3. Connect to the cluster using bin/redis-cli with the option -c and there will be errors when fetching keys that reside on other nodes of the cluster:

```
redis@192.168.1.65:~> bin/redis-cli -h 192.168.1.65 -p 6379 -c
192.168.1.65:6379> RANDOMKEY
"key:50375"
192.168.1.65:6379> get "key:50375"
-> Redirected to slot [6890] located at 192.168.1.66:6380
(nil)
```

4. To fix it, we issue the fix command of redis-trib.rb. After that, we issue the DBSIZE command to every node of the cluster:

```
redis@192.168.1.65:~> script/redis-trib.rb fix 192.168.1.65:6379
redis@192.168.1.65:~> script/redis-trib.rb call 192.168.1.65:6379
dbsize
>>> Calling DBSIZE
192.168.1.65:6379: 329674
192.168.1.67:6381: 328536
192.168.1.66:6380: 341790
```

5. Now, we can fetch the key successfully:

```
redis@192.168.1.65:~> bin/redis-cli -h 192.168.1.65 -p 6379 -c
192.168.1.65:6379> get "key:50375"
-> Redirected to slot [6890] located at 192.168.1.66:6380
"value:50375"
```

 You can utilize this method to migrate the data from one small Redis Cluster to another cluster with more nodes. The steps are almost the same, except that you need to copy multiple AOF persistence files to different nodes of the destination cluster.

Instead of copying the persistence file, we can utilize `redis-trib.rb` to perform the data migration directly:

```
redis@192.168.1.65:~> script/redis-trib.rb import --replace --from
192.168.1.7:6379 192.168.1.65:6379
...
Migrating key:974823 to 192.168.1.66:6380: OK
Migrating key:518820 to 192.168.1.66:6380: OK
Migrating key:704034 to 192.168.1.67:6381: OK
Migrating key:497427 to 192.168.1.65:6379: OK
Migrating key:349208 to 192.168.1.66:6380: OK
Migrating key:681758 to 192.168.1.67:6381: OK
Migrating key:190685 to 192.168.1.67:6381: OK
Migrating key:509235 to 192.168.1.66:6380: OK
Migrating key:635418 to 192.168.1.65:6379: OK
```

How it works...

In this recipe, we first introduced three methods to do data migration from one instance to another instance.

The first two methods are master-slave synchronization/loading persistence data files. Both methods are quite self explanatory.

The third one is the command MIGRATE. As stated in the Redis command documentation, this command actually executes a DUMP in the source instance, and a RESTORE in the target instance. There are two options, COPY and REPLACE, for one to decide the behavior of this command. If the COPY option is specified, the data from the source instance won't be deleted after the migration. Moreover, with the REPLACE option, you can overwrite the existing key of the target instance during migration.

We then introduced three methods to perform data migration from one instance to a Redis Cluster. The first two methods took advantage of AOF persistence as data migration media. The third method actually used SCAN and MIGRATE internally to copy the keys from the source Redis instance to a node of the cluster. By calculating the mapping of the key and slot, the redis-trib.rb script will send the key directly to the corresponding slot. So there is no need to relocate the keys or do the slot resharding.

There's more...

There are several excellent third-party tools to make the Redis data migration. One is redis-port from CodisLabs. Another is redis-migrate-tool from VIPShop. Both of the projects are open source and can be obtained from GitHub. Due to the space limitations of this book, we won't go into their details here.

See also

- For a complete reference of the data migration of Redis Cluster, you can refer to the *Migrating to Redis Cluster* section at https://redis.io/topics/cluster-tutorial
- For the MIGRATE command, you can learn more from the command reference at https://redis.io/commands/migrate
- For more about the project redis-port, you can refer to its GitHub repository at https://github.com/CodisLabs/redis-port
- For more about the project redis-migrate-tool, you can refer to its GitHub repository at https://github.com/vipshop/redis-migrate-tool

10
Troubleshooting Redis

In this chapter, we will cover the following recipes:

- Health checking in Redis
- Identifying slow operations/queries using the SLOWLOG
- Troubleshooting latency issues
- Troubleshooting memory issues
- Troubleshooting crash issues

Introduction

We introduced Redis production deployment and routine administration tasks in the previous chapters. Even if you have carefully deployed Redis instances and done the administration, troubleshooting is inevitable once the Redis service is online. This chapter will detail the most critical troubleshooting mechanisms of Redis.

First, we will start with daily health checking. This could give us early warnings before a disaster happens. Then, we will introduce how to identify the slow queries or operations using the SLOWLOG Redis command. After that, we will discuss how to handle latency and memory issues in detail. Finally, we will cover the debugging mechanisms when a Redis instance crashes.

Health checking in Redis

Checking the Redis Server's health status is important in troubleshooting issues. By monitoring the metrics and statistics information, we can often see what has happened or is happening on the server and may deduce the root cause of the issues. In this recipe, we will introduce a couple of Redis Server metrics or statistics that you should keep an eye on when troubleshooting issues.

Getting ready...

You need to finish the installation of Redis Server as we described in the *Downloading and installing Redis* recipe in `Chapter 1`, *Getting Ready with Redis*.

How to do it...

The steps for health checking in Redis are as follows:

1. To get Redis metrics and statistics information, use the `INFO` command with the following section:

```
127.0.0.1:6379> INFO stats
# Stats
total_connections_received:1
total_commands_processed:18
instantaneous_ops_per_sec:0
total_net_input_bytes:671
total_net_output_bytes:13183
instantaneous_input_kbps:0.00
instantaneous_output_kbps:0.00
rejected_connections:0
sync_full:0
sync_partial_ok:0
sync_partial_err:0
expired_keys:0
evicted_keys:0
keyspace_hits:0
keyspace_misses:0
...
latest_fork_usec:415
...
127.0.0.1:6379> INFO clients
# Clients
```

```
connected_clients:1
client_longest_output_list:0
client_biggest_input_buf:0
blocked_clients:0
127.0.0.1:6379> INFO persistence
# Persistence
loading:0
rdb_changes_since_last_save:0
rdb_bgsave_in_progress:0
rdb_last_save_time:1514662415
rdb_last_bgsave_status:ok
rdb_last_bgsave_time_sec:-1
rdb_current_bgsave_time_sec:-1
rdb_last_cow_size:0
aof_enabled:0
aof_rewrite_in_progress:0
aof_rewrite_scheduled:0
aof_last_rewrite_time_sec:-1
aof_current_rewrite_time_sec:-1
aof_last_bgrewrite_status:ok
aof_last_write_status:ok
aof_last_cow_size:0
```

2. To monitor basic Redis statistics continuously, use `redis-cli --stat`:

```
$ bin/redis-cli --stat
------- data ------ -------------------- load -------------------- -
child -
keys      mem     clients blocked requests                  connections
680765    27.04G  541     0       60853686691 (+0)          2012384429
AO
680961    27.04G  541     0       60853687586 (+895)        2012384431
AOF
681162    27.04G  539     0       60853688521 (+935)        2012384433
AOF
681362    27.04G  539     0       60853689496 (+975)        2012384435
AOF
681549    27.04G  543     0       60853690312 (+816)        2012384442
AOF
...
```

How it works...

`INFO STATS` returns the general statistics information of the Redis Server. The metrics you should pay attention to are:

- `total_connections_received`: Total number of connections that are accepted by the server. If these metrics increase quickly in a short period of time, your Redis Server may suffer from high CPU usage.
- `instantaneous_ops_per_sec`: Number of commands processed per second.
- `rejected_connections`: Number of connections rejected because of the `maxclients` limit. If these metrics increase, you should pay special attention to your memory usage of Redis.
- `sync_full`: Number of times slaves have fully synchronized with this master.
- `sync_partial_ok`: Number of times partial synchronizations have completed.
- `sync_partial_err`: Number of times partial synchronizations failed to complete.
- `evicted_keys`: Number of evicted keys due to `maxmemory` limit.
- `keyspace_misses`: Number of failed lookup of keys in the main dictionary. If this metric is too high, you should consider optimizing your application to reduce the number of missing key queries.
- `latest_fork_usec`: Duration of the latest fork operation in microseconds.

In the `Clients` information section, you should monitor the following two metrics:

- `client_longest_output_list`: The longest output list among current client connections. You need be vigilant when the value of this metric becomes greater than 100,000.
- `client_biggest_input_buf`: The biggest input buffer among current client connections. Be cautious when the biggest input buffer size is more than 10MB.
- `blocked_clients`: Number of clients pending on a blocking call (`BLPOP`, `BRPOP`, `BRPOPLPUSH`).

In the persistence section, what you should be interested are `rdb_last_cow_size` and `aof_last_cow_size`, which are the **Copy-On-Write** (**COW**) buffer size of the last operation of `BGSAVE` (saving RDB dump) and `BGREWRITEAOF` (AOF rewrite).

We have introduced memory monitoring of Redis in `Chapter 9`, *Administrating Redis*. You should definitely watch for memory usage by Redis. Another thing people often forget to check is the disk usage and the disk quota of the Redis data directory. If the disk space is full, Redis is unable to save RDB or AOF dumps.

The `--stat` option of `redis-cli` prints out the basic server metrics in real time, so that you can get a big picture of what's happening with memory usage, clients connected, and so on. By default, it prints out a new line every second, but the interval can be specified by the `-i <interval>` option.

See also

- The official documentation for the `INFO` command:
  `https://redis.io/commands/info`

Identifying slow queries using the SLOWLOG

When there are performance issues in Redis, for example, queries to Redis get timed out frequently, we may want to check why Redis is not able to serve a query request in a timely fashion. One possible reason is that there are some queries or operations that take a very long time to complete.

In this recipe, we will introduce how to use the Redis SLOWLOG feature to identify slow queries or operations.

Getting ready...

You need to finish the installation of the Redis Server as we described in the *Downloading and installing Redis* recipe in `Chapter 1`, *Getting Started with Redis*.

How to do it...

1. For the purpose of demonstration, let's set `slowlog-log-slower-than` to a very small value:

```
127.0.0.1:6379> CONFIG SET slowlog-log-slower-than 5
```

2. Execute a couple of test commands:

```
127.0.0.1:6379> SET foo bar
OK
127.0.0.1:6379> HGETALL bighash
...
127.0.0.1:6379> HMSET new_hash aaa bbb ccc ddd eee fff
OK
```

3. To read all slow logs, use `SLOWLOG GET`:

```
127.0.0.1:6379> SLOWLOG GET
1) 1) (integer) 6
   2) (integer) 1514613453
   3) (integer) 6
   4) 1) "HMSET"
      2) "new_hash"
      3) "aaa"
      4) "bbb"
      5) "ccc"
      6) "ddd"
      7) "eee"
      8) "fff"
   5) "127.0.0.1:46142"
   6) ""
2) 1) (integer) 5
   2) (integer) 1514613413
   3) (integer) 5
   4) 1) "HGETALL"
      2) "bighash"
   5) "127.0.0.1:46142"
   6) ""
```

4. To get the number of records in the slow log, use `SLOWLOG LEN`:

```
127.0.0.1:6379> SLOWLOG LEN
(integer) 2
```

5. To clear all records, use SLOWLOG RESET:

```
127.0.0.1:6379> SLOWLOG RESET
OK
127.0.0.1:6379> SLOWLOG LEN
(integer) 0
```

How it works...

The Redis slow log is a feature that records queries or operations with an execution time that exceeded the threshold specified by slowlog-log-slower-than in microseconds.

In our preceding example, we set the threshold to five microseconds, which means that all queries or operations that take more than five microseconds will be recorded by the slow log. The default value of slowlog-log-slower-than is 10000 (10 milliseconds), a negative value of this option means disabling slow log, while setting the option to 0 will log all queries.

The recorded slow queries or operations are pushed into a FIFO queue, the maximum size of which can be specified by slowlog-max-len, with the default value of 128. SLOWLOG GET prints all records in the queue. Alternatively, you can use SLOWLOG GET N to get the most recent N records.

The slow log record queue is in memory only and never persisted to disk, therefore the slow log system is very fast.

In our preceding example, there are two slow log records. Each slow log record is composed of six fields (four fields for Redis versions before 4.0):

- A unique progressive identifier for every slow log entry
- The unix timestamp at which the logged command was processed
- The amount of time needed for its execution, in microseconds
- The array composing the arguments of the command
- Client IP address and port (4.0 only).
- Client name if set via the CLIENT SETNAME command (4.0 only)

There's more...

It is worth noting that the Redis slow log sub-system only considers the actual execution time of the command, because that is the time the server thread is blocked and unable to serve other requests. The disk I/O or network transmission time is not considered. It is possible that you see increased latency or timeouts on the application side, but cannot find any slow logs in Redis. In this case, the bottleneck is not the slow queries or operations, but other factors such as increased network latency.

See also

- The official documentation for the SLOWLOG command: https://redis.io/commands/slowlog

Troubleshooting latency issues

Redis is designed to serve a large number of queries at an extremely fast speed. In most scenarios, there is a strict requirement for the response time between a client and the Redis Server. Therefore, high latency becomes the most fatal problem for the Redis online service. In this recipe, we will see how to measure and detect the latency of Redis, and also give you several possible clues to where the latency issue happens.

Getting ready...

You need to finish setting up the replication of the Redis Server as we described in the *Setting up Redis replication* recipe in Chapter 5, *Replication*.

For demonstration purposes, we populate a large amount of data:

```
for i in `seq 10`
do
nohup node generator.js hash 1000000 session:${i} &
done
```

How to do it...

The first action is to do the baseline latency measurement:

1. Before you put the Redis service online, run an `intrinsic-latency` test on the host where the Redis Server is running:

```
$ bin/redis-cli --intrinsic-latency 60
Max latency so far: 1 microseconds.
Max latency so far: 8 microseconds.
Max latency so far: 21 microseconds.
Max latency so far: 29 microseconds.
Max latency so far: 38 microseconds.
Max latency so far: 39 microseconds.
Max latency so far: 40 microseconds.
Max latency so far: 44 microseconds.
Max latency so far: 56 microseconds.
1867256801 total runs (avg latency: 0.0321 microseconds / 32.13
nanoseconds per run).
Worst run took 1743x longer than the average latency.
```

2. Another form of latency you should measure before starting the Redis service is the network round-trip latency. Use the `redis-cli` tool with the `-latency` option to obtain this kind of latency:

```
redis@192.168.1.68:~> bin/redis-cli -h 192.168.1.7 --latency
min: 0, max: 27, avg: 0.23 (5180 samples)
```

3. After you put your Redis service online, you may want to be notified if your Redis is suffering from high latency. You can use the `--latency-history` and `-i` options of `redis-cli` to monitor the PING latency of your Redis Server. You can further use a `log` collector, such as Logstash or Flume, to collect the latency log for your alerting:

```
$ bin/redis-cli --latency-history -i 10 >>latency.log &
$ tail -n10 latency.log
0 1 0.14 334
0 1 0.15 335
0 1 0.15 336
0 1 0.15 337
0 1 0.14 338
0 1 0.14 339
0 1 0.15 340
0 1 0.15 341
0 1 0.15 342
```

After you get the alerts, you can first detect if the root cause of the latency came from the `slow` commands:

1. Check the command processing statistics using `INFO COMMANDSTATS`:

```
$ bin/redis-cli INFO COMMANDSTATS
# Commandstats
cmdstat_hmset:calls=10000000,usec=1018137090,usec_per_call=101.81
cmdstat_select:calls=10,usec=7,usec_per_call=0.70
cmdstat_dbsize:calls=7,usec=8,usec_per_call=1.14
cmdstat_info:calls=9,usec=307,usec_per_call=34.11
cmdstat_monitor:calls=2,usec=4,usec_per_call=2.00
cmdstat_config:calls=6,usec=38,usec_per_call=6.33
cmdstat_slowlog:calls=2,usec=51,usec_per_call=25.50
cmdstat_command:calls=4,usec=1012,usec_per_call=253.00
```

2. When Redis is running, monitor the `SLOWLOG` from time to time as described in the previous recipe:

```
127.0.0.1:6379> SLOWLOG GET 10
1) 1) (integer) 268
   2) (integer) 1514429456
   3) (integer) 12026
   4) 1) "HMSET"
      2) "session:4e8c04b5-43bd-4d70-8071-82cae9792228"
      3) "field_0"
      4) "ullamco"
      5) "field_1"
      6) "anim"
   5) "127.0.0.1:52644"
   6) ""
 . . .
```

Apart from the `slow` commands, the latency may be due to excessive CPU use:

1. Check the CPU usage of the `redis-server` process:

```
$ ps aux |head -1;ps aux |grep redis-server
USER        PID %CPU %MEM    VSZ    RSS TTY      STAT START   TIME
COMMAND
redis      8787 99.3  1.6 1104752 1069984 ?      RNsl 15:12   20:57
bin/redis-server 0.0.0.0:6379
```

2. Check the metric `total_connections_received`:

```
$ bin/redis-cli INFO STATS |grep total_connections_received
total_connections_received:380
```

Another factor which can lead to latency is the persistence of the Redis Server:

1. Check the time spent for last forking:

```
$ bin/redis-cli INFO |grep "fork"
latest_fork_usec:332096
```

2. Check if the metric `aof_delayed_fsync` is increasing and also check the metric `aof_pending_bio_fsync` to see if there is a pending `fsync` job for an AOF background rewrite:

```
$ bin/redis-cli INFO |grep aof_delayed_fsync
aof_delayed_fsync:31
$ bin/redis-cli INFO |grep aof_pending_bio_fsync
aof_pending_bio_fsync:1
```

3. Search the Redis running log to find out if there is a slow AOF `fsync`:

```
$ less log/redis.log
8787:M 29 Dec 11:41:54.942 * Asynchronous AOF fsync is taking too
long (disk is busy?). Writing the AOF buffer without waiting for
fsync to complete, this may slow down Redis.
$ sudo strace -p $(pidof redis-server) -f -T -tt -e fdatasync
[pid  8799] 11:42:00.549175 fdatasync(21 <unfinished ...>
[pid 12280] 11:42:00.578918 +++ exited with 0 +++
[pid  8787] 11:42:00.578941 --- SIGCHLD {si_signo=SIGCHLD,
si_code=CLD_EXITED, si_pid=12280, si_uid=10086, si_status=0,
si_utime=3454, si_stime=460} ---
[pid  8799] 11:42:00.631804 <... fdatasync resumed> ) = 0
<0.082599>
[pid  8787] 11:42:12.940408 --- SIGALRM {si_signo=SIGALRM,
si_code=SI_KERNEL} ---
[pid  8799] 11:42:12.941798 fdatasync(21) = 0 <0.023443>
[pid  8799] 11:42:13.042708 fdatasync(21) = 0 <0.065880>
[pid  8787] 11:42:16.827229 --- SIGALRM {si_signo=SIGALRM,
si_code=SI_KERNEL} ---
[pid  8799] 11:42:16.831017 fdatasync(21) = 0 <0.117848>
[pid  8799] 11:42:17.074308 fdatasync(21) = 0 <0.030427>
...
$ iostat 1
avg-cpu:  %user   %nice %system %iowait  %steal   %idle
          0.25    7.13   27.27   15.69    0.00   49.66
```

Device:	tps	kB_read/s	kB_wrtn/s	kB_read	kB_wrtn
nvme0n1 716		179.00	0.00	716.00	0
sda 122212		240.00	0.00	122212.00	0

 `strace` is the system call tracer for Linux. The performance overhead of `strace` is considerable; thus, it should be used with great caution in the production environment.

You should also check if the Redis instance used any swap space:

```
$ bin/redis-cli INFO|grep process_id
process_id:20116
$ awk '/VmSwap/{print $2 " " $3}' /proc/20116/status
0 kB
```

Finally, check the network utilization of the host using `dstat`:

```
$ dstat -nt
-net/total- ----system----
recv  send|     time
  0     0 |29-12 09:10:10
74k   179k|29-12 09:10:11
105k  235k|29-12 09:10:12
91k   209k|29-12 09:10:13
106k  238k|29-12 09:10:14
```

How it works...

Firstly, we performed a measurement of the baseline latency, including the system intrinsic latency and the network round-trip latency. The system intrinsic latency is a baseline by which we can determine the degree of latency for the system (not including the Redis instance latency). For the network latency, we started testing the client application's host to simulate the network conditions.

In our example, we have *0.26 (0.03+0.23) ms* latency as a baseline.

Later, we collected the latency metrics by `redis-cli` into a log. The result shows the `min`, `max`, and `average latency`, as well as the detection sequences of your Redis to respond to the `PING` command. You can index the content of the log into Elasticsearch for further analysis and alerting.

Once you catch something running slowly, you can follow the steps mentioned in the previous section to detect why the latency happened.

The first action we took is command latency detection using INFO COMMANDSTATS. This command gives us a brief idea of the request processing statistics. After that, we checked the slow log using the SLOWLOG command to see which command was processed slowly. If you see any problems in the aforementioned step, consider implementing your business logic with operations of less time complexity, or use a non-blocking operation such as SCAN or DEL.

Moving on, we checked the CPU utilization. Due to the single-threaded model of Redis, the main redis-server process is only able to utilize one core of the processor. So, if the ps command shows CPU utilization of the redis-server process is near 100%, it means the Redis instance has been overloaded. If there is a CPU processing bottleneck, you should pay attention to the Redis operations you called in your applications. Operations, such as sorting with a huge amount of data, may lead to CPU saturation issues, and a large number of connections to a Redis instance can cause the same issue. The next metric we checked is the total number of connections. If this metric is increasing dramatically in a short time, it indicates that some clients did not manage their connections to Redis properly. Frequent connections and disconnections may lead to a latency on both the client and the server side and also cause high CPU usage of the redis-server process. In this case, extreme caution must be taken in how your application manages the connections with the Redis Server.

Later, we checked if the persistence cost is the cause of the latency issue. The persistence mechanism of Redis may cause high disk I/O times. One is the forking latency. The RDB background saves and AOF rewrite operation will fork new processes and incur latency on the main process. A Redis Server with a big dataset (greater than 16GB) may suffer from high fork latency. Another one is slow AOF latency.

In our example, we can tell from the aof_delayed_fsync and aof_pending_bio_fsync metrics that the Redis Server has become slow due to the slow fsync call. Also, the Redis running log also indicated that the disk was slow for the AOF fsync operation. Another method for detecting these kinds of issues is to use strace to trace the fdatasync function. From the OS's point of view, we used the iostat command and found that there was an I/O wait, which is a signal of slow disk I/O.

In this case, you can set the configuration option `no-appendfsync-on-rewrite` to `yes` as a compromise. This guarantees the appended `fsync` operation will not be started if there is an ongoing rewriting process. However, no `fsync` means there is a possible risk of losing data if the `redis-server` process exits unexpectedly during background rewriting. If this option does not help too much, you may consider disabling the AOF or setting the option `appendfsync` to `none`.

Network congestion is another essential factor for Redis latency issues. We checked the network utilization with the tool `dstat` to see if the network is congested.

Lastly, we checked if the `redis-server` process used swap space. A process that needs swapping means it will be blocked by the kernel in order to wait for the movement of pages from swap space to memory.

There's more...

If you have checked all the preceding possible reasons for latency issues but still have no clue, you can turn to the help of the internal latency detection.

1. Use the `latency watchdog` to see what the call stacks looked like when the latency happened:

```
$ bin/redis-cli config set watchdog-period 500
OK
$ bin/redis-cli debug sleep 3
$ bin/redis-cli config set watchdog-period 0
OK
8787:signal-handler (1514447053)
--- WATCHDOG TIMER EXPIRED ---
EIP:
/lib/x86_64-linux-gnu/libc.so.6(+0x14e0eb) [0x7fe381eb40eb]
$ tail -n100 log/redis.log
...
Backtrace:
bin/redis-server 0.0.0.0:6379(logStackTrace+0x45) [0x46ab25]
bin/redis-server 0.0.0.0:6379(watchdogSignalHandler+0x1b) [0x46abfb]
/lib/x86_64-linux-gnu/libpthread.so.0(+0x11390) [0x7fe382141390]
/lib/x86_64-linux-gnu/libc.so.6(+0x14e0eb) [0x7fe381eb40eb]
bin/redis-server 0.0.0.0:6379(sdscatlen+0x59) [0x430869]
bin/redis-server 0.0.0.0:6379(feedAppendOnlyFile+0x373) [0x464863]
bin/redis-server 0.0.0.0:6379(propagate+0x5a) [0x42b86a]
bin/redis-server 0.0.0.0:6379(call+0x3c7) [0x42bd47]
bin/redis-server 0.0.0.0:6379(processCommand+0x3a7) [0x42c127]
```

```
bin/redis-server 0.0.0.0:6379(processInputBuffer+0x105) [0x43bc15]
bin/redis-server 0.0.0.0:6379(aeProcessEvents+0x13e) [0x42586e]
bin/redis-server 0.0.0.0:6379(aeMain+0x2b) [0x425c9b]
bin/redis-server 0.0.0.0:6379(main+0x4a6) [0x422866]
/lib/x86_64-linux-
gnu/libc.so.6(__libc_start_main+0xf0) [0x7fe381d86830]
bin/redis-server 0.0.0.0:6379(_start+0x29) [0x422b69]
8787:signal-handler (1514447053) --------
...
```

In this example, we can tell the function `feedAppendOnlyFile` is running slowly.
You can find this function in the source code of Redis.

2. Another latency detection framework you can use is the Redis `latency-monitor`:

```
127.0.0.1:6379> CONFIG SET latency-monitor-threshold 100
OK
127.0.0.1:6379> DEBUG SLEEP 1
OK
(1.00s)
127.0.0.1:6379> DEBUG SLEEP .25
OK
127.0.0.1:6379> LATENCY LATEST
1) 1) "command"
   2) (integer) 1514451674
   3) (integer) 250
   4) (integer) 1000
127.0.0.1:6379> KEYS session:1:*
127.0.0.1:6379> LATENCY LATEST
1) 1) "command"
   2) (integer) 1514510287
   3) (integer) 2445
   4) (integer) 26167
127.0.0.1:6379> LATENCY HISTORY command
1) 1) (integer) 1514451668
   2) (integer) 1000
2) 1) (integer) 1514451674
   2) (integer) 250
3) 1) (integer) 1514451721
   2) (integer) 26167
```

In this example, we turned on the internal watchdog by setting the latency threshold to 100 ms, slept for a while to wait for the information collection, and turned off the watchdog. The command LATENCY LATEST shows the latency event name, the UNIX timestamp when the latency event occurred, the latest event latency in milliseconds, and the all-time maximum latency for this event. The LATENCY HISTORY returns the latest 160 latency events that are being tracked.

The last thing to remember is that it is possible that the memory of your server has become slow due to some hardware failure that is not easy to find out. So, use a hardware testing tool to test your memory speed and it may give you some clue as to why your Redis instance is running slowly.

See also

- For a complete reference to Redis latency troubleshooting, you can refer to the official documents at: https://redis.io/topics/latency
- If you are interested in the Redis latency monitoring framework, you can refer to the official documents at: https://redis.io/topics/latency-monitor
- For how to use sysbench to test memory performance, you can refer to the following blog: http://tech.donghao.org/2016/11/30/using-sysbench-to-test-memory-performance/

Troubleshooting memory issues

As we mentioned at the beginning of this book, Redis is a memory-based, key-value data store. Therefore, apart from latency issues, memory utilization issues are another kind of fatal problem. In this recipe, we will see how to perform troubleshooting of memory issues in Redis.

Getting ready...

You need to finish setting up the replication of the Redis Server, as we described in the *Setting up Redis replication* recipe in Chapter 5, *Replication*.

How to do it...

You should make sure you are able to get alerted when the memory issues happen:

1. Firstly, watch out if the `used_memory_human` metric is greater than the metric `maxmemory_human`:

```
$ bin/redis-cli INFO MEMORY|egrep
"used_memory_human|maxmemory_human"
used_memory_human:1016.45M
maxmemory_human:1.00G
```

2. Test regularly to see if it's working properly by writing a simple key value pair into the Redis instance:

```
127.0.0.1:6379> SET foo bar
(error) OOM command not allowed when used memory > 'maxmemory'.
```

3. Take a note of when the metric `evicted_keys` has increased:

```
$ bin/redis-cli INFO Stats|grep evicted_keys
evicted_keys:382901
```

4. Next, check the system memory and swap space utilization of the `redis-server` process:

```
$ bin/redis-cli INFO MEMORY |grep used_memory_rss_human
used_memory_rss_human: 1.03G
$ bin/redis-cli INFO|grep process_id
process_id: 9909
$ awk '/VmSwap/{print $2 " " $3}' /proc/9909/status
0 kB
```

Once you think that there might be a memory issue in the Redis instance, check if the root cause of the issue is a big dataset or an abnormal internal memory usage:

```
$ bin/redis-cli INFO MEMORY  | egrep
"used_memory_dataset|used_memory_dataset_perc"
used_memory_dataset:980896614
used_memory_dataset_perc:91.43%
```

Perform the following actions to check dataset memory usage:

1. Search for the big keys in the Redis instance using `redis-cli` with the option `--bigkeys`:

```
$ bin/redis-cli --bigkeys
# Scanning the entire keyspace to find biggest keys as well as
# average sizes per key type.  You can use -i 0.1 to sleep 0.1 sec
# per 100 SCAN commands (not usually needed).
[00.00%] Biggest hash    found so far
'sessionB:1:a166b25c-6199-459f-843a-278a02303d61' with 5 fields
[00.00%] Biggest hash    found so far 'sessionB:5:ecd01063-
d25b-4335-8ebc-3fbbd5a63fae' with 6 fields
[00.00%] Biggest hash    found so far 'sessionB:10:ede50aa3-
ae13-4773-849c-22a0a1992f6d' with 7 fields
[00.00%] Biggest hash    found so far 'sessionB:8:87b7e610-
d756-45cc-b52e-2b19721adbc8' with 8 fields
[00.00%] Biggest hash    found so far
'sessionB:3:5399b960-3f77-40db-b0e1-1a66610ac669' with 9 fields
[00.01%] Biggest hash    found so far 'sessionB:8:311037ce-
a9ee-4a1c-b6c7-17cce52ebb0b' with 10 fields
```

2. Another way to find out the big keys is to use SCAN and DEBUG OBJECT/MEMORY USAGE commands iteratively:

```
$ cat scanbigkeys.sh
#!/bin/bash
BEGIN=0
TOPNUM=10
TMPFILE="/tmp/scan.out"
RESULTFILE="result.out"
> $RESULTFILE
bin/redis-cli --raw SCAN $BEGIN > $TMPFILE
while true
do
    for key in `sed '1d' $TMPFILE`
    do
        echo -n $key" " >> $RESULTFILE
        bin/redis-cli --raw DEBUG OBJECT $key | awk '{print $NF}' |
cut -d":" -f 2 >> $RESULTFILE
    done
    CURSOR=`head -n1 $TMPFILE`
    if [[ $CURSOR -eq $BEGIN ]]
    then
            echo "Scan ended!"
            echo "The Top $TOPNUM key in your Redis is"
            cat $RESULTFILE  | sort -nrk2  | head -n$TOPNUM
```

```
            exit
        fi
bin/redis-cli --raw SCAN $CURSOR > $TMPFILE
done

$ bash scanbigkeys.sh
Scan ended!
The Top 10 key in your Redis is
sessionB:1:c8b22ce6-1cc0-4d8c-8d44-ac8b2d5856a5 268
sessionB:1:c7df3b53-359d-4d02-aca6-33695f7c4463 268
sessionB:1:643e949f-6c83-4112-a722-67e0735a205e 268
sessionB:1:9fe5d654-dc4d-45db-bd62-64c16cf4332f 266
sessionB:1:864aa1a1-5a99-45cb-88c2-0921c2aa6df3 265
sessionB:1:eea29894-5061-4e6e-be0d-11977bfc4615 264
sessionB:1:71836c1c-032f-435d-901d-2ac976c9a354 263
sessionB:1:b9d8c5bf-e3cc-44f3-b3d9-d44152fb493f 262
sessionB:1:49a82365-5798-4726-aec4-d0136d4af422 262
sessionB:1:f966ef61-59fc-4d0f-adf2-05292524face 261
```

3. Generate a memory report with Redis RDB tools:

```
$ git clone https://github.com/sripathikrishnan/redis-rdb-tools
$ cd redis-rdb-tools
$ sudo python setup.py install
$ rdb -c memory dump.rdb --bytes 128 -f memory.csv
$ sort -t, -k4nr memory.csv | more
0,list,mylist,11149484,quicklist,2319,10000
0,hash,myset:000000020924,21036,hashtable,3,10000
0,hash,myset:000000000702,20844,hashtable,2,10000
...
```

Perform the following actions to check internal memory usage:

1. To simulate a query buffer memory issue, start the `redis-benchmark` tool:

```
$ bin/redis-benchmark -q -d 102400000 -n 10000000 -r 25000 -t set
```

2. Check the memory metrics and pay special attention to the metrics
`used_memory_human`, `used_memory_dataset`, `used_memory_overhead`, and
`used_memory_dataset_perc`:

```
$ bin/redis-cli INFO MEMORY
# Memory
used_memory:6005338152
used_memory_human:5.59G
used_memory_rss:6092353536
used_memory_rss_human:5.67G
```

```
used_memory_peak:6005338152
used_memory_peak_human:5.59G
used_memory_peak_perc:100.00%
used_memory_overhead:5122882822
used_memory_startup:765576
used_memory_dataset:882455330
used_memory_dataset_perc:14.70%
total_system_memory:67467202560
total_system_memory_human:62.83G
used_memory_lua:37888
used_memory_lua_human:37.00K
maxmemory:1073741824
maxmemory_human:1.00G
maxmemory_policy:noeviction
mem_fragmentation_ratio:1.01
mem_allocator:jemalloc-4.0.3
active_defrag_running:0
lazyfree_pending_objects:0
```

3. Check the client query buffer memory occupancy and test if we can write a simple key to the Redis instance:

```
$ bin/redis-cli client list | awk 'BEGIN{sum=0}
{sum+=substr($12,6);sum+=substr($13,11)}END{print sum}'
5120032868
$ bin/redis-cli set foo bar
(error) OOM command not allowed when used memory > 'maxmemory'.
```

4. To simulate a client output buffer memory issue, stop the redis-benchmark tool using *Ctrl + C* and change maxmemory-policy to allkeys-lru

5. Start redis-cli with the option monitor, redirect the output into a log file, and then start redis-benchmark again:

```
$ bin/redis-cli config set maxmemory-policy allkeys-lru
OK
$ nohup bin/redis-cli monitor  >monitor.log &
[1] 25778
$ for i in `seq 5`
do
 nohup  bin/redis-benchmark -P 4 -t lpush -r 5000000 -n 10000000 -d
100 &
done
```

6. Wait for a while and use the following commands to fetch the memory related metrics:

```
$ bin/redis-cli dbsize;bin/redis-cli INFO MEMORY; bin/redis-cli
INFO CLIENTS
(integer) 0
# Memory
used_memory:1073795088
used_memory_human:1.00G
used_memory_rss:1253953536
used_memory_rss_human:1.17G
used_memory_peak:1073795088
used_memory_peak_human:1.00G
used_memory_peak_perc:100.00%
used_memory_overhead:13222706
used_memory_startup:765576
used_memory_dataset:1060572382
used_memory_dataset_perc:98.84%
total_system_memory:67467202560
total_system_memory_human:62.83G
used_memory_lua:37888
used_memory_lua_human:37.00K
maxmemory:1073741824
maxmemory_human:1.00G
maxmemory_policy:allkeys-lru
mem_fragmentation_ratio:1.17
mem_allocator:jemalloc-4.0.3
active_defrag_running:0
lazyfree_pending_objects:0
# Clients
connected_clients:252
client_longest_output_list:32248
client_biggest_input_buf:0
blocked_clients:0
```

7. Obtain the top 10 client output buffers' memory and test if we can still write a simple key to the Redis instance:

```
$ bin/redis-cli CLIENT LIST | awk '{print substr($16,6),
$1,$16,$18}'| sort -nrk1,1 | cut -f1 -d" " --complement | head -n10
id=62 omem=527221432 cmd=monitor
id=999 omem=0 cmd=lpush
id=998 omem=0 cmd=lpush
id=997 omem=0 cmd=lpush
id=996 omem=0 cmd=lpush
id=995 omem=0 cmd=lpush
id=994 omem=0 cmd=lpush
```

```
id=993 omem=0 cmd=lpush
id=992 omem=0 cmd=lpush
id=991 omem=0 cmd=lpush
127.0.0.1:6379> set foo bar
(error) OOM command not allowed when used memory > 'maxmemory'.
```

8. For memory fragmentation cost issues, check if the memory fragmentation ratio is higher than 1.5:

```
$ bin/redis-cli INFO MEMORY|grep mem_fragmentation_ratio
mem_fragmentation_ratio:1.03
```

How it works...

Before we dive into how to troubleshoot the memory issue, we first pay attention to how Redis calculates memory and checks if there are any **out-of-memory** (**OOM**) problems.

Generally speaking, the memory of a Redis instance includes the following parts:

B.Client Query Buffer	C.Client Output Buffer	D.AOF Buffer + AOF Rewrite Buffer	E.Dataset related cost Memory	F. Replication backlog	G. Lua
A.Dataset Memory			H.Memory Fragmentation		
Redis RSS Memory					
Operating System Memory					

We won't go into the details of each part of the preceding diagram, as you can find their meanings in the recipes of the previous chapters. For Redis version 4.0.1, one portion of memory that desires your considerable attention is the client query buffer. The metric used_memory includes this portion of memory, however, it may be extended as the client query buffer grows. Thus, if the query buffer grows abnormally, you may find that the used_memory is much greater than maxmemory.

In this case, the keys' eviction would start if the memory policy is configured properly. Another thing worth mentioning is that the monitor client output buffer is not included in the `used_memory_overhead` metric returned by the command `INFO MEMORY`. However, it's included in the `used_memory` metric. So, even if there is no key in the Redis instance, the OOM problem may still happen if there is client output buffer abuse.

Bear the following two formulas in mind. The first one shows how Redis determines whether the OOM problem might happen:

```
used_memory - AOF_buffer_size - slave_output_buffer_size >= maxmemory
```

The second one shows how the `used_memory_overhead` is calculated:

```
used_memory_overhead = server_initial_memory_usage + repl_backlog +
slave_clients_output_buffer + normal_clients_output_buffer +
pubsub_clients_output_buffer + normal_clients_query_buffer +
clients_metadata + AOF Buffer + AOF rewrite BUffer
```

The OOM problem is the most common issue in Redis. As we described in the previous recipes, once an OOM problem happens, Redis will try to evict some keys according to the eviction policy. If the eviction policy is `noeviction`, new incoming writing operations will be denied and clients will get the OOM error message.

In the previous section, the first thing we mentioned is how to get alerted when a memory issue happens. We have four ways to monitor the abnormal memory usage. In the first two ways, we tried to confirm whether there is a risk that the size of dataset stored in the Redis instance is larger than the configuration option `maxmemory`. In the last two ways, we checked if the **Resident Set Size** (**RSS**) of the `redis-server` process has taken too much memory, so that the OS may begin using swap space or even intend to start the Linux OOM Killer to kill the process.

After we have confirmed there is a memory issue, the next thing we should do is figure out the root cause of the issue, be it a big dataset or abnormal internal memory. By checking the metrics `used_memory_dataset` and `used_memory_dataset_perc`, we can tell whether the root cause of a memory issue is the big dataset, if the `used_memory_dataset_perc` is bigger than 90%, or if the internal memory cost that leads to the memory issue.

The prime aim for the big dataset issue is to dig out the big keys in the Redis instance. The easiest way to perform the search is to use the `redis-cli` tool with the option `--bigkeys`. An alternative way is to take advantage of the commands `SCAN` and `DEBUG OBJECT`. Another way to analyze your dataset is to use the third-party Redis RDB tool. It parses the RDB file and generates a memory report.

For the internal memory cost of a Redis Server, things are a little bit complicated. We first checked if the cost came from the client query buffer. For demonstration purposes, we started a `redis-benchmark` tool to populate data, and the payload of each key was 100 MB, which could cause the client query buffer to grow quickly. We noticed the metric `used_memory_human` was much greater than the metric `maxmemory` and also the metric `used_memory_dataset_perc` was less than 20%. Next, we added up the query buffers of all the clients and found out they took up around 4.6 GB (512,0032,868 bytes) of Redis memory. At this time, we were unable to write a simple key-value pair into the Redis instance due to the OOM issue. In this case, it is advisable to stop your applications or kill the connections.

Moving on, we showed the monitor client output buffer memory issue. For the purpose of monitoring, sometimes we can start the `redis-cli` tool with the monitor option. Sometimes, we may forget to stop the monitor process after the monitor data collection is done. We simulated such a situation by redirecting the output of `redis-cli monitor` into a log file. Under heavy traffic, the output buffer of the monitor client could take up a lot of memory of the Redis Server.

In our example, even though there is no key in the Redis instance (the only key in the testing was evicted due to the limited memory and the eviction policy), the OOM problem still came out. By checking the clients list, we can tell the root cause of this is the monitor's output buffer memory overhead. It should be noted that this kind of overhead is not included in the metric `used_memory_overhead`. To fix this issue, just stop or kill the monitor client.

Lastly, sometimes, due to the high frequency writing and deleting of keys, Redis may leave some memory fragments in its RSS memory. So, tracking the fragmentation ratio is important. If you find your memory fragmentation ratio is greater than 1.5, you can issue the command MEMORY PURGE to free up some memory fragments. If it doesn't help much, you have to fail over your Redis instance and plan a restart to release the memory fragments completely.

There's more...

In the previous section, we mentioned that, at the time of writing, for Redis 4.0.1, monitoring client output buffer memory usage is not included in the metric `used_memory_overhead`. There is a pull request to fix this. You can refer to issue #4502 in the Redis repository on GitHub.

See also

- There are quite a lot of things you could do to perform memory optimization of Redis. You can refer to these documents provided by the author of Redis at `https://redis.io/topics/memory-optimization`.
- You can find many tips for memory optimization at `https://github.com/sripathikrishnan/redis-rdb-tools/wiki/Redis-Memory-Optimization`.
- For RDB tools, you can refer to `https://github.com/sripathikrishnan/redis-rdb-tools`.
- Another popular memory analyzer is Redis Memory Analyzer `https://github.com/gamenet/redis-memory-analyzer`.

Troubleshooting crash issues

In rare cases, Redis may crash when it hits a bug. There are many things you can do when the Redis instance crashes. In this recipe, we will see how to perform troubleshooting of crash issues in Redis.

Getting ready...

You need to finish setting up the replication of the Redis Server, as we described in the *Setting up Redis replication* recipe in `Chapter 5`, *Replication*.

How to do it...

The steps for troubleshooting crash issues are as follows:

1. Simulate the crash using the `DEBUG SEGFAULT` command:

```
$ bin/redis-cli DEBUG SEGFAULT
Error: Server closed the connection
```

2. Check the log of the Redis instance after it crashes:

```
=== REDIS BUG REPORT START: Cut & paste starting from here ===
1710:M 07 Jan 20:58:01.324 # Redis 4.0.1 crashed by signal: 11
1710:M 07 Jan 20:58:01.324 # Crashed running the instruction at:
0x469cd0
1710:M 07 Jan 20:58:01.324 # Accessing address: 0xffffffffffffffff
1710:M 07 Jan 20:58:01.324 # Failed assertion: <no assertion
failed> (<no file>:0)
------ STACK TRACE ------
EIP:
bin/redis-server 0.0.0.0:6379(debugCommand+0x250)[0x469cd0]
Backtrace:
bin/redis-server 0.0.0.0:6379(logStackTrace+0x45)[0x46ab25]
. . .
bin/redis-server 0.0.0.0:6379(_start+0x29)[0x422b69]
------ INFO OUTPUT ------
# Server
redis_version:4.0.1
redis_git_sha1:00000000
redis_git_dirty:0
. . .
# Keyspace
------ CLIENT LIST OUTPUT ------
. . .
------ CURRENT CLIENT INFO ------
. . . .
------ REGISTERS ------
1710:M 07 Jan 20:58:01.344 #
RAX:0000000000000000 RBX:00007f16e9aaaa40
. . .
------ DUMPING CODE AROUND EIP ------
Symbol: debugCommand (base: 0x469a80)
. . .
=== REDIS BUG REPORT END. Make sure to include from START to END.
===
              Please report the crash by opening an issue on github:
                   http://github.com/antirez/redis/issues
          Suspect RAM error? Use redis-server --test-memory to verify
it.
```

3. If you are able to reproduce the crash, using the **GNU Project Debugger** (**GDB**) in your testing environment to debug the redis-server process can be a big help to learn what happened when the Redis instance crashed:

   First, we get the process ID of the redis-server:

   ```
   $ bin/redis-cli info | grep process_id
   process_id: 11239
   ```

4. Open another Terminal and then attach to the process using gdb:

   ```
   $ gdb /redis/bin/redis-server 11239
   GNU gdb (Ubuntu 7.11.1-0ubuntu1~16.5) 7.11.1
    . . .
   Reading symbols from /redis/bin/redis-server...done.
   Attaching to program: /redis/bin/redis-server, process 9611
   [New LWP 9612]
   [New LWP 9613]
   [New LWP 9614]
   [Thread debugging using libthread_db enabled]
   Using host libthread_db library "/lib/x86_64-linux-
   gnu/libthread_db.so.1".
   0x00007f0eddeed9d3 in epoll_wait () at ../sysdeps/unix/syscall-
   template.S:84
   84 ../sysdeps/unix/syscall-template.S: No such file or directory.
   ```

5. Make the process run continuously:

   ```
   (gdb) continue
   Continuing.
   ```

6. Crash the Redis instance and the segmentation fault log will be printed by the GDB:

   ```
   $ bin/redis-cli DEBUG SEGFAULT
   (gdb) c
   Continuing.
   Thread 1 "redis-server" received signal SIGSEGV, Segmentation
   fault.
   debugCommand (c=0x7f9e0b1b4200) at debug.c:313
   313                 *((char*)-1) = 'x';
   ```

7. Obtain the backtrace and processor registers information:

```
(gdb) bt
#0   debugCommand (c=0x7f9e0b1b4200) at debug.c:313
#1   0x000000000042ba26 in call (c=c@entry=0x7f9e0b1b4200,
flags=flags@entry=15) at server.c:2199
#2   0x000000000042c127 in processCommand (c=0x7f9e0b1b4200) at
server.c:2479
...

#5   0x0000000000425c9b in aeMain (eventLoop=0x7f9e14a36050) at
ae.c:464
#6   0x0000000000422866 in main (argc=<optimized out>,
argv=0x7ffd03cc8978) at server.c:3844
(gdb) info registers
rax            0x0          0
rbx            0x7f9e0b1b4200     140316767896064
...
gs             0x0          0
```

8. Check the value of a variable:

```
(gdb) p /s   (char*)c->argv[0]->ptr
$15 = 0x7f9e0b756e13 "DEBUG"
(gdb) p /s   (char*)c->argv[1]->ptr
$16 = 0x7f9e0b756e33 "SEGFAULT"
(gdb) p server
$1 = {pid = 11239, configfile = 0x7f9e14a1c093
"/redis/conf/redis.conf", executable = 0x7f9e14a2f003
"/redis/bin/redis-server",
   exec_argv = 0x7f9e14a21cd0, hz = 10, db = 0x7f9e14b4a000,
commands = 0x7f9e14a18060, orig_commands = 0x7f9e14a180c0,
   el = 0x7f9e14a36050, lruclock = 5383977, shutdown_asap = 0,
activerehashing = 1, active_defrag_running = 0, requirepass = 0x0,
   latency_events = 0x7f9e14a1a280, assert_failed = 0x506e30 "<no
assertion failed>", assert_file = 0x506e46 "<no file>",
   assert_line = 0, bug_report_start = 0, watchdog_period = 0,
system_memory_size = 67467202560, lruclock_mutex = {__data = {
            __lock = 0, __count = 0, __owner = 0, __nusers = 0,
__kind = 0, __spins = 0, __elision = 0, __list = {__prev = 0x0,
            __next = 0x0}}, __size = '\000' <repeats 39 times>,
__align = 0}, next_client_id_mutex = {__data = {__lock = 0,
            __count = 0, __owner = 0, __nusers = 0, __kind = 0,
__spins = 0, __elision = 0, __list = {__prev = 0x0, __next = 0x0}},
          __size = '\000' <repeats 39 times>, __align = 0},
unixtime_mutex = {__data = {__lock = 0, __count = 0, __owner = 0,
```

```
        __nusers = 0, __kind = 0, __spins = 0, __elision = 0,
   __list = {__prev = 0x0, __next = 0x0}},
        __size = '\000' <repeats 39 times>, __align = 0}}
```

9. Generate the `core` file:

```
(gdb) gcore
Saved corefile core.11239
```

10. Finally, quit `gdb`:

```
(gdb) q
A debugging session is active.
        Inferior 1 [process 11239] will be detached.
Quit anyway? (y or n) y
Detaching from program: /redis/bin/redis-server, process 11239
```

You can also send the logs and the core file to the author of Redis by emailing antirez@gmail.com.

How it works...

In the first step, we triggered a segmentation fault in the Redis instance using the command `DBBUG SEGFAULT`. The instance crashed immediately. It can be seen clearly from the running log of the Redis instance that the process has crashed and all the information, including the stack trace, the output of the `INFO` command, the clients' information, and the registers have been logged in the log file. If the crash can be reproduced, we could use GDB to attach to the Redis process for further debugging. Take note; you always perform debugging in your testing environment. After the GDB is attached to the `redis-server` process, just use the command `c` to let the Redis process continue running. For demonstration purposes, we crashed the Redis instance again using the `DEBUG SEGFAULT` command. The GDB caught the segmentation fault and printed out the message. We inspected the stack trace using the `bt` command of GDB and we took a look at the register information using teh `info registers` command. By checking the source code of Redis, we could also get the important variable's value using the `p` command of GDB. Finally, we generated a core file for further debugging and exited from the GDB using `q`.

Due to the limitations of the book, we won't go into the details of debugging. At this time, sending the core file and other information to the author of Redis is a good idea. You can also create an issue on GitHub if you believe you have found a real problem.

See also

- You can learn more about GDB at: `https://www.gnu.org/s/gdb/documentation`
- You can find out many details of Redis debugging at: `https://redis.io/topics/debugging`
- The author of Redis talked a lot about Redis debugging on his blog: `http://antirez.com/news/43`

11
Extending Redis with Redis Modules

In this chapter, we will cover the following recipes:

- Loading a Redis module
- Writing a Redis module

Introduction

Although Redis supports a good number of data types and great features, sometimes we may wish to add our own custom data types or commands to Redis. In Chapter 3, *Data Features*, we have learned that Lua scripts can be used to implement our customized logic on top of Redis built-in data types and commands. Additionally, starting from Redis 4.0, we can also extend Redis capabilities with Redis modules.

Redis modules are shared C libraries that can be loaded by the Redis server at startup or runtime. Redis modules have the following advantages over Lua scripts:

- As C libraries, Redis modules run much faster than Lua scripts
- New data structures can be created in Redis modules, while in Lua scripts we can only use existing Redis data types
- Commands created in Redis modules can be called from a client directly as if they were native commands, while Lua scripts have to be called with EVAL or EVALSHA

- Third-party libraries can be linked into Redis Modules, while what we can do in Lua scripts is very limited
- The APIs we can use in Redis modules are much richer than the APIs exposed to Lua scripts

In this chapter, we will first introduce how to load an existing Redis module and, then, we will show how to write a simple Redis module with the Redis module API.

Loading a Redis module

There are a lot of open-source Redis modules that can be used to extend Redis functionality. In this recipe, we will see how to load a module on Redis Server. We will load the ReJSON module, which adds JSON data type support to Redis.

Getting ready...

You need to finish the installation of the Redis Server, as we described in the *Downloading and installing Redis* recipe in Chapter 1, *Getting Started with Redis*.

How to do it...

The steps for loading a Redis module are as follows

1. Download the source code of ReJSON from GitHub:

```
$ git clone https://github.com/RedisLabsModules/rejson.git
Cloning into 'rejson'...
remote: Counting objects: 2066, done.
remote: Compressing objects: 100% (64/64), done.
remote: Total 2066 (delta 52), reused 83 (delta 43), pack-reused 1952
Receiving objects: 100% (2066/2066), 3.68 MiB | 0 bytes/s, done.
Resolving deltas: 100% (1114/1114), done.
Checking connectivity... done.
```

2. Go to the module source code directory and compile the module by running `make`:

```
$ cd rejson/src
~/rejson/src$ make
```

The module binary file will be generated as `rejson.so`:

```
~/rejson/src$ ls -l rejson.so
-rwxrwxr-x 1 user user 455888 Dec 29 17:56 rejson.so
```

3. To load a module in `redis-cli`, use the `MODULE LOAD` command with the path to the module binary:

```
127.0.0.1:6379> MODULE LOAD /redis/rejson/src/rejson.so
OK
```

4. Test if the module is loaded:

```
127.0.0.1:6379> JSON.SET jsonKey . '{"foo": "bar", "baz": ["aaa",
"bbb"]}'
OK
127.0.0.1:6379> JSON.GET jsonKey
"{\"foo\":\"bar\",\"baz\":[\"aaa\",\"bbb\"]}"
```

5. To unload a module, use the `MODULE UNLOAD` command with the module name:

```
127.0.0.1:6379> MODULE UNLOAD ReJSON
(error) ERR Error unloading module: the module exports one or more
module-side data types, can't unload
```

6. To list all loaded modules, use `MODULE LIST`:

```
127.0.0.1:6379> MODULE LIST
1) 1) "name"
   2) "ReJSON"
   3) "ver"
   4) (integer) 10001
```

7. Redis modules can also be loaded in a configuration file with the `loadmodule` directive:

```
loadmodule /redis/rejson/src/rejson.so
```

How it works...

Loading a Redis module is quite simple; when a module has been successfully loaded, we can also see it from Redis Server logs:

```
1960:M 29 Dec 18:31:07.403 # <ReJSON> JSON data type for Redis v1.0.1
[encver 0]
1960:M 29 Dec 18:31:07.403 * Module 'ReJSON' loaded from
/redis/rejson/src/rejson.so
```

The `MODULE UNLOAD` command takes the module name instead of the module library file path and it is good practice to keep the module library filename the same as the module name.

In the preceding example, since the `ReJSON` module created a new data type, it could not be unloaded at runtime. If a module is loaded by the `MODULE LOAD` command, it will be unloaded automatically when the server stops.

See also

- Here is a list of Redis modules that you can load and play with: `https://redis.io/modules`
- Redis modules Hub: `http://redismodules.com/`
- For more details about the Redis module, you can refer to the Redis module introduction at `https://redis.io/topics/modules-intro`

Writing a Redis module

Redis provides extensive C APIs for users to write a module. While Redis modules can be written in any language that has C binding functionalities, writing a Redis module in C language is the easiest and most straightforward method.

In this recipe, we are going to implement a Redis module, `MYMODULE`, in C language with a new command `ZIP`, which can be called as follows:

```
MYMODULE.ZIP destination_hash field_list value_list
```

The command takes two Redis lists and tries to create a Redis hash, whose fields are elements in `field_list` and corresponding values are elements of the same index in `value_list`.

For example, if `field_list` is `["john", "alex", "tom"]` and `value_list` is `["20", "30", "40"]`, `destination_hash` will be `{"john": "20", "alex": "30", "tom": 40}`. If the lengths of the two lists are not equal, the longer list will be truncated to the same length of the shorter one before creating the hash (the list itself will not change after that). If there are duplicate elements in `field_list`, the corresponding value of the right-most index will be kept in the hash. The command returns the length of the created hash.

Getting ready...

You need to finish the installation of the Redis Server, as we described in the *Downloading and installing Redis* recipe in `Chapter 1`, *Getting Started with Redis*.

How to do it...

The steps for writing a Redis module are as follows:

1. Create a `mymodule.c` file and include the header file, `redismodule.h`:

   ```
   #include "redismodule.h"
   ```

2. Create a `RedisModule_OnLoad()` function:

   ```
   int RedisModule_OnLoad(RedisModuleCtx *ctx, RedisModuleString
   **argv, int argc) {
      if (RedisModule_Init(ctx, "mymodule", 1, REDISMODULE_APIVER_1) ==
   REDISMODULE_ERR) {
         return REDISMODULE_ERR;
      }

      if (RedisModule_CreateCommand(ctx, "mymodule.zip", MyModule_Zip,
   "write deny-oom no-cluster", 1, 1, 1) == REDISMODULE_ERR) {
         return REDISMODULE_ERR;
      }

      return REDISMODULE_OK;
   }
   ```

3. Create a `MyModule_Zip()` function, which is the handler function of our new command:

```
int MyModule_Zip(RedisModuleCtx *ctx, RedisModuleString **argv, int
argc) {
  // MYMODULE.ZIP destination field_list value_list
  if (argc != 4) {
    return RedisModule_WrongArity(ctx);
  }
  RedisModule_AutoMemory(ctx);
  // Open field/value list keys
  RedisModuleKey *fieldListKey = RedisModule_OpenKey(ctx, argv[2],
REDISMODULE_READ | REDISMODULE_WRITE);
  RedisModuleKey *valueListKey = RedisModule_OpenKey(ctx, argv[3],
REDISMODULE_READ | REDISMODULE_WRITE);
  if ((RedisModule_KeyType(fieldListKey) !=
REDISMODULE_KEYTYPE_LIST &&
      RedisModule_KeyType(fieldListKey) !=
REDISMODULE_KEYTYPE_EMPTY) ||
      (RedisModule_KeyType(valueListKey) !=
REDISMODULE_KEYTYPE_LIST &&
      RedisModule_KeyType(valueListKey) !=
REDISMODULE_KEYTYPE_EMPTY)) {
    return RedisModule_ReplyWithError(ctx,
REDISMODULE_ERRORMSG_WRONGTYPE);
  }
  // Open destination key
  RedisModuleKey *destinationKey = RedisModule_OpenKey(ctx,
argv[1], REDISMODULE_WRITE);
  RedisModule_DeleteKey(destinationKey);
  //Get length of lists
  size_t fieldListLen = RedisModule_ValueLength(fieldListKey);
  size_t valueListLen = RedisModule_ValueLength(valueListKey);
  if (fieldListLen == 0 || valueListLen == 0) {
    RedisModule_ReplyWithLongLong(ctx, 0L);
    return REDISMODULE_OK;
  }
  size_t fCount = 0;
  size_t vCount = 0;
  while (fCount < fieldListLen && vCount < valueListLen) {
    //Pop from left and push back to right
    RedisModuleString *key = ListLPopRPush(fieldListKey);
    RedisModuleString *value = ListLPopRPush(valueListKey);
    //Set hash
    RedisModule_HashSet(destinationKey, REDISMODULE_HASH_NONE, key,
value, NULL);
    fCount++;
```

```
      vCount++;
    }
    while (fCount++ < fieldListLen) {
      ListLPopRPush(fieldListKey);
    }
    while (vCount++ < valueListLen) {
      ListLPopRPush(valueListKey);
    }
    //Get hash length
    RedisModuleCallReply *hlenReply = RedisModule_Call(ctx, "HLEN",
"s", argv[1]);
    if (hlenReply == NULL) {
      return RedisModule_ReplyWithError(ctx, "Failed to call HLEN");
    } else if (RedisModule_CallReplyType(hlenReply) ==
REDISMODULE_REPLY_ERROR) {
      RedisModule_ReplyWithCallReply(ctx, hlenReply);
      return REDISMODULE_ERR;
    }
    RedisModule_ReplyWithLongLong(ctx,
RedisModule_CallReplyInteger(hlenReply));
    RedisModule_ReplicateVerbatim(ctx);
    return REDISMODULE_OK;
}
```

4. Create a `ListLPopRPush()` function to read elements from a list.
   `ListLPopRPush()` and `MyModule_Zip()` should be placed before
   `RedisModule_OnLoad()`, or they have to be declared at the beginning of the file:

   ```
   static RedisModuleString *ListLPopRPush(RedisModuleKey *ListKey) {
     RedisModuleString *value = RedisModule_ListPop(ListKey,
   REDISMODULE_LIST_HEAD);
     RedisModule_ListPush(ListKey, REDISMODULE_LIST_TAIL, value);
     return value;
   }
   ```

5. Copy `redismodule.h` from the Redis source code package to the same directory
   of `mymodule.c` and compile it with `gcc`:

   gcc -fPIC -shared -std=gnu99 -o mymodule.so mymodule.c

6. Now, copy the generated module library file to a convenient location (such
   as `/redis`) and load our module in Redis:

   127.0.0.1:6379> MODULE LOAD /redis/mymodule.so
   OK

7. Let's try out the new command:

```
127.0.0.1:6379> RPUSH fields john alex tom
(integer) 3
127.0.0.1:6379> RPUSH values 20 30 40
(integer) 4
127.0.0.1:6379> MYMODULE.ZIP myhash fields values
(integer) 3
127.0.0.1:6379> HGETALL myhash
1) "john"
2) "20"
3) "alex"
4) "30"
5) "tom"
6) "40"
```

How it works...

The `RedisModule_OnLoad()` function is called when a module is loaded in Redis. It must be implemented in every Redis module as it is the entry-point. Usually, we need to initialize the module first with the API `RedisModule_Init()` and specify the module name, version, and API version. Redis modules are designed to be agnostic of Redis Server versions, but they have to be compliant with an API version. That is, a module does not need to be recompiled in order to be loaded in a different version of Redis Server, as long as the server knows which API version the module is using. The current Redis module API version is 1 (`REDISMODULE_APIVER_1`). We also need to create commands for the module, which is done by the function `RedisModule_CreateCommand()`, in which we pass the command name, the pointer to the command handler, and a string of flags that specify the command behavior. In our command `MYMODULE.ZIP`, the command handler is implemented in the function `MyModule_Zip()`. The command may modify a Redis dataset and request new memory space that may incur **Out Of Memory** (**OOM**); it does not support Redis clusters. The full list of flags can be found in the API reference. The last three parameters of `RedisModule_CreateCommand()` denote first key index, last key index, and key step of the command. As our command has only one key (for the destination hash), we just pass (`1, 1, 1`). If you are creating a command such as `MSET` (`MSET key value [key value]...`), (`1, -1, 1`) should be used, as `MSET` takes infinite keys (last key index = -1). The return value of `RedisModule_OnLoad()` should be `REDISMODULE_OK` unless there are errors.

The command handler function `MyModule_Zip()` takes three arguments-module context, command argument vector, and the number of command arguments. As you may notice, almost every Redis module API takes the module context as the first argument. The context is used to get a reference to the module itself, like its commands, clients that are calling commands, and so on. This context will be passed by other module APIs, and the argument vector will be passed by a client who is calling the command.

Inside the function, first of all, we check the number of command arguments is correct. As the command is designed to take three arguments (`destination_hash`, `field_list`, `value_list`) including the command itself, the number of command arguments should be 4. We then ask Redis to automatically manage the resource and memory in our command handler. This is done by simply calling `RedisModule_AutoMemory(ctx)`.

Next, we start accessing Redis keys, which, in our example, are two Redis lists. Redis provides two sets of APIs for Redis modules to access the Redis data space. The low-level API can access Redis keys and manipulate data structures very fast. The high-level API enables the module code to call Redis commands and fetch the result, which is very similar to how Lua scripts access the Redis data space. In our example, we use a low-level API `RedisModule_OpenKey()` to open two input lists and the destination hash. This API returns a pointer to `RedisModuleKey`, which is a handler of the Redis key. We then check the key type by using `RedisModule_KeyType()` to make sure the inputs are lists or empty.

The next step consists of looping through two lists and assigning values to the hash. Here, we create a helper function `ListLPopRPush()` to read elements from a list. The function pops an element from the left end and then pushes it back to the right end of the list, returning the element value to the caller. We use `RedisModule_ValueLength()` to get the length of each list and `RedisModule_HashSet()` to set values in the destination hash. The iteration stops when we have read all the elements in one of the lists, but we still need to pop and push the remaining elements from the other list, which might be longer, in order to make the two lists unchanged.

As the command needs to return the length of the created hash, here we use `RedisModule_Call()` to call Redis command `HLEN`. `RedisModule_Call()` can be used to call any Redis command and the result will be returned as a pointer to `RedisModuleCallReply`. `RedisModule_CallReplyInteger()` returns the result value as an integer, which is then passed into `RedisModule_ReplyWithLongLong()` and returned to the caller of our command.

RedisModule_Call() takes a variable length of parameters. The first parameter is the module context and the second parameter is a null-terminated C string with the command name. The third parameter is a format specifier for the command arguments, as the arguments may originate from different kinds of strings-null-terminated C strings, RedisModuleString objects as received from the argv parameter in the command implementation, and so on. In our example, the argument for HLEN is from a RedisModuleString as received in argv, so we just put s in the format specifier. The rest of the parameters are the command arguments.

Here is the full list of format specifiers:

- c --: Null terminated C string pointer.
- b --: C buffer, two arguments needed-C string pointer, and size_t length.
- s --: RedisModuleString as received in argv or by other Redis module APIs returning a RedisModuleString object.
- l --: Long integer.
- v --: Array of RedisModuleString objects.
- ! --: This modifier just tells the function to replicate the command to slaves and AOF. It is ignored from the point of view of arguments parsing.

RedisModule_ReplicateVerbatim(ctx) means our command verbatim will be propagated to Redis replicas.

For example, if we execute MYMODULE.ZIP myhash field values on a Redis master, its slaves will receive the command verbatim as the same.

There's more...

You may have noticed that RedisModule_OnLoad() also takes an argument vector and the number of arguments. These are arguments for the module, which can be specified when loading the module, such as MODULE LOAD mymodule arg1 arg2 arg3. It is useful when you want your module to behave differently by passing different parameters.

See also

- For a complete reference of the Redis module API, check out: `https://redis.io/topics/modules-api-ref`
- The official introduction of the Redis module API: `https://redis.io/topics/modules-intro`
- Writing Redis modules by Dvir Volk: `https://redislabs.com/blog/writing-redis-modules/`
- There is a library called `RedisModuleSDK` that adds a couple of utility functions and macros for Redis module developers: `https://github.com/RedisLabs/RedisModulesSDK`

12
The Redis Ecosystem

In this chapter, we will cover the following recipes:

- The Redisson client
- Twemproxy
- Codis – a proxy-based high-performance Redis Cluster solution
- The CacheCloud Redis management system
- Pika – a Redis-compatible NoSQL database

Introduction

As Redis has become mature open source software, that has earned a great adoption rate in the database world. There are a lot of other open source projects that are based on Redis. This chapter will introduce some of the popular projects in the Redis ecosystem.

Redisson client is a Redis Java client with extended features. It reduces the developers' load of implementing distributed objects and services, by using Redis as the storage backend.

Twemproxy, developed by Twitter, is a proxy that supports both Redis and memcached protocol. It is often used as a Redis data sharding solution, which can also reduce the number of connections to the backend Redis Servers.

Similar to Twemproxy, Codis is another centralized Redis high-performance proxy. By routing the requests to Redis instances behind the proxy, Codis provides an easy-to-use and production-ready Redis sharding solution without the developers' extra effort.

Managing a massive number of Redis instances can be a big headache. The project CacheCloud developed by Sohu TV comes into play. From new Redis instance deployments to online Redis instance monitoring, CacheCloud offers you an out-of-the -box online administration solution for almost all Redis operations.

Although the cost of physical memory has decreased dramatically in recent years, it is possible to save costs by using solid state drives as Redis data storage backend. The project Pika from Qihoo 360 is a Redis interface-compatible storage service, which implements this idea.

The Redisson client

Redisson is an enhanced Redis Java client, which provides a more convenient and easier way to work with Redis. Redisson offers a series of distributed objects and services, which simplifies the design and implementation of large distributed systems with Redis.

The following diagram shows an excerpt of Redisson features:

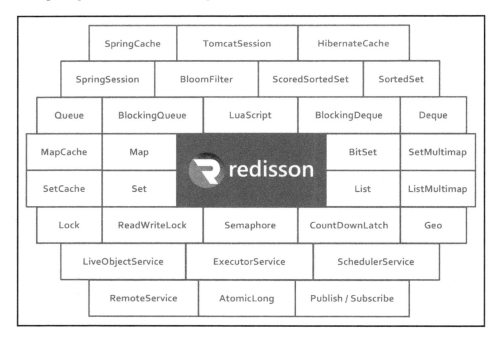

Redisson is based on the Netty framework in Java NIO. Not only can it be used as an extended Redis client on the database driver layer, it also provides more advanced features. Native Redis data types such as `hash`, `list`, `set`, `string`, `Geo`, and `HyperLogLog` are encapsulated into easy-to-use Java data structures or objects (`Map`, `List`, `Set`, `Object Bucket`, `Geospatial Bucket`, and `HyperLogLog`).

In addition, Redisson includes distributed data types such as Multimap, LocalCachedMap, and SortedSet. The Distributed lock, MultiLock, ReadWriteLock, FairLock, RedLock, Semaphore, and CountDownLatch objects are also implemented in the Redisson library. In short, Redisson is a useful library in building distributed systems with Redis.

With the distributed environment tools inside the Redisson library, Redisson also provides distributed services such as Remote Service, Executor Service, and Scheduler Service, for different use cases.

Redisson can also be viewed as an in-memory data grid. Redisson node, which is an independent task processing node, can be run as a system service and join a Redisson Cluster automatically.

Redisson aims to achieve separation of concerns for Redis users; therefore, developers can keep the focus on data modeling and application logic. It is easy to migrate to Redisson from other Redis Clients with the help of the Redisson *Redis commands mapping* table.

See also

- For more information about Redisson, you can refer to its GitHub page at
  `https://github.com/redisson/redisson`
- Redis command mapping table for Redisson client migration is available at
  `https://github.com/redisson/redisson/wiki/11.-Redis-commands-mapping`

Twemproxy

Twemproxy, also known as the **nutcracker**, is a fast and lightweight Redis proxy developed by Twitter. The purpose of this project is to provide a proxy and data sharding solution for Redis and to reduce the number of client connections to the backend Redis Servers.

As a proxy, Twemproxy supports both Redis and Memcached protocols. You could set up multiple Redis servers behind Twemproxy. Clients only talk to the proxy and do not need to know the details of backend Redis instances.

The following diagram shows the basic architecture of how **Twemproxy** works in the environment of multiple **Redis** instances:

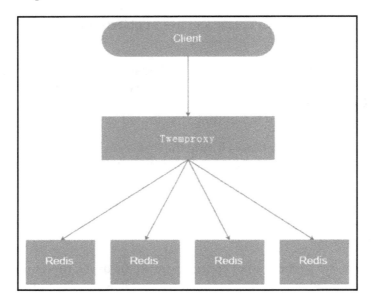

Twemproxy is able to shard data automatically across configured backend Redis instances. It supports multiple hashing modes. With consistent hashing supported, you can set up a reliable sharded Redis easily, using Twemproxy.

Twemproxy can be also configured to disable backend nodes on failure and retry after some time.

Using Twemproxy does not mean there is a single node failure problem. You can actually run multiple Twemproxy instances for the same group of backend Redis servers to prevent this problem.

Twemproxy does have limitations. It does not support all Redis commands. For example, PUB/SUB and transaction commands are not supported. In addition, adding or removing backend Redis nodes for Twemproxy is not convenient. First, the configurations will not be effective without restarting Twemproxy. Second, although consistent hashing is supported in Twemproxy, data won't be rebalanced automatically after adding or removing Redis nodes.

See also

- For more information about Twemproxy, you can refer to its GitHub page at `https://github.com/twitter/twemproxy`
- Refer to this page for all Redis commands supported in Twemproxy `https://github.com/twitter/twemproxy/blob/master/notes/redis.md`

Codis – a proxy-based high-performance Redis Cluster solution

In this chapter, we have introduced Twemproxy, a proxy-based sharding solution provided by Twitter. To solve the horizontal scalability limitation and the lack of the administration dashboard, the CodisLabs offers another Redis data sharding proxy called Codis. The performance, high-availability, and the usability of the Codis are highly superior to Twemproxy. Meanwhile, it's fully compatible with Twemproxy. In addition, a handy tool called the `redis-port` is provided along with this proxy to perform the migration from the Redis/Twemproxy to Codis.

The architecture of Codis is shown in the following image.

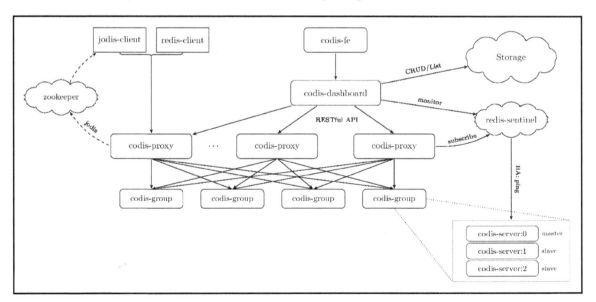

The codis-server is a special Redis instance based on the redis-3.2.8 branch. Additional data structures and instructions are added for the slot-related operation and data migration. In the preceding diagram, we have three codis-servers, one master, and two slaves.

The **codis-group** is a group of codis-servers working as a partial dataset. In a Codis Cluster, the dataset is divided into 1,024 slots by a CRC32 algorithm. Codis introduces the concept of the **codis-group**. Each group contains a master and at least one slave. Redis Sentinel manages the failover of the **codis-servers**.

The **codis-proxy** is the main proxy service implementing the Redis protocol for the client connection. Multiple Codis proxies could be deployed for the same product cluster. The state of these proxies can be synchronized.

The **codis-dashboard** is the cluster management tool by which the **codis-server** and the **codis-group** can be added and deleted.

The **jodis-client** is a smart client, which watches the Zookeeper to get the real-time available proxies and sends commands in a round-robin manner.

Since we have introduced various kinds of Redis data sharding solutions in the previous chapters and this chapter. Let's compare them to give you a basic understanding of which solution is the right solution for your scenario:

Feature / Product	Codis	Twemproxy	Redis Cluster
resharding without restarting cluster	Yes	No	Yes
pipeline	Yes	Yes	No
hash tags for multi-key operations	Yes	Yes	Yes
multi-key operations while resharding	Yes	No	No
Redis clients supporting	Any clients	Any clients	Clients have to support cluster protocol

See also

- For more details of Codis, you can refer to its GitHub page at
  `https://github.com/CodisLabs/codis`
- For more details of the Redis migration tool `redis-port`, you can refer to its
  GitHub page at `https://github.com/CodisLabs/redis-port`

The CacheCloud Redis management system

Deploying and managing a large number of Redis instances is cumbersome and time-consuming. In this section, we will introduce an open source project, CacheCloud developed by Sohu (NASDAQ: SOHU) TV to address this kind of problem.

CacheCloud is a Redis central management platform to perform Redis service provisioning, performance monitoring, and troubleshooting. It supports various kinds of Redis architecture, including Redis Standalone, Redis Sentinel, and Redis Cluster.

The architecture of Codis is shown in the following diagram:

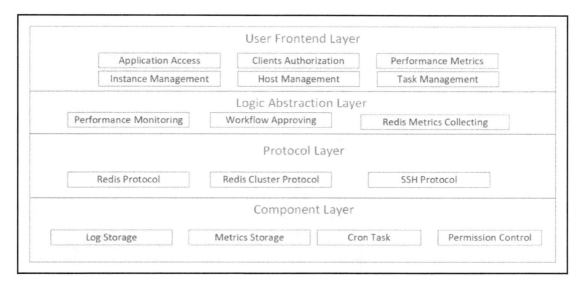

The following fantastic features are provided in CacheCloud:

- **Service Provisioning**: The user who wants to have a Redis in their application can apply the Redis data service with ease. The Redis standalone instance, Redis sentinel HA, and Redis Cluster are all supported and can be deployed automatically after the access application is approved.
- **Performance Monitoring**: The administrator can easily obtain the important performance metrics of all Redis instances managed by CacheCloud on one dashboard.
- **Issue Alerting**: The user will be notified if any issue happens in the Redis instance managed by CacheCloud.
- **Configuration/Admin Operation Management**: Nearly all the common admin operations and configuration changes can be performed in CacheCloud, eliminating the risk of the manual operation in the Terminal.
- **Client Access Management**: A special Java client is offered to help users collect the metrics of the Redis client, so that the troubleshooting can be performed without extra effort.

See also

- For more details of CacheCloud, you can refer to its GitHub page at `https://github.com/sohutv/cachecloud`
- The homepage of CacheCloud is available at `https://cachecloud.github.io/`

Pika – a Redis-compatible NoSQL database

Through the previous introduction, we have learned that if the dataset size of a Redis instance is too big, it is likely that the replication and persistence can be a big problem. Specifically, it always takes quite a long time to restore the dataset from a persistence file if the dataset of a Redis instance is large. In addition, the bigger is the dataset of a Redis, the longer it takes to perform the forking when the persistence is triggered. Worst of all, if the master Redis has a large dataset and owns multiple slaves, the full synchronization is a disaster. From the perspective of the storage cost, RAM is much more expensive than the **Solid State Drive (SSD)**.

To address these problems, Qihoo 360 developed Pika, which is a large-scale, high-performance, Redis-compatible storage system. Pika stores data on disks instead of memory, and the multithreaded design ensures considerable high performance. It supports multiple data structures and fully supports the Redis protocol. The user does not need to change the client-side code to migrate from Redis to Pika.

The architecture of Pika is shown in the following diagram:

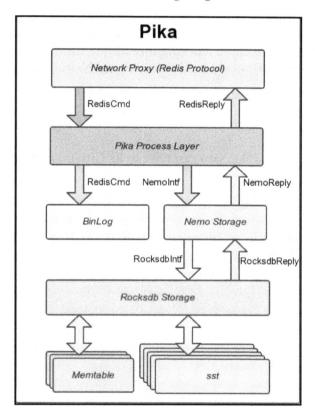

There are four main components in Pika, which are as follows:

- **Pink**: This is a network programming library, which is actually a wrapper of POSIX thread (`pthread`). It supports the proto buffer and Redis protocol. Developers can implement a high-performance server easily with Pink.
- **Nemo**: This is the storage engine for Pika, based on Rocksdb, to support the Redis data types such as `List`, `Hash`, `Set`, and `Zset`.
- **Binlog**: This is a sequence log of index and offset checkpoints. The synchronization between master and slave in Pika is accomplished by Binlog.
- **Working thread**: Multiple working threads are used to read and write, and the thread safety is guaranteed by the underlying Nemo engine.

See also

- For more details of Pika, you can refer to its GitHub page at `https://github.com/Qihoo360/pika`

Windows Environment Setup

For the readers who use Windows as the learning environment, it is strongly recommended to install VirtualBox (`https://www.virtualbox.org/`) and then set up the Ubuntu (`http://releases.ubuntu.com/16.04/`) 16.04 operating system on a virtual machine. If you would like to stick to Windows, this chapter will show you how to set up a Windows environment for your learning:

1. Install Ubuntu on Windows 10. In order to compile Redis from the source code and run the Bash shell scripts in this book, the Ubuntu subsystem of Windows 10 needs to be installed. You can follow the instructions at `https://docs.microsoft.com/en-us/windows/wsl/about` to get it installed.

2. Install Cygwin and the related packages. Install Cygwin (`https://cygwin.com/setup-x86_64.exe`) to `C:\tools\cygwin` and choose **Base** and **Devel** categories to install Make, Cmake, gcc, and bash:

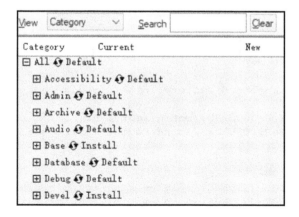

3. Install Redis by compiling the following code:

```
user@DESKTOP-JUTUKJS:~$ cd /mnt/c
user@DESKTOP-JUTUKJS:/mnt/c$ mkdir redis
user@DESKTOP-JUTUKJS:/mnt/c$ cd redis/
user@DESKTOP-JUTUKJS:/mnt/c/redis$ mkdir bin
user@DESKTOP-JUTUKJS:/mnt/c/redis$ mkdir conf
user@DESKTOP-JUTUKJS:/mnt/c/redis$ wget
http://download.redis.io/releases/redis-4.0.1.tar.gz
--2018-01-23 10:52:25--
http://download.redis.io/releases/redis-4.0.1.tar.gz
Connecting to 127.0.0.1:1080... connected.
Proxy request sent, awaiting response... 200 OK
Length: 1711660 (1.6M) [application/x-gzip]
Saving to: 'redis-4.0.1.tar.gz'

redis-4.0.1.tar.gz
100%[===============================================>]   1.63M
270KB/s    in 6.7s

2018-01-23 10:52:34 (249 KB/s) - 'redis-4.0.1.tar.gz' saved
[1711660/1711660]

user@DESKTOP-JUTUKJS:/mnt/c/redis$ tar zxf redis-4.0.1.tar.gz

user@DESKTOP-JUTUKJS:/mnt/c/redis/redis-4.0.1$ make
cd src && make all
make[1]: Entering directory '/mnt/c/redis/redis-4.0.1/src'
CC Makefile.dep
...
user@DESKTOP-JUTUKJS:~/redis-4.0.1$ make PREFIX=/mnt/c/redis
install
cd src && make install
make[1]: Entering directory '/home/user/redis-4.0.1/src'
CC Makefile.dep
...
make[1]: Leaving directory '/mnt/c/redis/redis-4.0.1/src'

user@DESKTOP-JUTUKJS:/mnt/c/redis$ cd ..
user@DESKTOP-JUTUKJS:/mnt/c/redis$ mkdir conf
user@DESKTOP-JUTUKJS:/mnt/c/redis$ cp redis-4.0.1/redis.conf conf/.

user@DESKTOP-JUTUKJS:~$ cd
user@DESKTOP-JUTUKJS:~$ ln -s bin /mnt/c/redis/bin
user@DESKTOP-JUTUKJS:~$ ln -s conf /mnt/c/redis/conf
```

4. Set up C programming IDE CLion. Download CLion, a C/C++ IDE, from `https:/ /download.jetbrains.8686c.com/cpp/CLion-2017.2.2.exe`. Then double-click on the setup file and follow the prompts to finish the installation.

5. Next, extract the `echodemo.tar.gz` file. The source code is provided along with this book (you can also find the source code in `Chapter 1`, *Getting Started with Redis*) to `c:\redis\redis-4.0.1` directory. The following screenshot shows the directory structure:

Name	Size	Type	Modified	Attr
.idea	12.5 KB	File Folder	Today 9:02	-----
cmake-build-debug		File Folder	Yesterday 15:17	-----
deps		File Folder	Yesterday 14:12	-----
echodemo		File Folder	星期日 18:26	-----
src		File Folder	星期日 18:26	-----
tests		File Folder	2017/7/24 21:58	-----
utils		File Folder	2017/7/24 21:58	-----
.gitignore	376 bytes	File	Yesterday 10:52	-a---
00-RELEASENOTES	124 KB	File	Yesterday 10:52	-a---
BUGS	53 bytes	File	Yesterday 10:52	-a---
CMakeLists.txt	3.19 KB	文本文档	星期六 2:08	-----
CONTRIBUTING	1.77 KB	File	Yesterday 10:52	-a---
COPYING	1.45 KB	File	Yesterday 10:52	-a---
INSTALL	11 bytes	File	Yesterday 10:52	-a---
Makefile	151 bytes	File	Yesterday 10:52	-a---
MANIFESTO	4.12 KB	File	Yesterday 10:52	-a---
README.md	20 KB	MD 文件	Yesterday 10:52	-a---
redis.conf	56.4 KB	CONF 文件	Yesterday 10:52	-a---

6. Open CLion and import the project. Make sure that you do not overwrite `CMakeList.txt`.

To prepare the build toolchains, set up the Cygwin environment by navigating to **Files**->**Settings**->**Build, Execution, Deployment**-> **Toolchains** as the shown in the following screenshot:

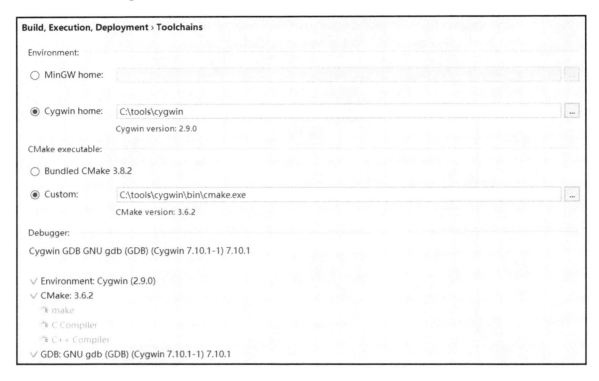

7. Open the Terminal in CLion and make a deps folder. Ignore the warnings during the compilation:

```
C:\redis\redis-4.0.1>cd deps
C:\redis\redis-4.0.1\deps>make CFLAGS=-D_WIN32 CPPDEFS=-D_WIN32
hiredis lua linenoise
(cd hiredis && make clean) > /dev/null || true
...
make[1]: Leaving directory '/cygdrive/d/redis-4.0.1/deps/linenoise'
```

8. Use **Build All** in CLion to build all the executable files. You can click on the **Build All** button, shown in the following screenshot:

9. Ignore the following warning and click on **Continue Anyway**:

You will find that the demo source code is being compiled, as shown in the following screenshot:

```
[ 92%] Building C object CMakeFiles/my-redis-server.dir/src/t_string.c.o
[ 93%] Building C object CMakeFiles/my-redis-server.dir/src/t_zset.c.o
[ 94%] Building C object CMakeFiles/my-redis-server.dir/src/util.c.o
[ 96%] Building C object CMakeFiles/my-redis-server.dir/src/ziplist.c.o
[ 97%] Building C object CMakeFiles/my-redis-server.dir/src/zipmap.c.o
[ 98%] Building C object CMakeFiles/my-redis-server.dir/src/zmalloc.c.o
[100%] Linking C executable my-redis-server.exe
[100%] Built target my-redis-server
```

By now, you have successfully compiled the source code of the demo program and redis-server. You can find all the executable files under the cmake-build-debug folder:

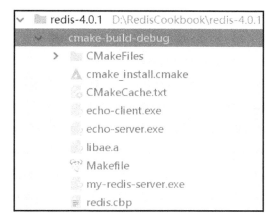

Run the `redis-server`, called `my-redis-server` in this book, by clicking on the target and then clicking on the arrow button:

The Redis Server will be started, as shown in the following screenshot:

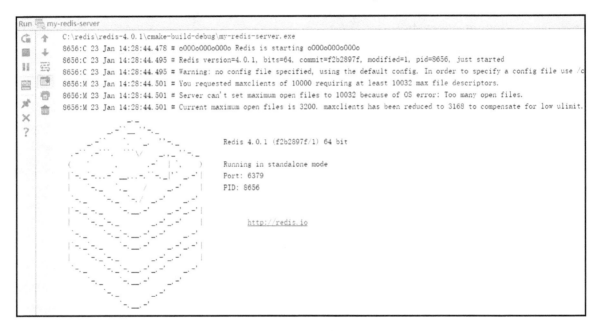

At this time, you can use the `redis-cli` we compiled in step 3 to connect to this `redis-server`. Perform some testing and then shut down the Redis instance:

```
user@DESKTOP-JUTUKJS:/mnt/c/redis$ bin/redis-cli
127.0.0.1:6379> set foo bar
OK
127.0.0.1:6379> get foo
"bar"

127.0.0.1:6379> get foo
127.0.0.1:6379> SHUTDOWN
not connected>
```

You can also debug the `redis-server` by setting a breakpoint, for example, in the `main()` function of `server.c`, as shown in the following screenshot:

```
3835                }
3836
3837                /* Warning the user about suspicious maxmemory setting. */
3838                if (server.maxmemory > 0 && server.maxmemory < 1024*1024) {
3839                    serverLog(LL_WARNING, "WARNING: You specified a maxmemory value
3840                }
3841
3842                aeSetBeforeSleepProc(server.el, beforeSleep);
3843                aeSetAfterSleepProc(server.el, afterSleep);
3844                aeMain(server.el);
3845                aeDeleteEventLoop(server.el);
3846                return 0;
3847            }
```

Click on the **Debug** button to start debugging:

You can then perform the debugging, as shown in the following screenshot:

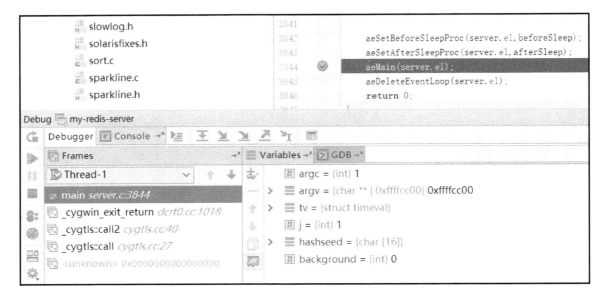

Other Books You May Enjoy

If you enjoyed this book, you may be interested in these other books by Packt:

Learning Neo4j 3.x - Second Edition
Jérôme Baton, Rik Van Bruggen

ISBN: 978-1-78646-614-3

- Understand the science of graph theory, databases and its advantages over traditional databases.
- Install Neo4j, model data and learn the most common practices of traversing data
- Learn the Cypher query language and tailor-made procedures to analyze and derive meaningful representations of data
- Improve graph techniques with the help of precise procedures in the APOC library
- Use Neo4j advanced extensions and plugins for performance optimization.
- Understand how Neo4j's new security features and clustering architecture are used for large scale deployments

Learning PostgreSQL 10 - Second Edition
Salahaldin Juba, Andrey Volkov

ISBN: 978-1-78839-201-3

- Understand the fundamentals of relational databases, relational algebra, and data modeling
- Install a PostgreSQL cluster, create a database, and implement your data model
- Create tables and views, define indexes, and implement triggers, stored procedures, and other schema objects
- Use the Structured Query Language (SQL) to manipulate data in the database
- Implement business logic on the server side with triggers and stored procedures using PL/pgSQL
- Make use of advanced data types supported by PostgreSQL 10: Arrays, hstore, JSONB, and others
- Develop OLAP database solutions using the most recent features of PostgreSQL 10
- Connect your Python applications to a PostgreSQL database and work with the data efficiently
- Test your database code, find bottlenecks, improve performance, and enhance the reliability of the database applications

Leave a review - let other readers know what you think

Please share your thoughts on this book with others by leaving a review on the site that you bought it from. If you purchased the book from Amazon, please leave us an honest review on this book's Amazon page. This is vital so that other potential readers can see and use your unbiased opinion to make purchasing decisions, we can understand what our customers think about our products, and our authors can see your feedback on the title that they have worked with Packt to create. It will only take a few minutes of your time, but is valuable to other potential customers, our authors, and Packt. Thank you!

Index

www.ingramcontent.com/pod-product-compliance
Lightning Source LLC
Chambersburg PA
CBHW080611060326
40690CB00021B/4660